ROMANCE MONOGRAPHS, INC.
Number 24

A STUDY OF JEAN-JACQUES BERNARD'S
THÉÂTRE DE L'INEXPRIMÉ

ROMANCE MONOGRAPHS, INC.
Number 24

A STUDY OF JEAN-JACQUES BERNARD'S
THÉÂTRE DE L'INEXPRIMÉ

BY

KESTER ADRIAN BRANFORD

UNIVERSITY, MISSISSIPPI
ROMANCE MONOGRAPHS, INC.
1 9 7 7

IMPRESO EN ESPAÑA

PRINTED IN SPAIN

I.S.B.N. 84-399-6422-6

DEPÓSITO LEGAL: V. 943 - 1977

ARTES GRÁFICAS SOLER, S. A. - JÁVEA, 28 - VALENCIA (8) - 1977

Library of Congress Cataloging in Publication Data

Branford, Kester Adrian, 1950-
    A study of Jean-Jacques Bernard's théâtre de l'inexprimé.

    (Romance monographs; no. 24)
    Bibliography: p.

    1. Bernard, Jean Jacques, 1888-1972—Criticism and interpretation.
I. Title.

PQ2603.E59Z62   842'.9'12   [B]   76-58424

CONTENTS

FOREWORD

JEAN-JACQUES BERNARD's attempt to free French drama from its en-
slavement to the strongly verbal and declamatory model, his efforts
to replace traditional rhetoric with a new and infinitely more subdued
rhetoric constituted a major challenge to the conventions of theatrical
expression. The challenge was not spectacular in appearance, and, to
a certain extent, Bernard's theatre has been overshadowed by more
audaciously iconoclastic undertakings. His *théâtre de l'inexprimé* represents a significant aspect of inter-war avant-garde drama, an important link in the chain of experimental drama that extends from
the late nineteenth century; but it has unjustly been neglected. This
has not always been the case. In the twenties and thirties Bernard
enjoyed a solid critical reputation and provoked much lively discussion; he was the subject of an excellent thirty-page monograph by
M. Paul Blanchart in 1928; more recently, Dr. May Daniels devoted
two chapters of her illuminating book *The French Drama of The
Unspoken* to Bernard. As yet, however, no full-length study has been
published on Bernard's theatre of the unexpressed. Equally regrettable is the fact that a number of misapprehensions continue to sur-
round this theatre — misapprehensions sometimes in evidence when
passing references are made to Bernard. This book seeks to dispel
false notions, and to rescue from a state of unjust neglect works which
are both valuable as experiments and admirable as pieces of drama;
it seeks also to show that Bernard's *théâtre de l'inexprimé* does not
belong exclusively to the past, to demonstrate the persistence in the
present day of ideas and techniques which he had championed.

This study, as the title indicates, does not aspire to be a com-
prehensive survey of Bernard the dramatist. Such a survey would

need to find room for his radio plays and his historical plays; it would need to take account of his movement away from the doctrine of Art for Art's sake, and of the mystical vein which runs through the later plays — in particular those that followed his conversion to Christianity. It is my view that the theatre of the unexpressed represents Bernard's most solid contribution to the renewal of twentieth-century French drama, but his work clearly admits of other approaches. Again, I have not attempted to explore systematically all the plays that belong to the category of *théâtre de l'inexprimé*; this would require an altogether more extensive study. I have chosen, instead, to centre my discussion on three plays which adequately demonstrate Bernard's use of the techniques of the unexpressed, and which are at the same time his most moving and persuasive plays: *Martine, Le Printemps des autres* and *L'Invitation au voyage*.

I wish to record my gratitude to Dr. M. M. Bowie of Clare College, Cambridge, to whose good judgement and meticulous care I owe countless improvements. I am also indebted to Professor Ll. J. Austin of Jesus College, Cambridge, and to Professor F. Scarfe of the British Institute in Paris for their valuable suggestions on particular portions of the manuscript.

My thanks are due to a number of others persons who helped in a variety of ways: M. Denys Amiel; M. Nicolas Bernard, son of Jean-Jacques Bernard; M. Raymond Bernard, brother of Jean-Jacques Bernard; Mlle Jacqueline Bossy; Mme Sylvie Chevalley, Archivist/Librarian at the *Comédie-Française*; Miss Linda Coles, Librarian at the Independent Broadcasting Authority; M. Gaspard de Condappa; M. Henri Crémieux, lifelong friend of Jean-Jacques Bernard and quondam Secretary to the reading committee of *Les Compagnons de la Chimère*; Dr. May Daniels; M. Jean-Jacques Gautier of the *Académie Française*; M. Paul Géraldy; Miss Veronica Griffiths; M. Paul-Louis Mignon of the International Theatre Institute; Miss Sally Peacock; Mr. Harold Pinter; M. Pierre-Aimé Touchard of the *Conservatoire National d'Art Dramatique*; the Staff at the Script Libraries of the B.B.C. and of the *Maison de l'O.R.T.F.*

I wish to acknowledge the courteous permission of M. Henri Crémieux to quote statements he made during my interview with him, and of MM. Jean-Jacques Gautier and Pierre-Aimé Touchard to quote from their respective letters.

I wish, finally, to express my appreciation of the financial assistance afforded by the University of the West Indies, and by the Leverhulme Trust and the British Institute in Paris.

K. A. B.

Wolfson College, Cambridge
March 1974

CHAPTER ONE

BACKGROUND AND PERSPECTIVES

AN INTERESTING, important and dauntingly complex study remains
to be written on the effect of war on the artist. In the nature of a
veritable cataclysm, the First World War was to modify radically the
material, spiritual and intellectual life of the Frenchman. A fresh
sense of insecurity gave rise to an anxious questioning of the values
which had hitherto been stoutly defended, and with whose sanction
so much carnage had resulted; for many the old ways were losing
their credit. The change of mood was affirmed after the Armistice
through an ardent desire for national revival, through a thirst for a
vibrant resurgence, and was consonant with the innovatory spirit that
began to animate with a special intensity all forms of artistic expression. No less than in poetry and in the novel, this spirit was felt
in the drama.

Of course the War did not occasion a definitive elimination from
French drama of its most spent ingredients; the post-war commercial theatre continued to prosper — much in the same way as during
the *Belle Époque*. It was outside this theatre, and on the fringe of the
established theatre in general, that the searching out of new ways
proceeded. This activity — part of a continual operation in any living
literature, but an activity which particularly befitted the beginning of
the new phase of history represented by the Armistice — was encouraged and accelerated by the formation of theatrical companies
of a basically non-commercial nature. The last years of the nineteenth
century had already witnessed the opening of experimental playhouses
such as *Le Théâtre Libre*[1] and *Le Théâtre de l'Œuvre*.[2] The post-

---

[1] Founded by André Antoine in 1887.
[2] Founded by Lugné-Poe in 1893.

war years were to see the reopening in Paris of Jacques Copeau's *Théâtre du Vieux-Colombier* in 1920,[3] the founding of Charles Dullin's *Théâtre de l'Atelier* in 1921, and the formation of Gaston Baty's *Compagnons de la Chimère* in 1922.

Jean-Jacques Bernard has remarked on the motley produce of post-war dramatists:

> C'est l'époque où Lenormand introduisait la psychanalyse au théâtre, Jules Romains l'unanimisme, Charles Vildrac les résonances de la poésie quotidienne, Paul Raynal un sens renouvelé du tragique, Crommelynck sa truculence colorée. Je ne cite ici que quelques-uns parmi les plus illustres, mais des tempéraments significatifs, et en même temps différents, dont la diversité même atteste la richesse de cette génération.[4]

The leading preoccupation of many members of this generation was to infuse new blood into an art form that had ceased to renew itself. The talent for manipulating in appealing fashion well-designed intrigues, the constant searching for striking theatrical effects, the exploitation of the stage for the propagation of ideas were still prominent in ensuring the success of the commercial theatre — a theatre over which Scribe, Sardou, Augier, Dumas *fils* and Sarcey continued, from beyond the grave, to preside. But in this theatre there was little that could kindle Bernard to enthusiasm. To him too much of it appeared over-concerned with financial profit, old-fashioned, and brilliant in a superficial way. By reaction, he was to attach little importance to the mechanics of dramatic action, to avoid meretricious ornaments, gaudy colours and boisterous gaiety, to reject the problem play, and to aim at a sober dialogue without frills.

Intimism

In various ways Bernard covered common ground with Denys Amiel,[5] Charles Vildrac[6] and Paul Géraldy,[7] and the plays of the

---

[3] Originally founded in 1913, but interrupted by the War.

[4] Bernard, 'La "Théorie du Silence",' *La Revue Théâtrale*, juin-juillet-août 1947, pp. 280-281.

[5] Born 1884.

[6] 1882-1971.

[7] Born 1885.

four authors have at times been grouped under the heading: *Théâtre intimiste*. This designation at once brings to mind the *Intima Teatern*, the playhouse which Falck and Strindberg managed between 1907 and 1910, and for which the 'chamber plays' were specifically composed. Setting out what an Intimate Theatre wanted to achieve and what was meant by chamber plays, Strindberg said, among other things, that the aim was to avoid "all calculated effects, places for applause, star roles, solo numbers." [8] In this respect, Strindberg anticipated Amiel, Géraldy, Vildrac and Bernard — in particular the latter two. Generally speaking, however, the term 'intimate' as it was applied to Strindberg's playhouse and to the other Intimate Theatres that sprang up in its wake, especially in Germany, was intended rather to indicate the size of the theatre than to denote the character of the plays produced. The earliest record that we find of the use of the phrase *théâtre intimiste* in reference to the four French authors is in an article by Benjamin Crémieux in 1925:

> L'école dramatique française contemporaine [...] qui suscite des imitateurs hors de nos frontières, c'est ce qu'on pourrait appeler le théâtre intimiste, [...] qui a pour tenants aux yeux de l'étranger quatre dramaturges [...]: Charles Vildrac, Paul Géraldy, Jean-Jacques Bernard, Denys Amiel. [9]

Bernard and Amiel worked together on the reading committee of the *Compagnons de la Chimère*; [10] Bernard was a friend of Vildrac's, and the two, along with writers like Giraudoux and Romains, made up the company at a number of secret *dîners des dix* between the wars. [11] But Amiel, Bernard, Géraldy and Vildrac did not formally constitute a school, as Crémieux's article might lead one to believe. Nor did they ever describe their plays as 'intimist.' Géraldy for one has registered his objection to this designation, and has warned against the use of labels under which writers without sufficient personality or authority to stand alone attempt to group themselves. [12] This notwith-

---

8 Strindberg, *Letters to the Intimate Theatre* (Translated by Walter Johnson), London, Peter Owen, 1967. p. 19.
9 Benjamin Crémieux, 'Le Théâtre,' *La Nouvelle Revue Française*, 1er déc. 1925, p. 745.
10 See below, p. 61.
11 See Bernard, *Mon Ami le Théâtre*, Paris, Albin Michel, 1958, pp. 125ff.
12 Paul Géraldy, letter to the author, January 1972.

standing, *intimisme* is, to our mind, a term that aptly signifies an inspirational vein from which some of the most outstanding plays of the four dramatists, certain poems, and certain paintings appear to derive.

Indeed there are a number of what one might call tonal resemblances between plays like *Martine* [13] or *Le Paquebot Tenacity* [14] and paintings in the intimist style. At the turn of the century this style was represented mainly by two of the *Nabis*: Pierre Bonnard and Édouard Vuillard. [15] In Vuillard's art Bernard discerned a reflection of the painter's nature:

> Il avait l'âme de son œuvre, intime, pénétrante, familiale, attachante. [...] Cet artiste au ton discret était comme un paradoxe. On le voyait rester des heures immobile, observant, portant en lui les œuvres à venir, ou bien il disparaissait pour travailler loin du bruit, dans le silence qui lui convenait et qu'il savait exprimer dans ses toiles. [16]

The intimism of Vuillard and Bonnard involved the use of subdued colouring, giving the effect of soft, dreamy light, and a preference for serene interiors and ordinary scenes of domestic life. In this, and in their attention to the unobtrusive, lies their affinity with the intimist playwrights.

The term *intimiste* also designates a poet attempting to express familiar, intimate emotions, and the humbler events and details of day-to-day life, in a mood of tranquillity and in a discreet, restrained language. Vildrac, qua poet, is often an Intimist; [17] but he was preceded by certain nineteenth-century figures; intimist qualities are to be found intermittently in the poetic work of Sainte-Beuve and Hugo. It is with good reason that Émile Henriot has referred to Hugo as "le tendre intimiste des *Voix intérieures* et des *Feuilles d'automne*," [18]

---

[13] The following chapter will be devoted to this play, which is perhaps Bernard's best-known, and which is one of the earliest of his pieces to show a sustained interest in unexpressed sentiment.

[14] By Vildrac.

[15] The *Nabi* group appeared towards the end of the 1880s, and professed a common opposition to Impressionist naturalism.

[16] Bernard, *Mon père Tristan Bernard*, Paris, Albin Michel, 1955, p. 158.

[17] See, for example, 'Visite' in *Livre d'Amour*, Paris, Éditions de Minuit, 1946, pp. 111-116.

[18] Émile Henriot, *Les Romantiques*, Paris, Albin Michel, 1953, p. 34.

and Hugo himself in the preface to the latter work seems to define accurately the intimist character of a large portion of the collection:

> Des feuilles tombées, des feuilles mortes, comme toutes feuilles d'automne. Ce n'est point là de la poésie de tumulte et de bruit; ce sont des vers sereins et paisibles, des vers comme tout le monde en fait ou en rêve, des vers de la famille, du foyer domestique, de la vie privée; des vers de l'intérieur de l'âme. [...] C'est l'écho de ces pensées, souvent inexprimables, qu'éveillent confusément dans notre esprit les mille objets de la création qui souffrent ou qui languissent autour de nous. [19]

There are four main points of similarity here with the *théâtre intimiste*: it is not a theatre of sound and fury; it rejects the uncommon and the extraordinary in favour of the ordinary aspects of everyday life; it attempts to capture pure emotion from the depths of the soul; it often reflects the notion of the incommunicability of impressions.

The intimism of Amiel, Bernard, Géraldy and Vildrac was marked by a special conception of what constitutes the action of a play. Géraldy, for instance, stated:

> Depuis que j'aime le théâtre, [...] je m'entends répéter cette lassante formule: 'Au théâtre il faut de l'action!' Évidemment, il faut de l'action! Sans *action*, que ferait *l'acteur?* Mais je demande qu'on s'entende sur le sens de ce mot-là. On appelle toujours action ce qui est mouvement extérieur. La seule *action* véritable au théâtre, c'est celle qui se passe dans les cœurs. [20]

There are "mouvements extérieurs" which are essential — or at least unobtrusive — and there are "mouvements extérieurs" which might be considered gratuitous. Géraldy was here disdaining them *en masse*. [21]

---

[19] Victor Hugo, 'Préface,' *Les Feuilles d'automne*, pp. 714-715 in *Œuvres Poétiques I*, Paris, Gallimard, 1964.

[20] Quoted by Robert de Beauplan, '*Christine* à la Comédie-Française,' *La Petite Illustration*, 31 déc. 1932, page not numbered.

[21] We are well entitled to question the validity of such a conception. It is perhaps more acceptable to one nurtured on Racine than to one nurtured on Shakespeare, the latter being less likely to feel that *Hamlet* and *Othello* suffer from their duels, or *Julius Caesar* from its battle-scenes.

Without putting forward their views so forcibly on this matter, the other three dramatists shared Géraldy's bias against the impressive, earth-shaking external events of the action-packed drama. Their common desire was to remove from the rôle of kingpin striking misfortunes, such as sudden death and financial disaster, to eliminate the physical contact of fights, duels and murders, to dispense with the unexpected reversals and the fanciful *coups de théâtre*, such as the finding of a long-lost parent. They wanted nothing as sensational as the mention of 'unmentionable' diseases, no strange occurrences, nothing that was too overtly dramatic. Theirs, in a word, was a movement towards quietude.

Speaking of the theatre, Vildrac declared:

> Erreurs et tricheries:
> Mettre en scène des personnages-psychologues qui s'analysent eux-mêmes à la perfection et font avec à-propos des citations puisées dans les lectures de l'auteur. [22]

Vildrac's wariness of conspicuous authorial intervention, either through witty *mots d'auteur* or through the introduction of a *raisonneur*, and his reluctance to portray characters who provide excellent self-portraits were signs of a reaction against the verbal exuberance that has figured so prominently in Western drama. A similar reaction is visible in the plays of Amiel and Bernard; but it is here that Géraldy diverged widely from the other three, for the elaborate analysis of sentiment in which he indulged is of the exact type that they frowned upon in the theatre. Furthermore, there are occasions on which the strains of lyricism, the sophisticated nothings which managed to titillate so many readers of his poems — in particular his highly successful collection *Toi et Moi* — drifted into his plays with less delightful results. [23] We easily sympathize with François Mauriac when he writes:

---

[22] Charles Vildrac, 'Réflexions sur le théâtre,' *Théâtre* (ed. Paul Arnold), Paris, Éditions du Pavois, 1945, pp. 22-23.

[23] According to Lucien Dubech, "de tous les ouvrages de la poésie française, *Toi et Moi* est sans doute celui dont il a été vendu le plus grand nombre d'exemplaires. On raconte que dans les lieux appelés *dancings,* après la guerre, quand un jeune homme voulait poser sa candidature auprès d'une femme, il lui offrait *Toi et Moi.*" *Les Chefs de File de la Jeune Génération,* Paris, Plon, 1925, pp. 147-148.

> C'est ennuyeux que les personnages de M. Géraldy parlent
> comme il écrit: je veux dire qu'ils parlent trop bien; ils
> parlent comme des livres. [24]

or with André George when he writes:

> Comme l'auteur supprime ici des personnages et des aven-
> tures, il emplit son cadre vide avec des mots, des mots, des
> mots. C'est la rhétorique, souvent hélas la plus banale, qui
> s'étale partout. [25]

It is important, then, to try to dispel the notion that the expressions
théâtre intimiste and *théâtre de l'inexprimé* are interchangeable. [26] Far
from being a pretext for hair-splitting, the distinction is essential if
we are not to imply that Géraldy's intimist theatre is a theatre of the
unexpressed; in fact the latter term properly applies to plays by
Bernard and Amiel, and, to a lesser degree, to Vildrac's plays. [27]

Placed beside Géraldy's theatre, that of Vildrac strikes one by its
sober, restrained, unembellished language. It is not of the characters
of *Le Paquebot Tenacity* that one can truthfully say:

> Ils parlent [...] une langue soignée, et s'expriment avec
> élégance et distinction, en personnages de comédie qui se
> savent admis à exposer leurs affaires de cœur sur les plan-
> ches de la Comédie-Française et qui sont, comme il convient,
> pénétrés et respectueux de l'honneur qui leur est fait. [28]

Vildrac's characters do not automatically and consistently attempt to
put their deepest thoughts into words. Vildrac, however, was far less
preoccupied than either Bernard or Amiel with the technical problem
of conveying unspoken thoughts, and he remained aloof from the
theorizing on the value of the unexpressed in drama in which they
were engaged.

---

[24] François Mauriac, 'Les Spectacles,' *La Nouvelle Revue Française*, 1er
janv. 1926, p. 123.

[25] André George, 'La Vie Théâtrale,' *Les Lettres*, janv. 1926, p. 118.

[26] Cf. Paul Surer, *Le Théâtre Français Contemporain*, Paris, Société d'Édition d'Enseignement Supérieur, 1964, p. 149.

[27] May Daniels has made a useful and illuminating study of this aspect
of Vildrac's theatre in *The French Drama of The Unspoken*, Edinburgh at
the University Press, 1953, pp. 121-143.

[28] René Doumic (reviewing Géraldy's *Aimer*), 'Revue Dramatique,' *Revue
des Deux Mondes*, 15 déc. 1921, p. 946.

The Unexpressed

Amiel envisaged an experimental drama based almost exclusively on the use of silence, though not in the sense of a total absence of words. The silence which interested him was that of people who "se taisent en parlant":

> Pour moi, garder le silence ne signifie pas se taire. Certes, les gens 'polis et sociables' parlent ... baguenaudent, s'expriment jusqu'à la verbosité et leurs bavardages peuvent être pourtant d'un *silence* angoissant, s'ils *se taisent* précisément sur leurs préoccupations principales, celles-là mêmes qui les ont fait se réunir. [29]

Such a situation is to be found in his *Le Voyageur.* The play, which begins when Paul returns from the United States to learn that his girl-friend Madeleine is in love with his best friend Jacques, deals with Paul's reconquest. The two men do not exchange virulent words, do not openly dispute Madeleine's love, do not even admit that a rivalry exists; but the atmosphere is highly charged with the bitterness of a battle which Paul eventually wins. An apt description of the process has been provided by May Daniels:

> The action here is on two levels. On the surface is the exchange of urbane conversation on the part of three civilized human beings; below, but very close to the surface, is the conflict of elemental passions. Beneath conventional phrases a friendship between two men is broken, an old love is reborn, a new love is destroyed and a woman chooses between two rivals. [30]

Towards the end of the play Paul reflects:

> Ah! l'admirable et la poignante chose que la vie!... Les minutes les plus insignifiantes sont peut-être grosses de drames intérieurs. [...] On voit des gens paisiblement assis... qui causent [...] avec calme... leurs gestes sont ceux de tous les autres hommes polis et sociables... et peut-être

---

[29] Denys Amiel, 'Les Œuvres par Leurs Auteurs,' *Gazette des Sept Arts,* 10 mai 1923, p. 3.

[30] May Daniels, *The French Drama of The Unspoken,* p. 149.

que dans leur cœur s'agitent en remous . . . la convoitise . . .
la haine . . . la passion de la bête ancestrale. [31]

These reflections appear to sum up the play as a study of the possibilities of duplicity which are inherent in social relationships. In
fact Amiel's characters frequently adopt false attitudes and try to use
their natural facility with words for purposes of deception. Bernard,
on the other hand, was more inclined to present inarticulate people,
or people who are not entirely aware of their real personality, or
people whose silences are motivated by inner uncertainty rather than
by a desire to mislead.

Brief mention may be made at this point of Jean-Victor Pellerin,
who was like Bernard and Amiel a member of the reading committee
of the *Compagnons de la Chimère*, [32] and whose *Intimité* (which had
its first performance on the same evening as *Martine* — 9 May 1922)
is often described as an 'unexpressed' play. [33] Pellerin's play is an
attempt to show what takes place in the mind behind the verbal
façade, the author's starting-point being that

> Un grand nombre d'hommes et de femmes [. . .] vivent deux
> vies souvent distinctes: l'une qui parle, gesticule, rit, pleure,
> crie, fait beaucoup de bruit, tient beaucoup de place; l'autre
> (la *vraie* peut-être) qui pense et rêve en sourdine, tout au
> fond de nous-mêmes, qui ne veut ou ne peut s'exprimer au
> grand jour, qui n'ose, qui se cache, — qui est notre silence. [34]

Pellerin was preoccupied, to a greater extent than Bernard, with the
externalization of secret thought: in *Intimité,* the spectator is allowed
to hear the 'hidden' thoughts which the couple confide to the characters that appear in ghostly fashion at the rear of the stage; these
characters are at times personified representations of the couple's unspoken thoughts. Bernard was more concerned to suggest the existence
of such thoughts without the precise, concrete, material indications
that are found in a play like Pellerin's.

---

[31] Denys Amiel, *Le Voyageur*, sc. 6, p. 69 in *Théâtre I*, Paris, Albin
Michel, 1925.

[32] See below, p. 61.

[33] This expression will serve as a shorthand equivalent of "play belonging
to the category of *théâtre de l'inexprimé*."

[34] Jean-Victor Pellerin, 'A propos d'*Intimité,*' *La Chimère. Bulletin d'Art
Dramatique,* mai (2) 1922, p. 70.

Bernard has always maintained that with *Martine* he had inclined by temperament towards a form of drama which he began to define only a few days before the play's première. This occurred when he was asked by Gaston Baty, who staged *Martine,* to write an introduction to the play for the official *Bulletin* of the *Compagnons de la Chimère.* In the article Bernard made known his dislike for ornate or analytical rhetoric in the theatre, and his view of drama as an art of suggestion and of the unexpressed. [35] The title of the article and Bernard's profession of his belief in the value of silence no doubt assisted the propagation of the label *théâtre du silence* — a label to which Bernard objected.

An artist using the verbal medium who stresses the virtues of silence is exposed to the charge of breaking the silence he so admires. It may be argued that even if one does not consider Vigny's 'La Mort du Loup' to be inspired by his mother's death and his painful breach with Marie Dorval, the poem still appears tinged with a note of personal suffering (however muted and discreet). In that case, Vigny frustrated his desire to emulate the wolf's stoic silence as soon as he put pen to paper, and the words "Seul le silence est grand; tout le reste est faiblesse" have rebounded upon him. [36] But the drastic alternative was for him to refuse to write, to leave in the place of 'La Mort du Loup' a blank page. A frivolous critic might suggest that the best way of underlining the value of silence in the theatre would be to compose dumb-shows. Bernard's conception of silence was broader. Silence in his plays is of two main types: first, pure silence as a form of expression, conveying according to a particular context particular moods and emotions; secondly, what might be termed wordy silence, which occurs when dialogue functions primarily as an impediment to pure silence. It would be wrong to imagine that his belief in the value of silence implied a call for a complete elimination of words from the drama, or that his technique consisted merely in using pauses effectively. The skilful use of the pause constituted only one of the various methods employed by him to convey to the audience the unexpressed matter at the core of plays like

---

[35] Bernard, 'Le silence au théâtre,' *Ibid.,* pp. 66-68.
[36] Alfred de Vigny, 'La Mort du Loup,' p. 200 in *Œuvres Complètes I,* Paris, Gallimard, 1950.

Martine, Le Printemps des autres and *L'Invitation au voyage.* [37] By
the unexpressed he meant the virtual dialogue underlying the surface
dialogue, and the sentiments which the characters are unable or
reluctant to formulate. The unexpressed, in his words,

> C'est toute la série des pensées ou des désirs qui échappent
> aux mots, qui ne peuvent s'échanger que par allusion in-
> directe, voire par le regard ou l'attitude, c'est toute la gamme
> des sentiments inexprimés, inavoués ou inconscients. *Et c'est
> pourquoi, rejetant l'expression de théâtre du silence, j'ai tou-
> jours préféré celle de théâtre de l'inexprimé, que j'avais
> d'ailleurs employée dès la première fois.* [38]

What Bernard sensed developing around him was a legend founded
on misapprehensions which were showing signs of persisting. One
thinks in this connection of the legend according to which Artaud
recommended butchery on the stage. Apparently one is to believe
that all plays written within the last three decades in which characters perpetrate atrocities on one another derive from his conception
of a *théâtre de la cruauté.* [39] In like manner, around an initial misunderstanding of what Bernard understood by 'silence' a legend was
born, and, as a result, the author's name too often conjures up the
vision of a strange extremist strongly advocating pantomime. The
fault lies partially in the failure of Bernard, as of Artaud, to take
stock at the outset of the opportunities for distortion and misrepre-
sentation afforded by careless terminology; as we have seen, Bernard's
'Le silence au théâtre' bears a large portion of responsibility. [40] Yet

---

[37] The two last-mentioned plays will hereafter be referred to as *Printemps*
and *L'Invitation.*

[38] Bernard, *Témoignages,* Paris, Coutan-Lambert, 1933, p. 27. My emphasis. In the order of things, Bernard's plays do not all reflect the same
degree of preoccupation with the unexpressed; some are in no important
way concerned with the unexpressed. *La Maison épargnée, Martine, Printemps, L'Invitation, Le Secret d'Arvers, L'Ame en peine, Nationale 6* and *Le
Jardinier d'Ispahan* are among those that belong to the category of *théâtre
de l'inexprimé.*

[39] "Je propose un théâtre de la cruauté. — Avec cette manie de tout ra-
baisser qui nous appartient aujourd'hui à tous, 'cruauté,' quand j'ai prononcé
ce mot, a tout de suite voulu dire 'sang' pour tout le monde. Mais *'théâtre de
la cruauté'* veut dire théâtre difficile et cruel d'abord pour moi-même." Antonin Artaud, *Le Théâtre et son Double,* Paris, Gallimard, 1964, p. 121.

[40] Above, p. 20.

the protests which he began to voice in March 1923 indicate the depth of the naïveté that marked some of the interpretations of his statements:

> Certains m'ont reproché, d'autres m'ont félicité de vouloir écrire des pièces avec des silences. Comme si le silence, ailleurs que dans la pantomime, avait une valeur en soi. [41]

> J'espère que personne ne prend plus à la lettre ce qu'on a appelé un peu trop simplement la 'théorie du silence'. Si un architecte exprimait ainsi l'importance des portes et des fenêtres: 'Les trous ont une grande valeur dans une maison', que dirait-on des gens qui lui reprocheraient de construire des maisons en trous? [42]

At virtually every subsequent discussion of his techniques Bernard has tried to dispel the original misinterpretation, to destroy the false myth of a theatre of silence in the narrow and simplistic sense the label was being given.

Which is not to say that the misconception has been universal. Henry Bidou and Paul Blanchart in France, James Agate and John Palmer in England promptly recognized the import of Bernard's plays, and many others have shown an excellent understanding of the issues underlying his dramatic practice. Ronald Peacock, remarking how Bernard could present within a realist framework a psychological crisis which was never actually uttered, but which was "suggested by a system of references and hints dropped in quiet, almost unobtrusive daily conversation and by those famous silences which made his work a centre of controversy", proposed that the theatre of the unexpressed was a symptom of the problem created by the endeavour to fulfil simultaneously the demands of naturalism and those of a fuller psychology. [43] Una Ellis-Fermor, examining Bernard's technique together with other efforts made "to overcome one of the most serious technical limitations of the dramatic form," to tackle the "problem of the intractable matter that will not be spoken and yet must be conveyed," observed:

---

[41] Bernard, 'Le Théâtre de Demain,' La Revue Mondiale, 1er mars 1923, p. 9.

[42] Bernard, 'Quelques précisions, après deux récentes expériences,' Comœdia, 7 avril 1924, p. 1.

[43] Ronald Peacock, The Poet in the Theatre, London, Macgibbon & Kee, 1961, pp. 11-12.

Everything in the [Bernard] play points towards some essential motive, experience or emotion which is never openly
acknowledged. It is an extremely subtle technique, difficult
to practise and not always easy for an audience to follow,
but it is a penetrating comment upon the nature and function
of the hidden life and unspoken thought of modern civiliza-
tion. It mirrors a world in which what is of deepest significance is indicated only by implication, and the playwright,
contending with almost insuperable difficulties, subdues even
this material to dramatic form. [44]

Notwithstanding, one is justifiably dismayed by the dogged longevity
of the misapprehensions concerning the *théâtre de l'inexprimé,* and
by the persistent reiteration of the narrowest interpretation of Bernard's technique. Pierre Brisson, speaking of the "naïve but salutary
excesses" of writers like Bernard, remarks: "L'essentiel d'un dialogue
devait être constitué par des points de suspension." [45] Pierre-Aimé
Touchard writes of

La *théorie du silence* d'après laquelle les acteurs devaient de
temps en temps s'interrompre et laisser le spectateur écouter
en silence toutes les résonances de la pensée qu'on venait
d'énoncer. Toute une littérature de points de suspension s'est
aussitôt présentée aux lecteurs de manuscrits. Il devenait
évident que chaque auteur jugeait son texte bourré de sentences ou de situations dignes de la réflexion silencieuse des
spectateurs. [46]

Bamber Gascoigne claims that Bernard's theatre "was based on the
dramatic possibilities inherent in the gaps between bits of dialogue." [47]
    A word needs to be said about the innumerable pause-dots which
no reader of Bernard's plays could fail to notice. It appears that
Bernard was one of the first French dramatists to make such extensive
use of pause-dots, which, as Touchard suggests, have since become
commonplace. In fact, an important concomitant of the rise to prom-

---

[44] Una Ellis-Fermor, *The Frontiers of Drama,* London, Methuen, 1964,
pp. 125, 117, 118.
    [45] Pierre Brisson, *Le Théâtre des années folles,* Genève, Éditions du Mi-
lieu du Monde, 1943, p. 41.
    [46] Pierre-Aimé Touchard, *Dionysos* suivi de *L'Amateur de Théâtre,* Paris,
Seuil, 1968, p. 96.
    [47] Bamber Gascoigne, *Twentieth-century Drama,* London, Hutchinson
University Library, 1963, p. 13.

inence of the stage direction in much of modern drama [48] has been
the ever-increasing presence of pause-dots in the published text of
plays; these dots have largely replaced the dash, which in Britain, if
not in France, so often signified a pause. [49] With Bernard, the three
periods frequently occur where the voice is supposed to trail off into
silence in the middle of, or at the end of, a sentence; at other times,
they mark a fleeting moment of hesitation between words, phrases or
syllables — an interval far briefer than that which would be indicated
by *un silence* or *un temps*. Bernard's abundant pause-dots (and other
rest-indications) are of course conditioned by an anxious desire to
transpose to the drama the speech patterns of life, and reveal the
author's profound concern with the whole rhythmic design of the verbal score; moreover, such indications evidently multiply in importance
in plays where words are employed with such tight economy, and
where there is a perpetual cross-illumination between brief utterance
and pregnant silence. Indeed, from this dramatically powerful sym-
biosis derives much of the poignancy of Bernard's plays, and it is at
the risk of destroying the author's intended effects that actor and
director may disregard his notations. In spite of all this, it seems to
us that to imply that Bernard's total achievement lay in his scrupulous
attention to the duration and value of the rest is to allow oneself to
be misled by the *théâtre du silence* label, and to engage in the spread-
ing of an erroneous belief.

The Inspiration of the Cinema

It is significant that the expression *théâtre du silence* had already
been used to refer to the contemporary cinema. In 1921, for example,
Séverin-Mars, playing on different meanings of *théâtre*, was arguing
in defence of the new form:

> Ce peut être un art. Ce peut même être un très grand art,
> car il met en œuvre deux forces, dont l'une est une des

---

[48] Cf. below, p. 174.

[49] Pinter once observed jokingly: "In *The Birthday Party* I employed a
certain amount of dashes in the text, between phrases. In *The Caretaker* I
cut out the dashes and used dots instead. [...] It's possible to deduce from
this that dots are more popular than dashes and that's why *The Caretaker*
had a longer run than *The Birthday Party*." 'Writing for the Theatre,' *Evergreen,* August-September 1964, p. 80.

plus puissantes parmi celles qui agissent directement sur
l'imagination: l'image; et l'autre, la plus subjective de toutes,
peut-être, la plus troublante: le silence. Le cinématographe,
c'est le théâtre du silence. C'est la mise en action de toutes
ses forces et de tout son mystère. C'est son langage. [50]

Bernard must surely have been sensible of the silent film's skilful
exploitation of non-verbal language, and there seems little reason to
doubt that the early cinema's use of silence and image helped to
fasten on his mind the eloquence of movement and gesture as an
alternative to purely verbal eloquence.

Bernard has left on record his admiration for the suggestive power
of the silent film. In a lecture delivered in November 1930 he revealed
that he entertained the oft-cherished wish for an ideal complementary
relationship between play and spectator:

> La mission du théâtre est d'éveiller des échos dans l'âme du
> spectateur. Et il y parviendra d'autant mieux qu'il laissera
> plus de place à ce besoin de rêve qui existe, à l'état clair
> ou à l'état latent, en chaque être humain. Et cela est vrai
> pour tous les arts. [51]

A play, he argued, should not attempt to impose uniformity of response; instead, the creative, imaginative activity which it stimulated
in the spectator should be in accordance with his sensibility, his
intelligence, his personality, his needs. Bernard felt that the silent film
left room for man's "besoin de rêve." He described the film as "un
art plastique en mouvement," which could speak, in the manner of a
picture or a cathedral, directly to the soul of the contemplator;[52] he
recognized in it the non-prescriptive generator of multiple responses
that he wanted the theatre to be. "Le film muet," he continued,
"renfermait une part illimitée de suggestion et cette suggestion dif-
férait d'un spectateur à l'autre. [...] Cette puissance de suggestion
qui était en lui, du fait même de son silence, suffit à expliquer son

---

[50] Séverin-Mars, 'Le théâtre du silence,' *Anthologie du cinéma* (ed. Marcel
Lapierre), Paris, La Nouvelle Édition, 1946, p. 131.

[51] Bernard, 'De la Valeur du silence dans les arts du spectacle,' *Témoignages*, Paris, Coutan-Lambert, 1933, p. 31.

[52] *Ibid.*, p. 21.

succès mondial. Le film muet, c'était l'art qui pouvait parler à chaque homme le langage même qu'il souhaitait entendre." [53]

One detects a note of envy for the resources of the film mingling with a note of nostalgia for its disappearing silence. In fact these pronouncements were made at the time when the talking film was being developed, and when there were fears that sound-recording might turn out to be a two-edged invention. It was widely felt that the cinema, which drew so much of its effectiveness from sequences of images, should be wary of excessive wordiness. When Bernard, in the same lecture, declared that the film, though no longer silent, would eventually learn not so say everything, [54] he was anticipating the remarks René Clair was to make in 1932:

> Le film, même parlant, doit créer des moyens d'expression très différents de ceux dont use la scène. Au théâtre, l'action est conduite par le verbe; ce qu'on y voit est d'une importance secondaire auprès de ce qu'on y entend. Au cinéma, le premier moyen d'expression est l'image, et la partie verbale ou sonore ne doit pas être prépondérante.
>
> On pourrait presque dire qu'un aveugle devant une véritable œuvre dramatique, un sourd devant un véritable film, s'ils perdent l'un et l'autre une part importante de l'œuvre représentée, n'en doivent pas perdre l'essentiel. [55]

It would be difficult to deny the general historical validity of René Clair's statement about the theatre; but the statement would not, we believe, be applicable to Bernard's theatre of the unexpressed. Rather such plays, seeming as they do to embody an aspiration towards the condition of images, would tend to fall into the category of those better appreciated by the deaf than by the blind.

It is relevant to recall here the attitude of Diderot, who, like Bernard, had repeatedly stressed that the drama should not rely exclusively on words, and who sometimes used to block his ears on viewing a play:

---

[53] *Ibid.*, p. 32.
[54] *Ibid.*, p. 34.
[55] René Clair, 'Du Théâtre au Cinéma,' *Anthologie du cinéma* (ed. Marcel Lapierre), p. 265.

Aussitôt que la toile étoit levée, & le moment venu où tous les autres spectateurs se disposoient à écouter, moi, je mettois mes doigts dans mes oreilles, non sans quelqu'étonnement de la part de ceux qui m'environnoient, & qui, ne me comprenant pas, me regardoient presque comme un insensé qui ne venoit à la comédie que pour ne la pas entendre. [56]

One would hesitate to recommend the indiscriminate adoption of this practice. By his own admission, Diderot was well acquainted with the plays that prompted this experiment, in which he was testing the appropriateness of the actors' movements and gestures. What needs to be underlined is that Diderot had many of the qualities ideally required for appreciating Bernard's *théâtre de l'inexprimé* (and the silent film). He responded well to the visual, and with him we already have the silent image being considered as a rival of, and alternative to, words. He spoke, for instance, of Lady Macbeth's rubbing of her hands during the sleep-walking scene as a sublime gesture which oratory could not equal: "Je ne sais rien de si pathétique en discours que le silence & le mouvement des mains de cette femme. Quelle image du remords!" [57] But the wonderment of Diderot's neighbours is a good indication of the extent to which, throughout the ages, theatre-goers have been conditioned to consider themselves primarily as an *audience,* that is to say, primarily as *listeners.* [58]

That *le public* (a conveniently neutral word) ought to be regarded as a body composed of as many *spectateurs* as *auditeurs* was the proposition made by Bernard's theatre of the unexpressed. This theatre can rightfully be described in terms of an audio-visual synthesis. Without denying words their essential rôle, it combated verbal hypertrophy and called for a careful attention to visual detail. In *Martine,* as May Daniels has noted, "the beginnings of love show in little instinctive movements and hesitations; dismay at its hopelessness, agitation at the sight of her cultured rival, anguish at the torments thoughtlessly inflicted on her by the one she loves — all appear in

---

[56] Denis Diderot, *Lettre sur les sourds et muets,* (*Diderot Studies VII*), Genève, Librairie Droz, 1965, p. 52.

[57] *Ibid.,* pp. 47-48.

[58] What Giraudoux has said, in a slightly different connection, is perhaps worth bearing in mind: "[Le Français] vient à la comédie pour écouter, et s'y fatigue si on l'oblige surtout à voir. En fait, il croit à la parole et il ne croit pas au décor." *Littérature,* Paris, Bernard Grasset, 1941, p. 280.

attitude, gesture and expression." [59] It cannot be denied that the spectator at times labours under a disadvantage; the demands made on his sight are sometimes too great. When, in *Printemps*, Maurice teasingly refers to Clarisse as "chère maman," the reader will no doubt notice her "mouvement de crispation qu'elle domine." [60] But however ingenious the lighting effects, such a movement will probably be lost upon the spectator without opera-glasses who is sitting at the back of the gallery of a vast theatre. Instances such as this suggest in Bernard a failure to take proper account of the limitations of the playhouse, and betray his envy for the resources of the psychological novel as well as those of the cinema. In the theatre, lighting is the solitary and insufficient non-verbal way of focussing attention on an unrepeated, unexaggerated, vaguely perceptible motion. Close-up, on the other hand, can perform this function much more effectively, and underline the significance of the unobtrusive. Yet it would be equally misleading to imply that Bernard habitually miscalculated. Few spectators (if any) are likely to miss the mobile and immobile images in *L'Invitation*, [61] the photographic shots of Martine, [62] the final image in *Martine* with its low-pitched intensity: a frustrated but resigned Martine, secluded in her suffering by the insensitivity of a well-intentioned Alfred, who is puffing away contentedly at his pipe. [63]

The Unconscious

Bernard chose as his watchword the following lines:

> To name is to destroy
> To suggest is to create. [64]

---

[59] May Daniels, *The French Drama of The Unspoken*, Edinburgh at the University Press, 1953, p. 184.

[60] Bernard, *Printemps*, Act II, p. 214 in *Théâtre I*, Paris, Albin Michel, 1925. Cf. Hedda Gabler, "suppressing an almost imperceptible smile" as she alleges that she burnt Lövborg's manuscript for Tesman's sake. *Hedda Gabler*, Act IV, p. 255 in *The Oxford Ibsen. Volume VII* (Translated by Jens Arup and James Walter McFarlane), London, Oxford University Press, 1966.

[61] See below, pp. 147-148.

[62] See below, p. 95.

[63] *Martine*, tableau 5, p. 184 in *Théâtre I*.

[64] See Bernard, 'Réflexions sur le théâtre. De la suggestion et de l'artifice,' *Le Théâtre Contemporain*, oct. 1952, p. 47; and Bernard, *Mon Ami le Théâtre*, Paris, Albin Michel, 1958, p. 48.

We have been unable to find the origin of these lines (according to Bernard they are from Shakespeare); but their flavour is strikingly Mallarmean, and Bernard's watchword might easily have been couched in the following terms:

> *Nommer* un objet, c'est supprimer les trois quarts de la jouissance du poëme qui est faite de deviner peu à peu: le *suggérer*, voilà le rêve.

Or:

> Évoquer, dans une ombre exprès, l'objet tu, par des mots allusifs, jamais directs, se réduisant à du silence égal, comporte tentative proche de créer. [65]

The Symbolist heritage is indeed clearly visible in Bernard. Apart from believing that the work of art should not seek to supply everything to the senses but should leave the last word to the imagination, apart from preferring the use of allusion to direct statement and descriptive eloquence, he shared the Symbolists' interest in the deep, inner, secret life of the soul, and their preoccupation with aspects of experience which are elusive, intangible, and, because they defy verbal analysis, inexpressible.

The distance is small between that which is inexpressible because of the inadequacy of the language, or because of an insufficient command of words, and that which is inexpressible because it is hidden from awareness. Not surprisingly, the concept of the unexpressed made an easy marriage with that of the unconscious. It is difficult to say at what precise point Bernard discovered Freud. Yves Le Lay's translation, *La Psychanalyse*, was published by Payot only in 1921; but before then Parisian literary circles, and, more particularly, the circles in which Bernard moved, had been engaged in the discussion of basic Freudian concepts. The man of letters had quickly realized that far from being relevant and important only to medical science, Freud's theories bade fair to leave a mark in every theatre of life, and in effect to alter the course of cultural history; the literary public had quickly realized that the insights into the human mind

---

[65] Stéphane Mallarmé, *Œuvres Complètes*, Paris, Gallimard, 1945, pp. 869, 400.

being proposed by Freud were worthy, even if not of instantaneous approbation and consecration, certainly of scrutiny and debate. It is this debate which gave currency in post-war France to notions such as that of the unconscious, and which would have allowed any aware and alert person to acquire at least a smattering of Freudian psychology.

Fundamental to Freud and to Bernard is the belief that a diagnosis of personality is unlikely to be accurate if one takes into account only deliberate words and actions, and conscious sentiments; one should also consider the actions that are impulsive, the words which slip out by accident or which are carefully avoided, and the unconscious sentiments. The individual is not always competent to provide self-portraits because he may well be unaware of the workings of his inner self. With this in mind Bernard argued:

> Il faut élargir le sens du mot [inexprimé] jusqu'à y englober tout ce qui relève de l'inconscient. Si les hommes n'expriment pas toujours leurs sentiments profonds, ce n'est pas uniquement parce qu'ils les cachent, par honte, par pudeur ou par hypocrisie. C'est encore plus souvent parce qu'ils n'en ont pas conscience, ou parce que ces sentiments arrivent à la conscience claire sous une forme tellement méconnaissable que les mobiles réels n'en sont plus perceptibles. [66]

The question that naturally arises is to what extent one may speak of Freud's influence on Bernard.

'Influence' is a much used term in literary criticism, and too frequently its use betrays a misleading confusion between sequence and causation. Irrefutably, there are instances where a decisive encounter has initially driven a person to write, or has helped to transform a writer's view of his art. Yet we tend perhaps not to pay sufficient attention to the fact that a state of receptivity often prefaces such opportune encounters; the principal effect of these could be to give sanction. In this regard, Gide's comments must surely be echoed by many:

> Il est bien téméraire d'affirmer que l'on aurait pensé de même sans avoir lu tels auteurs qui paraîtront avoir été vos initiateurs. Pourtant il me semble que, n'eussé-je connu ni

---

[66] Bernard, *Témoignages*, Paris, Coutan-Lambert, 1933, p. 29.

Dostoïevsky, ni Nietzsche, ni Freud, ni X. ou Z., j'aurais pensé tout de même, et que j'ai trouvé chez eux plutôt une autorisation qu'un éveil. [67]

One finds that Henri-René Lenormand is often cited as an example of a dramatist who immediately placed himself under the patronage of Freud, and, it is true that in addition to pronouncing on the rôle of the subconscious in the theatre, [68] Lenormand wrote plays which have an unmistakable psychoanalytical content. In one, *Le Mangeur de rêves*, [69] he even went so far as to offer the psychoanalysis of a psychoanalyst, the protagonist deriving morbid pleasure from bringing to the surface the secrets of his disturbed clients. But however great the rôle of psychoanalysis in his theatre, Lenormand (as Bernard pointed out) had written several of his essential plays before his discovery of Freud. Bernard concluded about the Lenormand-Freud relationship: "Il y eut moins là influence que rencontre heureuse." [70] What he failed to add is that a pre-existing state of receptivity in himself, his previous interest in the unconscious facilitated his own "rencontre heureuse" with Freud.

Bernard was decidedly a man who believed in the virtues of the unexpressed, as much in real life as in the drama. His modesty would never have permitted him to proclaim, like Gide, that he had anticipated Freud. [71] But his reticence on this point does not make it less obvious that his interest in the unconscious, though coinciding with the contemporary fashion, was not engendered by it, and that he belonged to the legion of those who did not need Freud to discover the unconscious. In January 1914, for example, Bernard had published a collection of short stories; one of these ('L'Épicier') dealt with the unconscious jealousy and smouldering revolt of a grocer which led him, in spite of himself, to an apparently causeless crime. [72] As Paul Blanchart has observed,

---

[67] André Gide, *Journal: 1889-1939*, Paris, Gallimard, 1955, p. 781.

[68] See, for example, Henri-René Lenormand, 'L'Inconscient dans la littérature dramatique,' *La Chimère. Bulletin d'Art Dramatique*, mai (2) 1922, pp. 74-80.

[69] First performed in January 1922.

[70] Bernard, *Mon Ami le Théâtre*, p. 140.

[71] "Freud. Le freudisme...," wrote Gide in 1922. "Depuis dix ans, quinze ans, j'en fais sans le savoir." *Op. cit.*, p. 729.

[72] Bernard, *L'Épicier*, Paris, Ollendorff, 1914.

Le récit a été construit sur la 'prolongation troublante dans la vie de l'homme des tristesses inavouées de l'enfant': par conséquent, nous sommes dans le domaine familier à la psychanalyse, et ce bien avant qu'il ait été question dans nos lettres du Professeur Freud et de ses théories. [73]

Again, the first of Bernard's experiments with unconscious sentiment in the theatre was *La Maison épargnée*, and, as far as our information goes, he was not at the time of composition acquainted with Freud. [74]

In the play, a German officer is lodged in the house of Fabien Costile, an influential man in an occupied village. When the Germans depart they burn down the village, sparing only Fabien's house. In the spared house the homeless are sheltered, the hungry are fed, the naked are clothed; yet a ground swell of suspicion and envy begins to rise. In the minds of the villagers, Fabien soon becomes a spy whom the Germans have rewarded by leaving his house standing. Finally Fabien and his family, ostracized despite their charitableness, decide to leave the village, and at the last moment Fabien runs back to his house and sets it afire.

Léon Lemonnier remarks that Fabien, on burning his house, is acting like "un criminel cherchant à détruire la preuve de sa mauvaise action." [75] Indeed what leads to this final impulsive act of destruction is Fabien's sense of guilt, which is irrational in so far as he has not committed any act for which he may reproach himself. During the Occupation he had to remember that complete non-cooperation would have made the Germans more severe in their dealings with the village as a whole; but he successfully walked the tightrope and was never more helpful than absolutely necessary. He and his family were civil to their uninvited guest without being cordial. On this score, therefore, his conscience is clear and the villagers' suspicions are unfounded. Nevertheless, while Fabien does not take upon himself the offences attributed to him, the villagers' unfounded suspicions precipitate the formation of his guilt complex. This is where the rôle of the un-conscious is capital, the author's premiss being that a wish can be

---

[73] Paul Blanchart, *Jean-Jacques Bernard*, Paris, Coutan-Lambert, 1928, p. 31.
[74] The play was composed between 1916 and 1919; first performed 5 November 1919 at the *Théâtre Antoine*.
[75] Léon Lemonnier, 'Le Théâtre de M. Jean-Jacques Bernard,' *Choses de théâtre*, mars 1923, p. 270.

unconscious and that remorse can follow such a wish. Irrational as Fabien's guilty feeling may appear, it is none the less motivated from within: it springs from the unconscious wish that he and his family could remain immune to the wrath of the Germans. Though he has done nothing, such as actually collaborating, with a view to having the wish fulfilled, once it is fulfilled his 'inexplicable' remorse ensues. His remark to his daughter: "Je n'ai rien fait de mal, pourtant! Et j'ai comme des remords," [76] and his statement after setting fire to his house: "Ce qu'il fallait, c'était effacer la tache inexplicable," [77] show his act of destruction to be an instinctive gesture of atonement for having had the wish and having benefited from its accomplishment.

Fabien's case bears a certain resemblance to that of Halvard Solness. The master builder realizes that he has acted unrighteously, having smashed Knut Brovik because he needed room for himself, having hindered Ragnar's progress, and having in a sense stolen Ragnar's fiancée. On letting himself be persuaded by Hilde to hang the wreath over the spire of the new house, though he knows full well that he suffers from a morbid dread of heights, he is yielding to an incitement to expiate his misdeeds through self-destruction. He is in fact obsessed throughout with the idea of atonement, explaining to Dr. Herdal why he allows his wife to harbour unjust suspicions in the following terms: "I somehow... enjoy the mortification of letting Aline do me an injustice. [...] It's rather like paying off a tiny instalment on a huge immeasurable debt." [78] A major part of his guilt complex has to do with the wrong he *feels* he has done to his wife, and it is here that his remorse resembles that of Fabien Costile. "I've never done you any wrong. Never knowingly, never deliberately, that is," he says to Aline. "And yet — I feel weighed down by a great crushing sense of guilt." [79] The retraction he makes is instructive: he admits the possible existence of past offences, but denies premeditation. Aline, however, does not feel wronged, and, like Dr. Herdal, she finds Solness's compunction difficult to fathom.

---

[76] Act II, p. 63 in *La Maison épargnée*, Paris, Librairie Théâtrale, Artistique et Littéraire, 1920.

[77] Act III, p. 84.

[78] *The Master Builder*, Act I, p. 372 in *The Oxford Ibsen. Volume VII* (Translated by Jens Arup and James Walter McFarlane), London, Oxford University Press, 1966.

[79] Act II, p. 396.

We learn subsequently, from his lengthy confession to Hilde, that his guilty conscience with regard to his wife derives from no concrete act but from a wish. Having noticed the crack in the chimney and willed a fire to destroy the house, he is convinced of his responsibility for the fire, although it has been established that there was no connection between the crack and the fire.

Solness has engaged in soul-searching, has sought out the sources of his guilty feeling, has forced repressed memories to the surface. The play begins when he is in a state of relative self-awareness. The moment is right for him to ventilate the fruits of his introspection. His confessions to Dr. Herdal and to Aline are not brought to completion; the former is absorbed in his own bewilderment, the latter thinks Halvard is mad. But there is Hilde. "Oh, Hilde," Solness bursts out, "you don't know how glad I am that you've come! At last I have somebody I can talk to." [80] Thanks to her we hear the results of his self-enquiry. Bernard captures his protagonist at a completely different phase. Fabien has reached the primary stage of detecting his remorse. The main reason why he does not promptly go beyond this stage to achieve self-knowledge is that the 'guilty' wish to find favour with the Germans is entombed in the unconscious. Fabien clearly did not relentlessly will that the village be burnt down and that his house be left standing, in the way that Solness willed the fire. Another probable reason is that his fear of what he might discover makes him reluctant even to begin to examine himself. We do not at all get the impression that Fabien has delved into himself, found the motive for his compunction, and carefully concealed it from all (though such a process is not alien to Bernard's theatre). Fabien is Bernard's archetypal unconscious man, who feels remorse without knowing the cause, and who goes through the motions of atonement without fully realizing it. Bernard inverts the procedure followed by Ibsen and creates, as it were, a Halvard Solness in a less communicative, less introspective and less conscious miniature.

We do not know for certain how much first-hand knowledge Bernard had of Freudian psychology, or how much was gleaned from the discussions taking place in Parisian literary circles in the early twenties. A number of statements made by him around this time indicate that he was aware of the debate and of its significance, and

---

[80] Act II, p. 402.

that he considered psychoanalysis to be a useful new tool for the dramatist. [81] He certainly did not try to minimize the Freudian implications of *Printemps*, [82] a play in which conduct is motivated by repressed sentiment, and one instinct hidden from awareness by its opposite:

> Il importe en effet de ne pas perdre de vue que jusqu'à la fin Clarisse s'ignore. Les plus purs d'entre nous peuvent porter dans leur cœur des desseins monstrueux qu'ils ne soupçonnent pas. Pour que Clarisse se comprenne, il faudra que ne se produise pas une catastrophe préparée par elle à son propre insu. Tout le deuxième acte est fait de ses manœuvres inconscientes. Quand elle oublie de faire à son gendre une commission dont dépend peut-être le bonheur de sa fille, on s'est demandé s'il s'agissait d'un oubli volontaire. Certainement oui, si l'on admet aussi qu'il n'est pas conscient. Y a-t-il donc des oublis volontaires inconscients? Pourquoi pas? C'est d'ailleurs sur cette question que Freud a écrit ses pages les moins discutables. Qu'on m'excuse d'introduire Freud là-dedans, mais ces pages-là sont précisément l'A B C de la psychanalyse. [83]

We should not now have to emphasize that *Printemps* was not an attempt to be fashionable. Bernard was principally concerned to use situations where characters do not put what they are thinking into words, and where the essential is communicated to the audience without being expressed. But already in *La Maison épargnée* the distinction was present in the author's mind between sentiments which are known but not formulated, and the inexpressible unconscious. Whether he would have continued along the lines of 'L'Épicier' and *La Maison épargnée* and arrived at *Printemps* had he never heard of Freud, is a matter for inexhaustible speculation. What does appear to have resulted from his "happy encounter" with Freud was a crystallization of various inklings into ideas which could be examined. Freud's theories, and the vocabulary of psychoanalysis, afforded Ber-

---

81 Witness Henri Rambaud et Pierre Varillon, 'Enquête sur les maîtres de la jeune littérature: Les Auteurs dramatiques' (Bernard's reply), *La Revue Hebdomadaire*, 16 déc. 1922, pp. 334-335.

82 First performed in March 1924.

83 Bernard, 'Quelques précisions, après deux récentes expériences,' *Comœdia*, 7 avril 1924, pp. 1-2.

nard and others a proper framework for considering what had been unorganized, ill-defined, intuitive notions.

Freud, then, brought to Bernard consciousness of the unconscious content of *La Maison épargnée*, and consciousness of the unconscious as a potential source of revitalization for a genre which was increasingly being described as moribund. One of his compelling interests was in renewal, and the possibilities offered by the unconscious for the renewal of the material of the drama were no less considerable than those offered for the renewal of method. Further, the choice of 'unconscious material' not only provided him with a supreme justification for the method he favoured, but also helped him in his movement towards quietude in the drama; for to treat of subconscious motives, repressed instincts and unknown desires operating in stealthy and silent fashion was one way of 'internalizing' violent action and eliminating sound and fury.

Antecedents

The habit of expatiating on intimate sentiments had long remained unquestioned in the French theatre, and occasionally had the most awkward results. It is true that Henry Becque, in his 'slices of life,' avoided the sermon-like tones of a Dumas *fils*; it is true that his repudiation of lengthy tirades lent to his dialogue an authenticity which was usually absent from plays in the Scribe tradition. Yet the language of his plays is not always as 'natural' as it is reputed to be, and in *Les Corbeaux* there is a conspicuous example of unnatural wordiness and its adverse effects. In Act II Madame Vigneron moans the death of her husband:

> MADAME VIGNERON. (*Pleurant, son mouchoir à la main.*) Excusez-moi, madame, je suis honteuse de pleurer comme ça devant vous, mais je ne peux pas retenir mes larmes. Quand je pense qu'il n'y a pas un mois, il était là, à la place où vous êtes, et que je ne le reverrai plus. [84]
>
> ... ...
>
> MADAME VIGNERON. (*Pleurant, son mouchoir à la main.*) Quel malheur, monsieur Teissier, quel épouvantable malheur! Mon pauvre Vigneron. C'est le travail qui l'a tué! Pourquoi

---

[84] Henry Becque, *Les Corbeaux*, Act II, sc. i, p. 101 in *Théâtre Complet II*, Paris, Charpentier, 1890.

travaillait-il autant? [...] Ah! il voulait voir ses enfants heureux pendant sa vie et leur laisser une fortune après sa mort. [85]

... ...

MADAME VIGNERON. *(Pleurant, son mouchoir à la main.)* Quel malheur, monsieur Bourdon, quel épouvantable malheur! Mon pauvre Vigneron! Ce n'est pas assez de le pleurer nuit et jour, je sens bien là que je ne lui survivrai pas. [86]

... ...

MADAME VIGNERON. *(Pleurant, son mouchoir à la main.)* Quel malheur, monsieur Lefort, quel épouvantable malheur! Mon pauvre Vigneron! Je ne me consolerai jamais de la perte que j'ai faite. [87]

The type of repetition which Becque employs here is effective as a comic device, and would be natural and understandable if he had at all any comic intentions at this point. As an attempt to impress upon us Madame Vigneron's sorrow at the death of her husband, the repetition of her lament fails, and has the effect of making us ask how genuine her grief is; and yet there is no evidence in the rest of the play to suggest that her affliction is a pretence. Bernard was to apply himself to the task of exploring less artificial ways of translating emotions which lyricism, rhetoric and grandiloquence had helped to falsify. This endeavour was based on a number of self-evident truths: that people do not habitually seek to clothe in words everything that passes through their minds, that their words sometimes bear little direct relation to their most urgent preoccupations, that at moments of intense emotion they often react with a few disjointed words, if not with complete silence.

It would appear that the First War brought in its wake a heightened awareness of these axioms and a heightened mistrust of oratorical virtuosity. Maurice Coindreau points out that during the war years one had heard — to satiety — all manner of cheap and brassy utterance:

Les cuivres entonnaient des hymnes à des héros éphémères. C'était à qui vanterait ses hauts faits, à qui ferait parade de

---

[85] Act II, sc. 2, pp. 107-108.
[86] Act II, sc. 7, pp. 126-127.
[87] Act II, sc. 9, p. 132.

ses souffrances. On jouait à la mère spartiate, au père cor-
nélien, on versait ses angoisses dans des lettres à effet, dans
le secret espoir qu'elles seraient un jour publiées. [88]

Étienne Guilhou, for his part, says that the War taught a love of
simplicity and a distaste for empty phrases. He proceeds:

> L'épouvante des attentes mornes sous le ciel fracassé d'obus
> nous a enseigné la valeur du silence, et nous avons appris à
> lire dans les yeux de nos compagnons, sans qu'ils aient besoin
> de parler. [89]

It is worth stressing, though, that the War accelerated rather than
initiated these trends; well before the War, in a different cultural
context, W. B. Yeats had remarked on the tendency of "educated and
well-bred people" not to wear their hearts upon their sleeves, and to
look silently into the fireplace when deeply moved. [90]

Undeniably, the features of conduct on which Bernard concentrated have ancient antecedents. Not unexpectedly, various elements
of his *théâtre de l'inexprimé* are prefigured in various places. The
Bible itself yields instances of the techniques of the unexpressed; in
comparing Homer's use of direct discourse with the style of the account of the sacrifice of Isaac, Auerbach aptly observes:

> The personages speak in the Bible story too; but their speech
> does not serve, as does speech in Homer, to manifest, to
> externalize thoughts — on the contrary, it serves to indicate
> thoughts which remain unexpressed. God gives his command
> in direct discourse, but he leaves his motives and his purpose
> unexpressed; Abraham, receiving the command, says nothing
> and does what he has been told to do. The conversation
> between Abraham and Isaac on the way to the place of
> sacrifice is only an interruption of the heavy silence and
> makes it all the more burdensome. The two of them, Isaac
> carrying the wood and Abraham with fire and a knife, 'went
> together.' Hesitantly, Isaac ventures to ask about the ram,

---

[88] Maurice Coindreau, *La Farce est jouée*, New York, Éditions de la Maison Française, 1942, p. 219.

[89] Étienne Guilhou, *Quelques tendances du théâtre d'après-guerre en
France*, Paris, Boivin & Cie, 1926, p. 22.

[90] W. B. Yeats, 'Discoveries,' *Collected Works. Vol. VIII*, Stratford-on-
Avon, Shakespeare Head Press, 1908, p. 20.

and Abraham gives the well-known answer. Then the text
repeats: 'So they went both of them together.' Everything
remains unexpressed. [. . .] Thoughts and feeling remain unexpressed, are only suggested by the silence and the fragmentary speeches. [91]

Bernard has often stressed that he did not devise the notion of
the unexpressed. "J'ai été frappé," he said, "de la valeur dramatique
des sentiments inexprimés et, loin de présenter cela comme une nou-
veauté, j'ai puisé un exemple dans Marivaux, comme j'aurais pu aussi
facilement le trouver dans Racine." [92] Doubtless, unexpressed sentiments do help at times to increase dramatic intensity in Racine; we
have only to think of Phèdre's avowal to Œnone. Doubtless, one can
agree with Frédéric Deloffre when he says of Marivaux:

> Dans les comédies, les mots valent moins par ce qu'ils ex-
> priment que par ce qu'ils impliquent. Ils sont moins riches
> de sens exprimé que de sous-entendus, et ces sous-entendus
> eux-mêmes sont encore à interpréter par rapport à une
> réalité inconsciente. [93]

Obviously, however, it is not a matter of taking away the confidants
from Racine and the emotional tirades from Marivaux and obtaining
a theatre of the unexpressed. What formed just a part of the dramatic
instinct of Racine and Marivaux, what can be found in germ in
myriad plays, was consciously pursued and given sustained emphasis
by Bernard.

There are clear signs of a similar emphasis on the unexpressed in
some of Maeterlinck's plays, and it is significant that Bernard, in
his introductory note to *Martine,* should have sought sanction for
his technique by quoting Maeterlinck:

> 'Dès que nous avons vraiment *quelque chose à dire* nous
> sommes *obligés* de nous taire.' [94] On n'a peut-être rien écrit
> qui s'appliquât plus strictement au théâtre. [95]

---

91 Erich Auerbach, *Mimesis* (Translated by Willard Trask), New York,
Doubleday Anchor Books, 1957, pp. 8-9.
92 Bernard, 'Avant-Propos,' *Théâtre I,* Paris, Albin Michel, 1925, p. 6.
93 Frédéric Deloffre, *Une Préciosité nouvelle. Marivaux et le Marivaudage,* Paris, Société d'Édition Les Belles Lettres, 1955, p. 194.
94 From Maurice Maeterlinck, *Le Trésor des humbles,* Paris, Société du
Mercure de France, 1896, p. 9.
95 Bernard, 'Le silence au théâtre,' *La Chimère. Bulletin d'Art Dramatique,* mai (2) 1922, p. 67.

Nevertheless, Bernard never specifically admitted an indebtedness to Maeterlinck; he reserved his tribute for Jules Renard: "Mon père mis à part, qui en tant que père était un cas spécial, Renard fut le seul écrivain vivant qui eut sur moi une influence profonde." [96] To this statement may be juxtaposed a remark by Amiel:

> Il est un autre écrivain dont je ne crois véritablement pas avoir subi l'influence, mais dont j'ai toutefois beaucoup appris: c'est le grand Jules Renard. Cet écrivain considérable et qu'on ne connaît pas assez est, il faut le dire, le maître de la synthèse, du raccourci. [97]

Indeed it is not merely that Renard's playlets tended towards the concise, unadorned, restrained language that was to mark the *théâtre de l'inexprimé,* but that *Poil de Carotte* presented an imposing model of reticent fortitude in the person of M. Lepic — a man so devoted to the practice of keeping his own counsel that for some sixteen years he has abstained from revealing the chagrin caused by his unhappy marriage, a man who, when eventually brought to give expression to this chagrin, does so in the least expansive of terms, a man whom Poil de Carotte depicts as follows:

> C'est un homme préoccupé et taciturne. [...] Il aime mieux se faire comprendre par un geste que par un mot. S'il veut du pain, il ne dit pas: 'Annette, donnez-moi le pain.' Il se lève et va le chercher lui-même, jusqu'à ce que vous preniez l'habitude de vous apercevoir qu'il a besoin de pain. [...] Il m'aime à sa manière, silencieusement. [98]

When one considers the whole of Renard's dramatic output, however, it becomes plain that he was not preoccupied, to as high a degree as Maeterlinck, with silence within and outside the drama.

As May Daniels has observed, "Maeterlinck's *Théâtre de l'Inexprimé* consists [...] of the eight plays from *La Princesse Maleine*

---

[96] Bernard, *Mon père Tristan Bernard,* Paris, Albin Michel, 1955, p. 115.

[97] Henri Rambaud et Pierre Varillon, 'Enquête sur les maîtres de la jeune littérature: Les Auteurs dramatiques' (Amiel's reply), *La Revue Hebdomadaire,* 16 déc. 1922, p. 340.

[98] Jules Renard, *Poil de Carotte,* sc. 3, p. 108 in *Théâtre Complet,* Paris, Gallimard, 1959.

to *La Mort de Tintagiles,* written between 1889 and 1894. [99] In these plays he endeavours to communicate philosophical truths through the medium of the Unexpressed. [...] He is most effective when he communicates not the truth itself, but the intensity of feeling produced by this truth." [100] The main agent in these plays is the malevolent force of doom, translating itself into death and heralded by bad dreams, thunder and lightning, the appearance of strange birds, and other ominous signs. In the words of Maeterlinck,

> On y a foi à d'énormes puissances, invisibles et fatales, dont nul ne sait les intentions, mais que l'esprit du drame suppose malveillantes, attentives à toutes nos actions, hostiles au sourire, à la vie, à la paix, au bonheur. [101]

The author's tendency is to 'internalize' the action, which is reduced to the effect created by the invisible main agent on the persons visible on the stage. The characters' response to the doom which they sense is fear, and the dramatic interest centres on the attitudes and gestures which signal the intensive growth of this fear.

It is in this sense that the plays, revolving round a silent drama, fall into the category of theatre of the unexpressed, the over-simplified truths about the horrible nature of death and the relentless nature of destiny being conveyed without rhetoric. This also is the point at which Maeterlinck's dramatic practice coincides with his deliberations on silence:

> Si je vous parle en ce moment des choses les plus graves, [...] de la mort ou de la destinée, je n'atteins pas la mort, [...] ou le destin, et malgré mes efforts, il restera toujours entre nous une vérité qui n'est pas dite, qu'on n'a même pas l'idée de dire. [...] Cette vérité, c'est *notre vérité* sur la mort, le destin [...]; et nous n'avons pu l'entrevoir qu'en silence. [102]

---

[99] *La Princesse Maleine* (1889), *L'Intruse* (1890), *Les Aveugles* (1890), *Les Sept Princesses* (1891), *Pelléas et Mélisande* (1892), *Alladine et Palomides* (1894), *Intérieur* (1894), *La Mort de Tintagiles* (1894).

[100] May Daniels, *The French Drama of The Unspoken,* Edinburgh at the University Press, 1953, pp. 93-94.

[101] Maurice Maeterlinck, 'Préface,' *Théâtre I,* Paris, Fasquelle, 1929, p. ix.

[102] Maurice Maeterlinck, *Le Trésor des humbles,* Paris, Société du Mercure de France, 1896, pp. 21-22.

That Maeterlinck was obsessively attentive to the value of silence is revealed by various other statements in his book of essays *Le Trésor des humbles*. Inspired by Carlyle's "Speech is of Time, Silence is of Eternity," [103] he makes the contrast between the transitory nature of the spoken word and the ineffaceable quality of silence, which he claims is the sole depository of eternal truth. In matters of love, therefore, what resists the passing of time and defies oblivion is silence:

> Ce qu'avant tout vous vous rappellerez d'un être aimé profondément, ce n'est pas les paroles qu'il a dites ou les gestes qu'il a faits, mais les silences que vous avez vécus ensemble; car c'est la *qualité* de ces silences qui seule a révélé la *qualité* de votre amour et de vos âmes. [104]

Maeterlinck propounded various ideas which apparently were also at the roots of Bernard's theatre of the unexpressed. Apart from believing that it is silence which determines the flavour of love, Maeterlinck felt that there are several other occasions in life when silence is the most natural and spontaneous reaction; a departure, a return, great joy or, most of all, misfortune do not welcome rhetoric. His thesis was that given the inadequacy of words, one is obliged to be silent when one is gripped by deep emotion or when one really has something to say, and this proposition was in keeping with his theory of tacit communication between minds:

> Dès que les lèvres dorment, les âmes se réveillent et se mettent à l'œuvre. [...] Si vous voulez vraiment vous livrer à quelqu'un, taisez-vous. [105]

Lengthy discourse indicates an attempt to camouflage genuine states of mind by preventing that mystical tacit communication for which silence is an absolute prerequisite:

> Nous ne parlons qu'aux heures [...] où *nous ne voulons pas* apercevoir nos frères. [106]

---

[103] Thomas Carlyle, *Sartor Resartus* (ed. Rev. James Wood), London, Dent, 1902, p. 385. The first two pages of *Le Trésor des humbles* are a translation of part of Book III, ch. iii.

[104] *Le Trésor des humbles*, p. 11.

[105] *Ibid.*, p. 17.

[106] *Ibid.*, p. 10.

On a number of occasions in Maeterlinck's plays, characters echo
the author's ideas on tacit communication and on the inadequacy of
language. In *Alladine et Palomides* King Ablamore says to his daughter Astolaine:

> Il y a un moment où les âmes se touchent et savent tout
> sans que l'on ait besoin de remuer les lèvres. [107]

In *Aglavaine et Sélysette* Aglavaine says to her sister-in-law Sélysette:

> Parlons comme des êtres humains, comme de pauvres êtres
> humains que nous sommes, qui parlent comme ils peuvent,
> avec leurs mains, avec leurs yeux, avec leur âme, quand ils
> veulent dire des choses plus réelles que celles que les paroles
> peuvent atteindre. [108]

Often, though, one finds that Maeterlinck's characters spare no efforts
to analyse their feelings (especially their feelings of love), and to
communicate them as precisely as they can, while remaining conscious
of the vanity of their efforts. Witness Méléandre, in *Aglavaine et
Sélysette*, trying to explain to Aglavaine his complex emotions with
regard to her and to his wife Sélysette:

> Il me semble parfois que je l'aime presque autant que je
> t'aime, et parfois que je l'aime plus que toi, parce qu'elle
> est plus loin de moi ou plus inexplicable ... Et puis, lorsque
> je te revois, tout s'efface autour d'elle, je ne l'aperçois plus ...
> et cependant, si je la perdais pour toujours, je ne pourrais
> jamais t'embrasser sans tristesse. [...] Mais je ne puis l'aimer
> qu'en toi seule, et quand tu seras loin, je ne l'aimerai plus. [109]

Méléandre is the Maeterlinckian protagonist at his most garrulous,
and his outpourings help to cast an ironical shadow on Maeterlinck's
statements on silence and love in *Le Trésor des humbles*. The contradictions between the ideas presented in those essays and the
author's dramatic practice is further visible in his use of monologues
in which characters grapple with events and with themselves. [110] Such

---

[107] Act III, sc. 1, p. 182 in *Théâtre II*, Paris, Fasquelle, 1929.
[108] Act II, sc. 2, p. 44 in *Théâtre III*, Paris, Fasquelle, 1930.
[109] Act III, sc. 2, p. 78.
[110] Notably Le Médecin in Act III, sc. 4, Le Roi in Act III, sc. 5, and
Maleine in Act IV, sc. 3 of *La Princesse Maleine* (*Théâtre I*); and Pelléas
in Act IV, sc. 4 of *Pelléas et Mélisande* (*Théâtre II*).

monologues were to be deliberately eschewed by Bernard, in whose plays self-analysis is rarely expressed verbally. It is important also to underline a fundamental difference in the use of the unexpressed by Maeterlinck and Bernard. Maeterlinck was concerned to evoke the imposing mysteries of the universe, to strike into our hearts an awe of the unknown, as he led us into a fabulous world of sombre forests and sinister castles; Bernard remained more firmly rooted in the immediate present, and chose to concentrate on the common manifestations of ordinary human existence.

Maeterlinck argued in favour of a *tragique quotidien*, which he felt to be more authentic, more profound, and more in accordance with our true being than the tragedy of impressive events. Deploring the tendency of other dramatists to introduce violent external action, he was drawn towards the concept of a drama of apparent immobility, to the concept of static theatre: [111]

> Il m'est arrivé de croire qu'un vieillard assis dans son fauteuil, attendant simplement sous la lampe, écoutant sans le savoir toutes les lois éternelles qui règnent autour de sa maison, interprétant sans le comprendre ce qu'il y a dans le silence des portes et des fenêtres et dans la petite voix de la lumière, [...] il m'est arrivé de croire que ce vieillard immobile vivait en réalité d'une vie plus profonde, plus humaine et plus générale que l'amant qui étrangle sa maîtresse, le capitaine qui remporte une victoire ou 'l'époux qui venge son honneur.' [112]

Maeterlinck's preference (at that particular stage of his career) for action reduced to the bare essentials was shared to a certain extent by Bernard, as witness the heavy dependence of the latter's plays on the non-event, and their avoidance of overtly dramatic scenes. It should be remembered, however, that violent external action is by no means absent from Maeterlinck's plays, and that occasionally it runs the risk of distracting the audience's attention from the more silent, internal drama. Such is the case of *La Princesse Maleine*, where

---

[111] Maeterlinck later dismissed this concept as an almost worthless theory of his youth. See *Le Double Jardin*, Paris, Fasquelle, 1904, pp. 119-120; and Barrett H. Clark, *A Study of the Modern Drama*, New York-London, D. Appleton-Century Company, 1938, p. 163.

[112] *Le Trésor des humbles*, pp. 187-188.

the strangling of Maleine and the killing of the madman, Prince Hjalmar's execution of Queen Anne and his own suicide all take place on the stage. [113] Yet Maeterlinck definitely moved in the direction of the simple and unspectacular subject-matter of the undynamic play. He reached his limit with *Les Aveugles*, which is of interest to the modern reader in that in two main ways it seems to prefigure *En attendant Godot*: the twelve blind men and women, awaiting a priest who is supposed to take them back to the Home and who sits dead right beside them, foreshadow the two tramps; the disintegration of action, in the traditional sense, which we see beginning in *Les Aveugles* progresses to a complete lack of cohesive action in *Godot*.

By the turn of the century Maeterlinck had both dismissed the concept of static theatre and considerably reduced the rôle of the unexpressed in his plays; it is uncertain whether in the twenties he would readily have accepted the title of grand initiator of the *théâtre de l'inexprimé*. [114] There are conspicuous differences between Maeterlinck and Bernard: Bernard's reflections and 'unexpressed' plays do not have the undertones of mysticism we find in Maeterlinck; Bernard's plays involve a more austere refusal of analysis and protracted verbalization than Maeterlinck's. Despite these differences, however, despite the changes in the character of Maeterlinck's work, the eight plays which he wrote between 1889 and 1894, and his deliberations on silence and on the theatre indicate that he was Bernard's most significant precursor writing in French. [115]

---

[113] Act IV, sc. 5; Act V, sc. 4 in *Théâtre I*.

[114] We have been unable to find any record of Maeterlinck's response to Bernard's plays.

[115] The rôle of precursor may also be attributed to the Polish poet and dramatist Cyprjan Kamil Norwid (1821-83). Norwid argued for poetic and dramatic forms which would derive their strength from the interplay of the spoken word, its concealed meanings and implications, the unspoken word, and silence. "His task as an excavator of deeper meanings was to show drama behind the stage, the inward action modestly hidden under the outward. His heroism was the heroism of silence and self-awareness" (Jerzy Pietrkiewicz, 'Introducing Norwid,' *The Slavonic and East European Review*, Dec. 1948, p. 236). Unfortunately, his plays, such as *Wanda* (1860) and *Krakus* (1860), remained buried in Poland for too long to make any discussion on his relationship with Maeterlinck, Bernard or Amiel anything more than conjectural.

Bernard and the 'Zeitgeist'

The cultural historian frequently notices similar developments occurring in different places at the same time. This common phenomenon often permits us to visualize the tendencies of a particular era; but it does not always offer a rigorously precise explanation. Bernard relates how certain affinities were noticed between his work and that of an Italian contemporary Cesare Lodovici, and how critics assumed that Chekhov was their common ancestor:

> A l'époque où nous écrivions l'un et l'autre les pièces où nos amis communs voyaient des sensibilités parentes, je ne connaissais même pas le nom de Lodovici, et Lodovici n'avait rien lu de moi. En parlant ensemble, nous eûmes la surprise de constater que nous avions passé à peu près à la même époque par les mêmes idées esthétiques, par les mêmes doutes aussi. Bien mieux, il me dit: 'En Italie, on considère que vous avez dû subir l'influence de Tchékhov.' Or, c'est exactement ce qu'en France on m'avait dit de Lodovici. J'ajoute que c'est ce qui me donna l'idée de lire Tchékhov, dont Lodovici, lui aussi, ne prit connaissance qu'après coup. [116]

Literary history is of course replete with hasty equations between resemblance and consanguinity, and Bernard's cautionary tale is gladly received. So while we propose to examine the most interesting of the resemblances which, undeniably, exist between Bernard and not only Chekhov but also Ibsen and Pirandello, this examination will serve to show how Bernard's drama stood in relation to a general drift of Western drama, rather than to prove cases of direct, conscious influence.

Familiar to all theatre-goers is the mechanism used by the dramatist as he leads us progressively to the carefully prepared climax of a crucial scene. A noticeable feature of Bernard's theatre is the habitual omission of the logical last term of such a progression. It is this procedure that operates when, in *L'Invitation,* Olivier and Marie-Louise fail to have the *explication* we were expecting, [117] or when Martine, on the point of declaring her love, appears suddenly to lose

---

[116] Bernard, *Témoignages*, Paris, Coutan-Lambert, 1933, p. 44.
[117] See below, pp. 138 ff.

her voice. [118] This Bernardian version of 'brinkmanship' shows his disregard for the exigencies of the well-made play, his disdain for the cult of the *scène à faire*; but the denial of sure dramatic effects is also a sign of an attempt to de-theatricalize the theatre and dramatize the undramatic — an attempt in which he was preceded by Chekhov. Secret illusions, unfulfilled desires, vague disappointments, boredom, dissatisfaction, langour and inertia provide the matter for Bernard's plays. To his penchant for seemingly eventless drama was added his alienation from the convention of a clearly-delineated, well-rounded plot, and, as in Chekhov, the final curtain tends to signal less a conclusion than an interruption in the course of non-events.

L'Invitation (to which we shall devote the fourth chapter) bears a number of resemblances to *The Three Sisters,* the first being the parallel between the Moscow theme in Chekhov's play and the Argentina theme in Bernard's. [119] The provincial wife living in a house surrounded by fir-trees, who longs to escape from what she feels is a dismal, rutty existence, would be perfectly at home with the sisters; the lingering rhythm of day-to-day life which Bernard captures, the portrayal of Marie-Louise's slow internal evolution would, one imagines, easily have passed muster with Chekhov. In both plays, one is confronted with the ordinary destinies of little, unheroic, forbearing people, whose aspirations remain aspirations because they lack the energy to realize them; we in the audience are faced with dialogue that often looks aimless, and with a penury of what we usually regard as dramatic action.

Chekhov and Bernard veered towards an elimination of striking peripeteias, and of the most theatrical and spectacular aspects of the genre. But their method involved not so much an abolition of action as a displacement of the centre of gravity towards a deeper level of action; the action visible on the surface becomes an outward sign of the complex patterns of activity below the surface.

Words assume special functions here. Sometimes they alternate with short evocative pauses, or yield entirely to a longer silence. Often they cease to attempt a direct translation of the characters' inner movement, acting instead as a smoke-screen of hesitant triviality behind which lies an unexpressed preoccupation. We may instance

---

[118] See below, pp. 75-77.
[119] The main difference is that Marie-Louise has never seen Argentina.

the abortive interview in *The Cherry Orchard* between Varya and Lopakhin — an interview which Mrs Ranevsky, Varya, and Lopakhin himself hoped would result in his proposing to Varya: [120]

> VARYA. (*Spends a long time examining the luggage.*) Funny, can't find it.
> LOPAKHIN. What are you looking for?
> VARYA. Packed it myself, and can't remember. (*Pause.*)
> LOPAKHIN. Where are you going now, Varya?
> VARYA. Me? To the Ragulins'. I've agreed to look after their house — to be their housekeeper, I suppose.
> LOPAKHIN. In Yashnevo, isn't it? About fifty miles from here. (*Pause.*) Aye.... So life's come to an end in this house.
> VARYA. (*Examining the luggage.*) Where can it be? Must have put it in the trunk. Yes, life's come to an end in this house. It will never come back.
> LOPAKHIN. I'm off to Kharkov by the same train. Lots to see to there. I'm leaving Yepikhodov here to keep an eye on things. I've given him the job.
> VARYA. Have you?
> LOPAKHIN. This time last year it was already snowing, you remember. Now, it's calm and sunny. A bit cold, though. Three degrees of frost.
> VARYA. I haven't looked. (*Pause.*) Anyway, our thermometer's broken. (*Pause. A voice from outside, through the door: 'Mr. Lopakhin!'*)
> LOPAKHIN. (*As though he had long been expecting this call.*) Coming! (*Goes out quickly.*)
> (*Varya sits down on the floor, lays her head on a bundle of clothes, and sobs quietly.*) [121]

In other cases, the words correspond more closely to the characters' preoccupations, while the dialogue becomes less of an interchange. What one speaker says becomes a spur to meditation in the other, and the bulk of the dialogue consists of more or less self-addressed remarks. Witness the following extract from Bernard's *Le Feu qui reprend mal*, in which the recently returned prisoner of war speaks with his wife:

---

[120] The interview also provides an example of that 'brinkmanship' which we associate with Bernard.

[121] Anton Chekhov, *The Cherry Orchard*, Act IV, pp. 240-241 in *Four Plays* (Translated by David Magarshack), London, Allen and Unwin, 1970.

BLANCHE. Tu vas trouver bien des changements autour de nous...

ANDRÉ. Le gros Lubin ne reviendra pas. Il est mort au camp. Ç'a été bien triste.

BLANCHE. Sa femme ne le sait pas. C'est affreux! Dieu! quand je pense que... Ah! je te dirai quels moments j'ai passés... Et si peu de nouvelles. Rien depuis trois mois.

ANDRÉ. On n'écrivait pas comme on voulait. C'était bien dur les derniers temps.

BLANCHE. Nous n'en pouvions plus. Je ne sais pas comment j'ai résisté.

ANDRÉ. Ce pauvre Lubin! Il en est mort beaucoup, comme lui, depuis quelques semaines.

BLANCHE. Le plus dur, ç'a été le début de la guerre, et puis la fin.

ANDRÉ. Ce n'est pas étonnant. Nous étions privés de presque tout. Il fallait une santé pour supporter cela!

BLANCHE. On n'avait jamais été aussi triste que cette année.

ANDRÉ. C'est comme nous. Nous avions fini par nous laisser aller.

BLANCHE. Des deuils dans toutes les familles, tu comprends.

ANDRÉ. Au début, nous organisions des petites fêtes, des jeux.

BLANCHE. On n'avait plus de goût à rien.

ANDRÉ. *(En écho.)* On n'avait plus de goût à rien. Nous nous laissions vivre, ou plutôt mourir.

BLANCHE. *(En écho.)* Mourir, oui. On se laissait mourir. *(Ils restent un moment silencieux. Blanche est appuyée contre André assis. Ils se tiennent la main, mais chacun suit sa pensée et leurs yeux sont baissés vers le sol de côtés différents.)* [122]

About this passage Paul Blanchart writes:

Sous la simplicité de ces mots dolents et humblement résignés, c'est non seulement toute la tragédie des années de guerre qui frissonne, mais c'est encore l'esseulement atroce de deux êtres ployés au même foyer alors que les événements les ont rendus si distants l'un de l'autre. Les mélodies discrètes et poignantes qui, sur un mode mineur, alternent et

---

[122] *Le Feu qui reprend mal*, Act I, pp. 32-33 in *Théâtre I*, Paris, Albin Michel, 1925.

> se répondent dans ce duo, aboutissent à ce double écho, sorte
> de point d'orgue verbal et sentimental à la fois, dont la
> résonance est infinie. [123]

It is plain that this "infinite resonance" results from the use of a
characteristically Chekhovian device; often in Chekhov one notices
characters simultaneously following individual lines of thought and
feeling, and thereby indirectly drawing attention to the spiritual distance which their physical proximity cannot reduce.

★ ★ ★

No one would care to imply that the non-verbal mode of expression predominates in Ibsen; yet it remains true that he did begin at
times to move along the course that Bernard was to pursue more
systematically. For instance, Ibsen's manipulation of the language of
image and gesture in parts of *A Doll's House* allowed him to create
a texture resembling in its composition the audio-visual synthesis
towards which the theatre of the unexpressed later tended. [124] A valuable illumination on this topic is provided by James Walter McFarlane in his discussion of "Ibsen's continuingly audacious experimentation in the dramatic use of language":

> There is [throughout *A Doll's House*] an exploitation of the
> dramatic resources of gesture and posture and movement so
> unrelenting and so ingenious as to make the accompanying
> words in many cases almost superfluous. The point has been
> made before that much of (for example) the first Act of *A
> Doll's House* would not merely have sufficient non-verbal
> quality to interest a deaf person, but would in fact be in
> unusually high degree intelligible to him. [125]

We have already remarked upon the prominence which Bernard
gave to the visual element, and we shall return later to the recurrence
in *L'Invitation* of the pictorial image contained in the following
passage:

---

[123] Paul Blanchart, *Jean-Jacques Bernard*, Paris, Coutan-Lambert, 1928,
pp. 16-19.

[124] Cf. above, p. 27.

[125] James Walter McFarlane, 'Introduction,' pp. 11-12 in *The Oxford
Ibsen. Volume V*, London, Oxford University Press, 1961.

JACQUELINE. Oui, tu as tout ce qu'il faut pour être heureuse: un bon mari, un bel enfant. Je ne vois pas de quoi tu te plaindrais.

MARIE-LOUISE. Mais je ne me suis pas plainte, Jacqueline... (*Elle remonte vers le fond et reste un moment rêveuse, les yeux fixés sur la forêt.*)

JACQUELINE. Qu'est-ce que tu regardes?

MARIE-LOUISE. Ces arbres...

JACQUELINE. Qu'est-ce qu'ils ont?

MARIE-LOUISE. Oh! une simple idée... Ne t'es-tu jamais dit qu'au lieu de ces arbres, qui ne changent jamais, nous pourrions en avoir d'autres qui perdraient leurs feuilles et en pousseraient de nouvelles chaque printemps? [126]

For the present, it is important to note the features which the scene above has in common with this scene from *Hedda Gabler*:

> (*The door stays half open, and we hear Tesman repeating his message of love to Aunt Rina, and thanking again for the slippers.*
> *While this is going on Hedda walks about the room, raises her arms and clenches her fists as though in a frenzy. Then she draws the curtains back from the verandah door, stands there and looks out.*
> *After a while Tesman comes back and shuts the door behind him.*)
> TESMAN. (*Picking up the slippers from the floor.*) What are you looking at, Hedda?
> HEDDA. (*Calm and collected once more.*) I'm just looking at the leaves on the trees. They're so yellow. And so withered.
> TESMAN. (*Rewraps the slippers and lays them on the table.*) Yes, well, it's September now, you know.
> HEDDA. (*Ill at ease again.*) Why yes... already it's... it's September. [127]

In his analysis of this play, John Northam states that "Hedda's aspirations, her actions, her language are all turned into fragmentary vagueness by the pressures that have driven them so deep. We have

---

[126] Act I, tableau I, pp. 274-275 in *Théâtre I*. See also below, pp. 147-148.
[127] *Hedda Gabler*, Act I, pp. 182-183 in *The Oxford Ibsen. Volume VII*, London, Oxford University Press, 1966.

no clear achievement to respect, no clear statement to admire." [128] In fact, like Bernard's 'unexpressed' plays, *Hedda Gabler* sets store by suggestive action and movement, and by the avoidance of direct, explanatory statements. Thus Hedda's pregnancy is alluded to, but never announced. We were able to infer from her impatient, irritated and curt contributions during Tesman's observations on her plumpness that she found the business of her pregnancy distasteful. Suspicions of reactions even stronger than distaste are now corroborated by her frenzied movements. She subsides after reaching her pitch, but the sense of repose which follows the drawing back of the curtains (this defiantly flagrant contradiction of her own command) is disturbed by Tesman's indeliberate reminder of her progressing condition.

The quality and quantity of Hedda's utterances in the scene above are fairly representative of her spoken contribution in the play as a whole. John Northam describes her as "a character whose main failing was inarticulateness — a poet denied self-expression," [129] and James Walter McFarlane as "one of the least eloquent heroines in the whole of the world's dramatic literature." [130] One way of looking at the play is as an investigation of the dramatic possibilities of a protagonist characterized by a tendency to silent self-communion, and by speech that is often disjointed and colourless. McFarlane has pertinently pointed to the complex, allusive texture of the ordinary-seeming linguistic material, and to the danger inherent in this method:

> The audience is continually being given slight indications, hints and suggestions that betray a state of mind or a habit of thought, many of them so slight that it is almost impossible to separate them out. [...] The price paid for this subtlety is great; for the strain on the audience then becomes almost intolerable. [131]

---

[128] John Northam, *Ibsen. A Critical Study*, Cambridge at the University Press, 1973, p. 181.

[129] John Northam, *Ibsen's Dramatic Method*, London, Faber and Faber, 1953, p. 171.

[130] James Walter McFarlane, 'Introduction,' p. 12 in *The Oxford Ibsen. Volume VII*.

[131] *Ibid.*, p. 13.

This is a pitfall which Bernard, on employing a similar method, managed to avoid in *Printemps*, and failed to avoid in *Le Jardinier d'Ispahan*. [132]

Hedda, then, like the protagonists of Bernard's 'unexpressed' plays, is not prone to much vocal self-analysis. Ibsen's emphasis on visual rather than verbal presentation obliges us to guess at her unformulated motivations — motivations which are sometimes unknown to her. She does not quite know how to explain her actions, she admits to Brack. Things just suddenly come over her. [133] A different procedure is discernible in *The Master Builder*, where the denouement, consisting of Solness's expiatory ritual, is preluded by an examination of conscience, many parts of which we hear. During the course of the play, there is a gradual exposure of the unexpressed ideas and sentiments that have been fermenting inside Solness's tormented conscience before the rise of the curtain. Foremost among these are the reasons for his guilty feeling, and here it is that Hilde's rôle as confidante is so cardinal. As well as bringing about his avowals, she anticipates and formulates, on more than one occasion, Solness's unspoken thoughts — as when she suggests that he should put some kind of tower on the houses he constructs, or when she tells him that no one but he should be allowed to build. [134]

Hilde participates thereby in the wordless communion between souls, which May Daniels rightly sees as one of "two characteristics of the *Théâtre de L'Inexprimé*, apparently contradictory, but in fact expressing two different aspects of the one reality." The other characteristic is "the sense of isolation of human souls." [135] Both characteristics are conspicuous in *The Master Builder:* Aline and Solness travel in insulated cabins along continuously equidistant lines, each claiming responsibility for the unforgettable misfortune of their life, each failing to respond sympathetically to the other's guilt complex. Solness confesses to Hilde his inability to talk to Aline, [136] but this deficiency is counterbalanced both by his occasional silent communion with Hilde, and by his privileged means of communication with Kaja

---

[132] See below, pp. 110 ff., 156-157, 188.

[133] See Act II, p. 210.

[134] *The Master Builder*, Act I, p. 387; Act II, p. 400 in *The Oxford Ibsen. Volume VII.*

[135] May Daniels, *The French Drama of The Unspoken*, Edinburgh at the University Press, 1953, p. 190.

[136] Act II, p. 402.

Fosli; she, we remember, fell under a wordless spell and fulfilled Solness's unvoiced wish when she joined his office:

> SOLNESS. I never dropped the slightest hint of this at the time. I just stood and looked at her wishing with all my soul that I had her here. [...] She came back here to me, and acted as though I had come to some sort of arrangement with her. [...] About the very thing I'd been wishing for. But about which I hadn't said a single word.
> ... ...
> Well, but what about that other matter? Her believing I'd *spoken* to her of things I'd only wished for — silently? Inwardly? To myself? [137]

✻ ✻ ✻

The reality/illusion conflict, the problem of multiple personality, the concept of the relativity of truth continue to be recurrent features of a substantial portion of twentieth-century literature. They have been made popular in the theatre largely through Pirandello, and, in particular, through plays like *Six Characters in Search of an Author*, *Henry IV* and *Right You Are!* (*If You Think So*). These three plays are among the nine that between 1922 and 1926 were introduced by Dullin and Pitoëff to an enthusiastic Paris — an enthusiasm sanctioned by the French government when it officially honoured Pirandello during his visit to Paris in 1923. [138] The impact of these plays on the French theatre has been durable, and echoes of the techniques they employ are ubiquitous. Nevertheless, these 'echoes' do not automatically prove a prior acquaintance with Pirandello, and Bernard's *Le Feu qui reprend mal* is a case in point.

Le Feu qui reprend mal deals with the retrospective jealousy of a returned prisoner of war André Mérin, who learns that during his absence his wife Blanche had billeted an American officer. The play is not, however, a study of jealousy along the lines of *Othello*; Othello at least is convinced that he has real grounds for discontent. [139] Rather

---

137 Act I, pp. 371-372.

138 Between December 1922 and May 1926 *The Pleasure of Honesty*, *Six Characters*, *All for the Best*, *Each in His Own Way*, *Right You Are!*, *The Imbecile*, *Henry IV*, *Naked* and *By Judgment of the Court* (*La Patente*) had their Paris premières. At one time during the 1924-25 season, the last five mentioned were playing simultaneously at three theatres in Paris.

139 So also is Leontes in *The Winter's Tale*, though the reasons for his conviction remain invisible to the audience.

Le Feu qui reprend mal is a study of the preliminary anguish of uncertainty, and of the inability to distinguish falsehood from truth.
André's search for the truth involves a disquieting, ever-increasing
awareness of the impenetrable side of personality, an awareness which
contributes to his mistrust of appearances and of words. He is particularly conscious of the fact that words can as easily befog the truth
as reflect it. For he knows that Jeanne, Blanche's close friend, has
successfully concealed from her husband her extra-marital affair; the
question that torments him is how to believe Blanche, who insists
that she has never erred, when Jeanne can so skilfully practise duplicity, and when, in addition, she dupes him into thinking for a
moment that she had made a full confession to her husband. Henry
Bidou remarks that the tragedy lies in the terrifying resemblance between sincerity and dissimulation; [140] indeed if we did not know that
Bernard had composed the play before his acquaintance with Pirandello and his ideas, we would be tempted to speak of Pirandellian
inspiration. [141]

To be sure, the divergences between Pirandello and Bernard are
many. The plays of the latter still reflect, for instance, a strong basic
belief in the verifiable nature of events, situations and feelings. By
concentrating on personages who are unaware of the character of their
sentiments, or who are unable or reluctant to formulate them, by
consistently calling into play the hidden springs of human conduct,
Bernard often surrounded his creations with a halo of mystery. But he
did not go as far in this direction as Pirandello, in whose plays the
essential mysteries of personality frequently remain intact. With one
author, the spectator is sent in pursuit of unexpressed but accessible
truth; with the other, he is sent in pursuit of a truth that is out of
reach. [142] For the rest, Pirandello's plays are loquacious and commonly

---

[140] Henry Bidou, 'La Semaine Dramatique,' *Journal des Débats,* 21 oct.
1929, p. 3.
[141] A full investigation of 'pre-Pirandellian Pirandellism' (as a full investigation of 'pre-Freudian Freudianism') would require a volume to itself.
Thomas Bishop has made some useful comments on this phenomenon in
France in *Pirandello and the French Theatre,* London, Peter Owen, 1961.
See, for example, pp. 52-53.
[142] This is especially true of *Right You Are! (If You Think So),* where
the verification of Signora Ponza's identity which we await at the end and
which does not materialize involves a flouting of our traditional expectations
that is akin to the Bernardian blend of brinkmanship.

feature an outspoken *raisonneur*. On the other hand, however, it is true that the Manager's advice to the Stepdaughter in *Six Characters* sound like guide-lines that Bernard was following on composing his 'unexpressed' plays:

> I am aware of the fact that everyone has his own interior life which he wants very much to put forward. But the difficulty lies in this fact: to set out just so much as is necessary for the stage, taking the other characters into consideration, and at the same time hint at the unrevealed interior life of each. I am willing to admit, my dear young lady, that from your point of view it would be a fine idea if each character could tell the public all his troubles in a nice monologue or a regular one hour lecture. [143]

Yet here again we should not speak too hurriedly of influence. "I had presented my early plays when I saw those of Pirandello," Bernard says in a letter to Thomas Bishop. "I therefore could not tell you that he influenced me, but I can assure you that I found myself naturally in accord with his work." [144]

Bishop sees the accord in three of Bernard's plays: in *L'Invitation* and *Nationale 6,* where the respective protagonists come to identify their illusions for what they are, discover "that illusions about faraway places may be less attractive than the realities around the corner," and in *Printemps,* in which the protagonist's temporary unawareness of her real personality yields finally to lucidity. [145] To those three we may add *Denise Marette,* a play that greatly reminds one of *Henry IV.* Having concealed from the outside world, for the sake of the reputation of her declining father, that the paintings bearing his signature are her productions, Denise eventually destroys her authentic artistic identity and enters the prison of her lie. A final point of correspondence is worth noting: both Pirandello and Bernard were inclined to have as protagonists characters on whom the spectator can seldom rely to give solid, straightforward information about themselves or

---

[143] *Six Characters in Search of an Author,* Act II, p. 52 in Pirandello, *Three Plays* (Translated by Edward Storer and Arthur Livingston), London, Dent, 1936.

[144] Quoted by Thomas Bishop, *Pirandello and the French Theatre,* pp. 72-73.

[145] *Ibid.,* p. 73.

about other characters, or to illuminate in a direct manner the situations in which they find themselves.

Of the tendencies of Western drama at the beginning of this century which are in evidence in Chekhov, Ibsen and Pirandello, at least two may be recalled here. The first involves an estrangement from the formula of the well-made play — an estrangement that was neither uniform nor total, Ibsen often betraying an ambivalence towards the technique of French intrigue drama. Still, placed beside the mechanically conducted intrigues of Scribe, many of the plays of Chekhov, Ibsen and Pirandello will reveal a striking lack of 'finish,' and, in the main, they represent a movement away from the traditions of form which Scribe and Sarcey had made sacrosanct. The second trend was towards a close attention to the undersurface of life, and mirrored a widening perception of the wealth of largely unexplored material that lay in the unconscious mind. Both trends are strongly marked in Bernard's *théâtre de l'inexprimé*. There, however, they have been compounded with what has become one of the major tendencies of this century: the tendency to call in question the rôles which the verbal medium has customarily played in drama.

The 'Metteur en scène'

We mentioned at the start of this chapter that the regenerative activity which took place after the First War was emboldened by the formation of theatrical companies of a basically non-commercial nature. At the head of each of these companies was a *metteur en scène,* a personage who was to become intimately connected with all the progressive currents in French inter-war drama. As far as Bernard is concerned, it is manifest that were it not for the example, advice and support of men like Antoine, Lugné-Poe, Copeau and Baty, his development as a dramatist would have been seriously retarded. Before proceeding, then, to an analysis of three of the main plays that Bernard has written in the vein of the unexpressed, we shall consider the figure of the *metteur en scène.*

The turn of the century had seen the dynamos of the stage yielding some of their territory. The names of Mounet-Sully, Henry Irving, Eleonora Duse and Sarah Bernhardt continued to resound, but beside these figures the hitherto obscure figure of the director was coming to prominence. He was busy pondering on the art of acting, theorizing on the theatre, formulating programmes for its reform, devising scenic innovations. Adolphe Appia and Max Reinhardt in Germany, Stanislavski and Danchenko in Russia, Gordon Craig and Granville-Barker in England, Antoine and Lugné-Poe in France were all engaged in this activity, which led to a radical modification of stage-presentation throughout Europe. The successors of Antoine and Lugné-Poe — Copeau, Baty, Dullin, Jouvet and Pitoëff — have left an indelible mark on twentieth-century French drama.

In September 1913, announcing the opening of the *Théâtre du Vieux-Colombier*, Copeau thundered from his tribune at the *Nouvelle Revue Française:*

> Si l'on veut que nous nommions plus clairement le sentiment qui nous anime, la passion qui nous pousse, nous contraint, nous oblige, à laquelle il faut que nous cédions enfin: c'est *l'indignation.*
>
> Une industrialisation effrénée qui, de jour en jour plus cyniquement, dégrade notre scène française et détourne d'elle le public cultivé; l'accaparement de la plupart des théâtres par une poignée d'amuseurs à la solde de marchands éhontés; partout, et là encore où de grandes traditions devraient sauvegarder quelque pudeur, le même esprit de cabotinage et de spéculation, la même bassesse; partout le bluff, la surenchère de toute sorte et l'exhibitionnisme de toute nature parasitant un art qui se meurt, et dont il n'est même plus question; partout veulerie, désordre, indiscipline, ignorance et sottise, dédain du créateur, haine de la beauté; une production de plus en plus folle et vaine, une critique de plus en plus consentante, un goût public de plus en plus égaré: voilà ce qui nous indigne et nous soulève. [146]

Driven by his stern sense of mission, aided by an enthusiastic and energetic troupe (which included Dullin and Jouvet), Copeau undertook to rehabilitate the theatre. As director, he firmly repudiated mechanical and electrical contrivances, and fostered a brand of austere and sober *décors* for which he is still remembered. The fruits of his efforts were not tardy. "Nous avons vu venir au théâtre," Vildrac recounts, "ceux-là mêmes qui le désertaient naguère: sur la scène les poètes, et dans la salle un public d'élite sans cesse accru, sans cesse

---

[146] Jacques Copeau, 'Un essai de rénovation dramatique. Le Théâtre du Vieux-Colombier,' *La Nouvelle Revue Française,* 1er sep. 1913, p. 338.

élargi. Nous avons vu et voyons encore prospérer, à la faveur de cette renaissance, des théâtres que les industriels du spectacle jugeaient plus ou moins inexploitables." [147] Vildrac himself had won acclaim as a dramatist thanks to Copeau's production of *Le Paquebot Tenacity*, [148] an event which marked a summit in the history of the *Vieux-Colombier*. [149]

In the words of S. A. Rhodes, Copeau

> aimed at drama that was pure theatre, that fused realistic and idealistic concepts on the literary and architectural plans. He aimed high, but his uncompromising idealism ultimately thwarted his efforts. It caused him to be too exacting toward the dramatists — so that he drove even such contemporary masterpieces as *La Souriante Mme Beudet*, *Martine*, *Knock*, and the plays of Pirandello to seek a haven elsewhere. [150]

Indeed the honour of being produced by Copeau was denied to many a worth-while play. If we are to believe Bernard, though, Copeau did not reject *Martine*:

> Il ne l'a pas refusée, comme certains l'ont dit; il n'a pas eu à la refuser, puisque je ne la lui ai pas apportée. [151]

Bernard has none the less been anxious to record his indebtedness to Copeau. He claims that he was inspirited in 1913 by 'Un essai de rénovation dramatique,' and that he was among the most fervent spectators at the *Vieux-Colombier's* first evening. [152] He then continues:

> J'eus moi-même un jour l'occasion de lui confier qu'en écrivant *Martine* j'avais devant les yeux le cadre du Vieux-Colombier. Si ce fut Baty et non lui qui créa la pièce [...],

---

147 Charles Vildrac, 'Jacques Copeau,' *Hommes et Mondes*, janv. 1950, p. 103.

148 First performed in March 1920 (together with Prosper Mérimée's *Le Carrosse du Saint-Sacrement*).

149 Copeau recalls that this is when they were discovered by the public authorities, assailed by snobs, and rumoured to be prosperous. *Souvenirs du Vieux-Colombier*, Paris, Nouvelles Éditions Latines, 1931, pp. 55-56.

150 S. A. Rhodes, 'France and Belgium,' *A History of Modern Drama* (eds. Barrett H. Clark and George Freedley), New York-London, D. Appleton-Century Company, 1947, p. 276.

151 Bernard, *Mon Ami le Théâtre*, Paris, Albin Michel, 1958, p. 20.

152 *Ibid.*, pp. 15 ff.

il n'en reste pas moins que sans Copeau *Martine* n'aurait pas été ce qu'elle fut. Je me plais à rendre à sa mémoire le témoignage de cette imprégnation. Je n'ai pas été — et je le regrette — un auteur de Copeau, mais ma fidélité lui est restée jusqu'au bout. [153]

Bernard's was not an isolated case, and his statements go a long way towards giving a more accurate measure of Copeau's importance than would be given by a list of dramatists discovered and plays staged. Copeau's rallying cry had by no means gone unanswered.

Antoine, Lugné-Poe and Pitoëff were all, at one time or other, of assistance to Bernard. Antoine had useful words of counsel for the young playwright, and the latter deeply respected the elder's opinions, whether unfavourable, as in the case of *La Maison épargnée*, or favourable, as in the case of *Le Feu qui reprend mal* and *Martine*. Lugné-Poe staged *Printemps* in 1924; he had previously hailed *Martine* as "[une] œuvre, si sobre et d'un pathétique si humain, [qui] achèvera de classer M. J.-J. Bernard parmi les premiers de nos jeunes auteurs," [154] and he had had to abandon his planned production at the *Théâtre de l'Œuvre* of *Le Feu qui reprend mal* because of a general dissatisfaction with the leading lady. [155] In 1926 Pitoëff produced *L'Ame en peine*. "J'avais remis le manuscrit à Pitoëff un soir dans sa loge, un peu avant minuit," Bernard recollects. "A 7 heures du matin, je fus réveillé par un coup de téléphone. 'J'ai lu, je joue'." [156] It is with Baty, however, that Bernard had the closest affinity, and with Baty that he had the most advantageous alliance.

In 1921, Bernard and a group of dramatists, "sentant la nécessité de s'unir pour mieux lutter contre les difficultés de l'industrie théâtrale," [157] joined forces. In obvious tribute to Ibsen they dubbed themselves *Le Canard sauvage*, and in April of that year they organized the production of Denys Amiel and André Obey's *La Souriante Madame Beudet* — a play which brought renown to its authors and was made into a film two years later. The *Canard sauvage* sensed, how-

---

[153] *Ibid.*, p. 20.
[154] Quoted by Gaston Sorbets, '*Martine*, au théâtre des Mathurins,' *La Petite Illustration*, 22 juillet 1922, page not numbered.
[155] The play was eventually produced at the *Théâtre Antoine* by *Le Cercle des Escholiers*, a group with which Lugné-Poe was also associated.
[156] *Mon Ami le Théâtre*, p. 87.
[157] *Ibid.*, p. 32.

ever, that they needed an *animateur,* and felt in general accord with
Baty's basic ideas; in 1922, after negotiations between Bernard and
Baty, they annexed themselves as a reading committee to the latter's
recently constituted group of actors, electricians, costume-designers,
painters and dancers — *Les Compagnons de la Chimère.* [158] The year
1922 was one of glory for the *Compagnons.* Baty's production in May
of Bernard's *Martine* and Pellerin's *Intimité* attracted the notice of
all those who were seeking an alternative to the tired routine of the
established theatres. In the autumn the *Alliance Française* sponsored
the company's tour of Belgium, Germany and Switzerland (which
turned out to be a highly encouraging success), and Baty declared
victoriously on his return:

> L'opinion commune est que notre théâtre est fort en retard
> sur celui des autres pays et que la scène française vit encore
> du vaudeville et de l'éternel triangle. La Chimère a apporté
> à l'étranger l'expression française d'un mouvement interna-
> tional. [159]

Enthusiasm in the company was at its apex. But as yet the *Compagnons* had no playhouse of their own. For *Martine* and *Intimité*
they had had to borrow the stage of the *Théâtre des Mathurins.* Re-
solved to rectify matters, the *Compagnons* took out a lease on a site
at 143 Boulevard Saint-Germain — opposite L'Église-Saint-Germain-
des-Près. A wooden building was constructed, was appropriately bap-
tized *La Baraque de la Chimère,* and was inaugurated on 2 May 1923
with a farce by Lucien Besnard and with Amiel's *Le Voyageur.* The
aphorism which appeared regularly on the group's *Bulletins* — "Les
œuvres que nous jouons n'ont pas été faites pour la Chimère: c'est
la Chimère qui a été faite pour elles" — was no empty statement;
Le Voyageur, which many saw as a play written according to Baty's
formula, had been written eleven years earlier.

---

[158] The original members of the reading committee were Denys Amiel,
Bernard, Lucien Besnard, Saint-Georges de Bouhélier, Edmond Fleg, Henri-
René Lenormand, Gabriel Marcel, Émile Mazaud, Adolphe Orna, Jean-Victor
Pellerin, Jean Sarment and Auguste Villeroy. Henri Crémieux later became
the Secretary.

[159] Quoted by France Anders, *Jacques Copeau et le Cartel des Quatre,*
Paris, A. G. Nizet, 1959, p. 137.

The agreement between Baty and the reading committee was that out of every three plays that the *Compagnons* were to present, he should select one and they two. Not unexpectedly, many of the pieces passed by the committee were composed by members; yet this did not happen automatically, and the fact that Bernard's *Le Secret d'Arvers* was vetoed [160] attests to the individual, independent scrutiny to which each play was subjected. The extent to which variety of opinion prevailed within the assembly is obvious from the following satirical comments on the *Compagnons'* intentions by Adolphe Orna, a member of the reading committee:

> A les entendre, on dirait que l'art théâtral sera d'ici peu changé de fond en comble. La foule comprendra par les gestes échangés entre les personnages; et nous, les spectateurs, rirons ou pleurerons rien qu'à regarder l'expression du visage de l'interprète ou en contemplant un décor. [...] La réplique sera remplacée par de la mimique. Les sourds eux-mêmes entendront. On n'aura plus besoin que de jumelles. Pourvu qu'on ne tousse pas dans la salle et qu'on entende le silence, tout sera pour le mieux dans le meilleur des mondes. Le public, un doigt au front, écoutera les acteurs; seulement il devra saisir, non pas ce qu'ils disent, mais surtout ce qu'ils ne disent pas. Ainsi, l'auteur exprimera la douleur et la joie par des sous-entendus. Quelle plaisanterie! [161]

Orna's comments are important for another reason: they contain the burden of the reproachful refrain that has not ceased to be directed at Baty, Bernard, Amiel, Pellerin and other *Compagnons.*

The *Baraque de la Chimère* functioned for only a few months; built on hope and enthusiasm, it was soon consumed by financial adversity. In the last issue of the company's official publication Baty broke the news:

> La Baraque de la Chimère ferme ses portes. Si modeste qu'elle soit, sa construction a absorbé toutes nos ressources; les prévisions de l'architecte se sont trouvées plus que doublées; nous n'avons plus d'argent.

---

[160] Baty had suggested the idea of the play.
[161] Adolphe Orna, 'Sur le Présent et l'Avenir prochain du Théâtre en France,' *Comœdia,* 11 août 1923, p. 1.

Toutes les demarches que nous avons faites pour en trouver sont restées vaines. Nous n'aurions pu durer qu'en acceptant les compromissions et les combinaisons trop coutumières; c'eût été mentir à notre principe même et devenir pareils aux autres; nous préférons disparaître. [162]

Though the closing of the *Baraque* coincided with the disbanding of the *Compagnons,* Bernard maintained his close association with Baty, and the latter continued his activity in the theatrical vanguard, constantly placing artistic merit before commercial prospects. In this, he was united in spirit with Dullin, Jouvet and Pitoëff, and the *Cartel des quatre* which on Jouvet's initiative the four directors formed in 1927 represented the consecration of a long-standing spiritual solidarity.

In our view, the vital contribution made to twentieth-century French drama by Copeau and the *Cartel des quatre* cannot be overstressed. It appears, nevertheless, that many others incline to the view that the *metteur en scène* has been less a benefit than a bane. It has for long been fashionable in France to talk of the crisis of the theatre, and, in the recurring discussions on the crisis, it has become customary to apportion most blame to the director. [163] A few years ago Fernand Crommelynck stated:

Le metteur en scène est une superfétation. Mais il s'arroge jusqu'au droit de modifier l'auteur. Il se substitue à lui. [...] Sous l'influence du metteur en scène, le théâtre n'est plus, à proprement parler, un art. [164]

More recently still, Claude Baignères was complaining:

Depuis quelques années, [les metteurs en scène] ont cessé d'être simplement les catalyseurs du spectacle. Chargés naguère de faire apparaître les intentions d'un auteur en assimilant son style et en indiquant aux comédiens les places et

---

[162] *La Chimère. Bulletin d'Art Dramatique,* no. 13, 1923, p. 203. In February 1924 the *Baraque* was sold by auction. It was later demolished, and in its place today there stands an hotel.

[163] It may not be superfluous to add that as a result of competition from cinema, radio and television, it is primarily from the financial point of view that twentieth-century theatre as a whole is in a state of perpetual crisis.

[164] Fernand Crommelynck, 'La crise?... Tout le mal est venu du metteur en scène,' *La Table Ronde,* mai 1966, pp. 29-30.

mouvements que le texte suggère, ils veulent désormais faire œuvre de créateur. Ils se forgent une manière, adoptent des tics, cherchent entre les lignes les prétextes qui leur permettront d'accrocher leur propre chapeau; et ils plient l'ouvrage tout entier à leur idéologie. [165]

Crommelynck and Baignères were thinking of the successors of the *Cartel*, but already in 1927 Benjamin Crémieux was sounding the alarm about "l'impérialisme du metteur en scène." [166] And when in 1952 Jean Vilar emphatically paid tribute to the work of the interwar director, his statement was taken to signify little more than disdain for the dramatist. Guy Leclerc recounts:

> Vilar avait déclaré:
> 'Les vrais créateurs dramatiques de ces trente dernières années ne sont pas les auteurs mais les metteurs en scène.'
> Georges Neveux s'exclama:
> 'Jean Vilar, vous exagérez!';
> Armand Salacrou dénonça les 'calembredaines de Vilar.'
> Roger Ferdinand, président de la Société des Auteurs, pria le directeur du T. N. P. de ne pas accabler les dramaturges 'd'un injuste dédain.' [167]

The question of the director's interpretation of the dramatist's intentions, that of the appropriateness of the *mise en scène*, the question whether the dramatist's text should in any way be altered are constantly mooted. Some believe that there are grave moral issues involved in abridging *Hamlet* or in shortening Théramène's *récit*. That school, seeing perhaps the theatre as the province of the dramatist alone, holds that once he has written his play, to make or even to suggest an alteration is sacrilegious. Needless to say, such would-be acts of sacrilege have often been performed with impunity. "Who are reputed the most eminent English actors of all time?" Harold Hobson asks. "Garrick and Irving, both of them men who would chop Shakespeare about, invent spurious endings, add their

---

[165] Claude Baignères, 'L'adaptation des pièces anglo-saxonnes peut-elle résoudre la crise du théâtre français?,' *Le Figaro littéraire*, 28 oct. 1972, p. vi.

[166] Benjamin Crémieux, 'Chronique Dramatique,' *La Nouvelle Revue Française*, 1er juillet 1927, pp. 96-100.

[167] Guy Leclerc, *Le T. N. P. de Jean Vilar*, Paris, Union Générale d'Éditions, 1971, p. 123.

own lines of dialogue, and generally behave as though the playwright's work were merely the raw material out of which they set themselves to fashion what they would." [168] With regard to the living writer, the demands of actors and directors have at times been as capricious as their obstinacy and self-righteousness have been immoderate. John Northam relates that "Hedwig Niemann-Raabe, a German actress, refused to play the part of Nora as originally written. She declared that she would never leave her children. As is well known, Ibsen was forced to provide an alternative ending for the German theatre." [169] One remembers also the numerous clashes during rehearsals of *Hernani* between Hugo and Mademoiselle Mars, and her persistence in replacing

> Vous êtes mon lion superbe et généreux!

by

> Vous êtes, mon seigneur, vaillant et courageux! [170]

Fortunately, though, requests for alterations have not always been unreasonable, and no such imputations of caprice can justifiably be made against the *Cartel*. The alterations which they requested have in most cases been positively to the advantage of the playwright in question. One has only to think of the joint endeavour of Jouvet and Giraudoux to prepare *Siegfried* for the stage:

> Tout au long des répétitions, [Jouvet] avait demandé à Giraudoux, dont le manuscrit était beaucoup trop long, des remaniements, des coupures, auxquels Giraudoux, attentif et convaincu, se plia de la meilleure grâce du monde. [171]

And, as René Lalou notes, "quatre volumes de variantes et de premières versions dans l'édition de son *Théâtre complet* montrent quels sacrifices [Giraudoux] consentit pour ajuster, avec le précieux con-

---

[168] Harold Hobson, *The French Theatre of To-day*, London, Harrap, 1953, p. 29.

[169] John Northam, *Ibsen's Dramatic Method*, London, Faber and Faber, 1953, p. 26.

[170] Victor Hugo, *Hernani* (ed. Alexandre Beaujour), Paris, Bordas, 1964, Act III, sc. 4, l. 1028.

[171] Luc Renaud, 'Notre Giraudoux,' *Paris-Théâtre*, déc. 1952, p. 8.

cours de Louis Jouvet, ses plus riches inventions au cadre d'une scène." [172] The renewal of French inter-war drama proceeded largely through collaborations, based on reciprocal trust, between dramatists and directors, the Giraudoux-Jouvet association being the most celebrated of a series: Salacrou and Dullin, [173] Lenormand and Pitoëff, Bernard and Baty. It would be a curious detour round the truth to consider as the instigators of decline and the subjugators of dramatists men who, courageously defying the prospects of bankruptcy, provided havens for plays that could not obtain access to the established theatres, men who by their patience and enterprise encouraged the development of a whole new breed of dramatists.

The member of the *Cartel* who is most often singled out as an example of a director who, by subjugating the dramatist, accelerated the supposed decadence is Baty; Robert Kanters is in this respect representative:

> La réduction du texte au prétexte, de l'auteur au rang de l'accessoiriste, est toujours le premier souci du metteur en scène. On en pourrait prendre des exemples déjà historiques chez M. Baty. [174]

The fact is that Baty has been haunted by the repercussions of his pronouncements against "Sire le Mot" in 1921. The models for Baty's ideal theatre came from the Athenian drama, the medieval *mistère* and the Elizabethan drama. In these he found a harmonious balance between the literary, the plastic and the musical, which was disturbed when in seventeenth-century France the verbal element became predominant. He underlined as a major contributory factor to the Word's predominance the practice (which developed after the success of *Le Cid*) of placing spectators on the stage; this hastened the end of the old decorative system and restricted the actor in his movements:

> L'exiguïté de la scène, la présence de maints fâcheux, l'encombrement des entrées gênent son mouvement et paralysent

---

[172] René Lalou, *Le Théâtre en France depuis 1900*, Paris, Presses Universitaires de France, 1951, p. 92.

[173] Salacrou, his denunciation of "les calembredaines de Vilar" notwithstanding, is undeniably indebted to Lugné-Poe and Dullin.

[174] Robert Kanters, 'De l'art de la mise en scène considéré comme un assassinat,' *La Table Ronde*, janv. 1948, p. 135.

ses gestes. Un seul moyen d'expression lui reste, la voix. Il déclame donc au lieu de jouer. Sire le Mot a achevé sa conquête. [175]

What he yearned for was the return to a form of drama where the Word would not stifle the play's other potential components. The following definition of his conception of drama is one with which Bernard was in complete agreement:

> Pour nous, l'art dramatique reste l'art suprême en qui tous les autres s'exaltent, plus beaux d'être réunis. La sculpture donne l'attitude, le geste, la danse; la peinture, le costume et le décor; la littérature, le texte; la musique, la voix de l'acteur, les bruits, le chant parfois et souvent la symphonie. Ces multiples moyens s'accordent pour donner du thème commun l'expression dont chacun est capable, dans un style qui doit varier avec chaque œuvre. La traduction visuelle et auditive accepte le même parti-pris que l'écriture. Au-delà des mots, la pensée achève de s'exprimer par le geste, la couleur et le son. [176]

The idea of combining various elements into an 'integral' spectacle did not, as is sometimes implied, originate with Artaud. [177] Wagner had already argued for a synthesis of the dramatic, the verbal and the musical, and Gordon Craig had expressed hopes for a total theatre:

> The Art of the Theatre is neither acting nor the play, it is not scene nor dance, but it consists of all the elements of which these things are composed: action, which is the very spirit of acting; words, which are the body of the play; line and colour, which are the very heart of the scene; rhythm, which is the very essence of dance. [178]

---

[175] Baty, 'Le Masque et L'Encensoir (1921),' *Rideau Baissé*, Paris, Bordas, 1949, p. 106.

[176] *La Chimère. Bulletin d'Art Dramatique*, fév. 1922, p. 3.

[177] Gaston Rageot states proudly: "Je tiens à réclamer la paternité de ce mot [drame intégral] que j'ai été le premier à employer en ce sens dans une étude sur Saint-Georges de Bouhélier." *Prise de Vues*, Paris, La Nouvelle Revue Critique, 1928, p. 187.

[178] Gordon Craig, *On the Art of the Theatre*, London, Heinemann, 1929, p. 138.

It is from Gordon Craig that Baty appears to have inherited many of his ideas, and where Craig argued that Shakespeare's dramatic poems are so complete in their written form, leave so little room for improvement through stage representation that they are not suitable for stage representation, [179] Baty argued:

> Racine: tout est dans le texte, non seulement chaque repli des caractères, chaque nuance des sentiments, mais aussi l'aspect physique des personnages, leur mimique, leur costume, mais encore le décor, le milieu, l'atmosphère. Réaliser tout cela sous une seconde forme, ne serait-ce pas accumuler d'inutiles et barbares pléonasmes? [180]

This estimate of Racine (with which Bernard disagreed), coupled with his comments on "Sire le Mot," doubtless helped Baty to acquire his reputation as an enemy of the text, and as a director who was most interested in works that allowed him scope for dazzling with his creative genius.

Bernard's plays are not of this type, and, appropriately, Baty's sets for *Martine* and *L'Invitation* were decidedly unspectacular. The same cannot be said of *Crime et Châtiment* and *Madame Bovary*, [181] which are often cited as examples of Baty's decorative virtuosity gone out of control. Recalling these productions, René Lalou confesses that he was unable to commune with either Dostoevsky or Flaubert. "Je me souviens seulement," he continues, "de l'art avec lequel Baty faisait s'éteindre, côté jardin, un réverbère, ou s'allumer, côté cour, une loge de théâtre." [182] Again, those who saw *Bérénice* at the *Comédie-Française* in 1946 were either enraptured or confounded by the unbridled ingeniosity of Baty's production, and Bernard himself has affirmed that Baty dangerously deformed Racine's play. [183]

The claim that Baty did at times engage in excesses of *mise en scène* is not easily dismissed. There seems, however, to be less ev-

---

[179] *Ibid.*, pp. 140-144, 281-285.

[180] Baty, 'Le rôle du décor,' *La Chimère. Bulletin d'Art Dramatique,* mai 1922, p. 49.

[181] Produced at the *Théâtre Montparnasse* in 1933 and 1936 respectively (Baty's adaptations).

[182] René Lalou, *Le Théâtre en France depuis 1900,* Paris, Presses Universitaires de Franc, 1951, p. 61.

[183] See Bernard, *Mon Ami le Théâtre,* Paris, Albin Michel, 1958, p. 69.

idence to buttress the contention that he showed arrogant disrespect for the dramatist's text. In querying the foundation of this facet of Baty's reputation, it is essential to consider not only his utterances, but also what he did in practice. The testimony of those whose works he staged (and who, we may add, never hesitated to decry what they felt were his excesses) is therefore specially useful. Bernard states:

> Il souffre encore de cette inquiétude qu'éprouvent les auteurs devant le metteur en scène. Les auteurs ne savent pas toujours discriminer celui qui les trahit de celui qui les sert. Ceux du moins qui ont travaillé avec Baty pourraient témoigner de son respect des textes qui lui étaient confiés. [184]

Lenormand, for his part, testifies:

> Il n'est pas vrai qu'il sabre à plaisir dans les textes. Personnellement, je l'ai plutôt vu me demander des ajoutés que des coupures. A part quelques suppressions abusives dans *Phèdre*, je ne crois pas qu'on puisse lui reprocher de mutilations dans son maniement des classiques. [185]

Ultimately, there lie at the bottom of Baty's reputation as an enemy of the text a number of imprudent statements by Baty himself which, taken in isolation, could suggest a petulant dislike for the Word. But apparently many of his detractors, not content with reading too literally some of his hyperboles, have visited upon him the 'sinful' statements of others. Gordon Craig, for instance, believed so firmly in the sovereignty of the director that he felt the latter should ignore the author's stage directions; for the author to dictate stage directions was to poach on the director's preserves, to tamper with his art. [186] Nowhere, though, does one find Baty pleading in favour of the overriding authority of the director or encouraging contempt for the dramatist's text. What he was saying was that French drama was afflicted by hypertrophy of the verbal element, and should aim at a more balanced synthesis of its latent constituents:

---

[184] *Ibid.*, p. 34.
[185] H.-R. Lenormand, *Les Confessions d'un auteur dramatique II*, Paris, Albin Michel, 1953, pp. 26-27.
[186] *On the Art of the Theatre*, pp. 149-151.

> Lorsque fut fondée *la Chimère,* son programme avouait l'am-
> bition d'orienter le théâtre de demain dans la voie du drame
> intégral, où le mot ne règne plus seul, mais où les autres
> éléments reprennent tout leur pouvoir d'expression. [...]
> *Cependant le texte reste la base de l'œuvre.* [187]
> ... ...
> *Le texte est la partie essentielle du drame.* Il est au drame
> ce que le noyau est au fruit, le centre solide, autour duquel
> viennent s'ordonner les autres éléments. [188]

After such repeated assertions one wonders at the irresponsibility of
a critic with as wide an audience as Lucien Dubech, who, it may be
on the basis of hearsay, put abroad the following idea:

> Baty joua le rôle de l'Ilote ivre, partant en guerre avec une
> innocente intrépidité contre l'ennemi qu'il baptisait: *Le Sei-
> gneur le mot.* [189] C'est-à-dire qu'il jugeait que, dans une pièce
> de théâtre, l'élément pernicieux est le texte. Inutile de perdre
> son temps à charger contre ce moulin à vent. [190]

As is only to be expected, Bernard and Baty were not completely
in unison, and, as we have mentioned, Bernard could not bring himself
to defend Baty's claim that Racine's plays do not lend themselves to
representation. Bernard saw, however, where Baty's reassessment of
the rôle which the Word should play in drama ran parallel to his.
Dramatist and director coincided in the realization that a domain
which does not belong to words could usefully be explored in the
drama, and in their willingness to undertake such an exploration.
Valiantly upholding the insufficiently appreciated axiom that drama
is not designed primarily for the solitary reader, they vindicated the
theatre's right to exploit a language beyond conceptual language, and
to develop an idiom particular to itself — an idiom composed of
equally active elements: movement, gesture, facial expression, bodily
attitude, *décor,* words and silence. Reacting thus against the tendency
to consider the drama as a province of written literature, Bernard and

---

[187] Baty, 'Un Comité de Lecture,' *La Chimère. Bulletin d'Art Dramatique,* avril 1922, p. 33. My emphasis.
[188] Baty, 'Le Texte,' *La Chimère,* oct. 1922, pp. 84-85. My emphasis.
[189] The exact phrase was of course *Sire le Mot.*
[190] Lucien Dubech, *La crise du théâtre,* Paris, Librairie de France, 1928,
p. 72.

Baty gave impulse to what has proved to be an irreversible movement away from the rhetorical tradition in the French theatre.

We have seen that Bernard's plays were reacting against certain aspects of pre-First-World-War theatre, and were part of a multiform movement of renewal in the French drama of the post-war years; we have reflected on the use of the term *intimisme* and outlined the tenets of the *théâtre de l'inexprimé*; we have considered the impact of the silent film on Bernard's conception of drama, and observed the opportune encounter between Freud's doctrines and the theatre of the unexpressed; we have discussed Maeterlinck's status as precursor of this theatre, and shown how Bernard's plays related to a general drift of Western drama; we have, finally, taken stock of the position of the inter-war director in France, and suggested that he is not entirely deserving of the strictures to which he is at times subjected. Our next task will be to examine in greater detail Bernard's *théâtre de l'inexprimé*; to this end we have selected the three plays which best show the unexpressed in operation, and in which Bernard is in finest form: *Martine, Printemps* and *L'Invitation*. The examination requires a particular sort of critical approach. The theatre of the unexpressed seeks to circumvent and transcend some of the limitations inherent in dramatic form, seeks to lend dramatic weight to that which fails to result in speech and action, abounds less in explicit statements than in allusions. Through the figures appearing in these plays, we will be investigating imperfectly delimited realms of mental and emotional activity; we will be trying to hold under the steady gaze of criticism mobile, fluid quantities, whose presence is at times only covertly suggested. The verbal standard for checking the inferences which may be deduced from the complex of impressions will frequently be absent; often we will have to be content with unverifiable conjecture. There is, admittedly, a danger here of excessive self-indulgence; but some measure of conjecture is required if one is to respond actively and creatively to the appeal Bernard makes to the imagination.

CHAPTER TWO

MARTINE

Une petite paysanne dont la souffrance est tout silence, parce qu'elle ne peut pas, parce qu'elle ne veut
pas, parce qu'elle ne sait pas l'extérioriser. [1]

THE CHARACTER OF MARTINE is a stereotype belonging to an era of
which we receive, by implication, a stereotyped vision. It is an era
preceding the mass-emigration of youth from the country village to
the city, when the country girl living on her father's farm never
emerges from her country village, marries a country boy, and bears
him many other country boys and girls. The pattern of Martine's life
is in this sense pre--established. It is taken for granted in Grandchin
that Alfred will one day marry her and continue the management of
her parents' farm. The fact that Martine is far from being passionately
in love with Alfred is, of course, of no great consequence to anyone
— not even to Martine herself, it appears.

Then came Julien, full of the usual empty complimentary phrases
of the gallant young man meeting a girl who catches his fancy. For
Julien Martine holds the attraction of the unspoilt, though there is
no suggestion in him of the preying seducer ready to despoil simple
innocence. In the case of Martine, a more serious and complicated
process has begun. For perhaps the first time ever she envisages the
possibility of a life outside the pre-established pattern; a life in

---

[1] Bernard's description of Martine in 'Théâtre radiophonique,' *Théâtre
VII*, Paris, Albin Michel, 1949, p. 200. *Martine* was first performed 9 May
1922 at the *Théâtre des Mathurins*.

the company of a smooth and cultured Julien, the very opposite of the boorish Alfred. It would have been better for her if she had never envisaged this possibility; her suffering lies in her awareness of a possibility which will never be converted to actuality, and then in her inability, once she has had her fateful glimpse of a cherished alternative, to accept readily her pre-ordained life.

The first blow to Martine is her discovery that Julien, the young man who has just met her and is showing an interest in her, is the grandson of her neighbour Madame Mervan. The flicker of hope that a fruitful relationship might develop between Julien and herself is dimmed for two reasons. First there is Martine's awareness of a social gap: in her position as the occasional unpaid assistant and companion to Madame Mervan, she is clearly conscious that Julien is in a higher social class. The ease with which Julien can address Martine by her Christian name contrasts sharply with Martine's inability, at any point in the play, to bring herself to call Julien by his Christian name. [2] Then again Martine knows, from her conversations with Madame Mervan, of Jeanne; the latter is, according to Madame Mervan, Julien's fiancée, an assertion which he attempts to deny.

During his first two weeks in Grandchin Julien sees Martine frequently, and is thrown into agitation when he notices her through his window. It seems, in fact, that he genuinely likes Martine. But the more he sees of her, the more he senses that in addition to the social difference, to which he attaches no importance, there exists a wide intellectual and spiritual divergence. Martine's lack of cultural sophistication prevents her from appreciating some of his compliments; unable to understand, she responds by nervous giggling to a symbol he evokes. It is at a moment when he is most disillusioned with Martine that Jeanne appears, displaying from the start a close spiritual and intellectual affinity with Julien. So much so that he soon remarks to Jeanne:

> Je parlais une langue étrangère et je retrouve un parler familier, une façon directe de comprendre les choses ... sans explications. Le langage de ce qui ne s'exprime pas ... (Il la

---

[2] In the fifth tableau (p. 173 in *Théâtre I*, Paris, Albin Michel, 1925) she addresses him as "monsieur Julien." Similarly, Perdican remains for Rosette in *On ne badine pas avec l'amour* "monseigneur" or "monsieur le docteur."

regarde.) Et il y a tant de choses qui ne s'expriment pas et qu'il faut comprendre ... comme ça ... n'est-ce pas? [3]

When at the end of the second tableau Jeanne, to Julien's delight, is able to complete a stanza from Chénier which Martine, a few minutes earlier, had failed to recognize as poetry, it becomes obvious to us that Madame Mervan's matchmaking is bearing fruit and that Martine's chances have vanished.

Julien, then, is no longer likely to disturb the pattern of Martine's life that has been rehearsed from generation to generation; there is now no issue for her from the life-style which she was apparently beginning to see as one not intended for her. This last statement calls for clarification. There seems little doubt that Martine enjoys the whole business of working on her father's farm. But the author implies that looming about her village is that cloddishness which Martine certainly does not possess, but which would directly threaten to spread to her in the event of an association with Alfred. In another age, perhaps, she would have displayed her independence by moving to another town. But she is tied to her village by family responsibilities. Alfred, in his clumsy way of wooing, rubs in facts which she would earnestly like to be untrue:

> Tu sais bien qu'on finira toujours par se marier. Tu te marieras, faut bien. Et qui que c'est que t'épouseras? [...] Toi et moi, on est fait pour se marier. [4]

In the meantime Julien and Jeanne get married and, after a while, they decide to go and live in Paris. A year later Madame Mervan dies, and the couple return to settle the sale of the house in Grandchin. By this time, Martine is married to Alfred and is having her first baby. To the casual observer, unacquainted with her story, she is just an ordinary farmer's wife rendering invaluable service to her husband and dutifully bearing his children. But we know that her hidden scars have not disappeared, and that her experience is preventing her from being completely happy now that she is resignedly

---

[3] Tableau 2, pp. 129-130.
[4] Tableau 3, pp. 133, 135.

following the foreordained undeviating course. Serge Radine aptly remarks:

> Julien a éveillé en son âme des besoins nouveaux, des goûts plus fins, plus délicats, qui ne lui permettront plus désormais de trouver la joie et l'apaisement dans une destinée adaptée à sa condition. [5]

Martine was Bernard's first attempt to tackle on the stage a vast and complex technical problem:

> Est-il possible de porter à la scène des sentiments que les personnages n'extériorisent pas, soit qu'ils ne puissent les avouer, soit qu'ils n'en aient pas conscience? Qu'on veuille bien se rappeler que l'amour secret de Martine n'a jamais échappé à aucun spectateur et que pourtant le mot d'amour n'est pas prononcé une seule fois dans la pièce. [6]

What is unusual about *Martine* is not the mere existence of the hidden love. Dramatists have long recognized the tension which can be produced in a character, and the interest which can be generated, by such a love. What is much more unusual in a play which centres on hidden love is the failure of the female protagonist ever to mention her love at all. The more common procedure is for the dramatist to find a means whereby the character may clearly disclose the long-standing secret. The false report of Thésée's death encourages Phèdre to make such a disclosure to her confidante and then to Hippolyte. In *Uncle Vanya* too, Sonia, a close relation of Martine's, secretly in love with Astrov for six years, manages to declare herself to her stepmother, though not to Astrov. But Martine, provided with no one in whom she can confide, is forced to take her own counsel, and, denied the convenience of a protracted soliloquy, she never lets us hear her declaration of love.

This does not mean that she never comes close to voicing her feelings. Witness the following exchange:

---

[5] Serge Radine, *Essais sur le théâtre* (1919-1939), Genève-Annemasse, Éditions du Mont-Blanc, S. A., 1944, p. 124.

[6] Jean-Jacques Bernard, 'Quelques précisions, après deux récentes expériences,' *Comœdia*, 7 avril 1924, p. 1.

JULIEN. Il est émouvant, ce champ de blé encore intact... Jusque-là je ne l'avais pas remarqué, parce qu'il était entouré d'autres champs de blé. Mais, aujourd'hui que tout est fauché autour de lui, sa forme se dessine. Et voyez quel symbole! Sa forme est exactement celle d'une corne d'abondance...

MARTINE. (*Riant.*) Une corne...

JULIEN. (*Lâchant sa main.*) ...Oui... (*Il s'écarte. Elle courbe la tête. Au bout d'un instant, il se retourne et la regarde.*) Qu'est-ce que vous avez? (*Il va vers elle.*)

MARTINE. Je ne sais pas... je ne sais pas... (*Elle tombe dans ses bras, sans forces.*)

JULIEN. (*Après un moment.*) Dites-moi, Martine...

MARTINE. Ce n'est rien... Je pense trop... Je pense trop. [7]

Martine is here patently overcome with emotion to which she will not or can not give utterance. We should consider this exchange in relation to the action that has taken place in the interval between the first two tableaux. During the two weeks separating the end of the first tableau and the beginning of the second, Julien and Martine have been seeing each other constantly, and we are left to imagine that during this time Martine's initial inclination has had the opportunity to mature into love. This appears to us a more accurate interpretation than that of Léon Lemonnier, who suggests a much quicker process in Martine:

> Comment sommes-nous sûrs qu'elle aime Julien? Dans tout le premier tableau, nous sentons quelle joie elle éprouve à se sentir auprès du jeune homme. Mais tout à coup, il lui dit: 'En route vers Grandchin, Martine... comme deux amoureux.' Et elle s'arrête brusquement, interdite: son amour s'est révélé à nous, non point par ses propres paroles, mais par l'écho éveillé en elle par les mots entendus. [8]

We believe instead that Martine is taken aback because Julien's words bring to a conscious state the yet half-perceived wish that they might in fact form a loving pair, a wish which she will nurture during her subsequent encounters with him.

---

[7] Tableau 2, p. 124.

[8] Léon Lemonnier, 'Le Théâtre de M. Jean-Jacques Bernard,' *Choses de théâtre,* mars 1923, p. 271.

Nevertheless, her frequent meetings with Julien do nothing to reduce her sense of inferiority. As Daniel Mornet says,

> Un autre instinct lui fait deviner, à chaque instant, que Julien ne peut pas l'aimer, qu'entre elle et lui il y a l'abîme qui sépare son ignorance, ses habitudes frustes de son intelligence raffinée, de son goût exigeant. Tout cela n'est en elle qu'impression puissante, mais obscure. [9]

The exchange we have quoted above follows immediately upon Martine's hopeless perplexity on hearing Julien quote Chénier, and his somewhat condescending promise to cultivate in her a love of poetry. She is intuitive enough to sense Julien's irritation and disillusion when, as she laughs without understanding the image of the cornucopia, he brusquely moves away, letting go her hand. Her love for Julien is obvious, but her feelings of rejection, unworthiness and inferiority are strong enough to defeat the urge to unbosom herself. Perhaps another heroine, in spite of herself, would have taken the opportunity to pronounce a tirade, without having to be coaxed. But Bernard, concerned with the problem of unexpressed sentiment in the theatre, manages to derive dramatic vigour from Martine's very absence of speech, and to provide plausible psychological justification for her evasive taciturnity.

It is doubtful whether Martine's failure to declare herself is intended by the author as a sign of natural inarticulateness. Certainly we should be careful not to overstress her simplicity and suggest that it constitutes a form of mental deficiency. Notwithstanding Bernard's patronizing treatment of the peasant (as is so manifest in his depiction of Alfred) it would be wrong to see Martine as a female François le Champi. At the age of ten, "le pauvre enfant ne montrait guère plus son raisonnement dans ses paroles que le jour où [Madeleine] l'avait questionné pour la première fois. Il ne savait dire mot, et quand on voulait le faire causer, il était arrêté tout de suite, parce qu'il ne savait rien de rien." [10]

---

[9] Daniel Mornet, *Introduction à l'étude des écrivains français d'aujourd'hui*, Paris, Boivin & Cie, 1939, p. 124.

[10] George Sand, *François le Champi*, Paris, Nelson-Calmann-Lévy, 1937, pp. 52-53.

The evidence does not suggest in Martine an inborn all-embracing reticence. In her initial encounter with Julien, before she learns who he is, she is fairly expansive on her daily activities, and is able to engage in normal polite conversation. [11] There is even less evidence to support the view that Martine is feeble-minded. The fact that she does not recognize Chénier's *Le Mendiant* when Julien recites from it does not make her a simpleton. Rather we should bear in mind that there is a definite progression in Martine's personality, and that it is only when Jeanne appears and wins Julien's preference that she stubbornly withdraws into herself.

She had of course always been aware of the existence of Jeanne, Julien's presumed fiancée; but feeding on Julien's reassurances as on her own self-persuasion, she had allowed herself to think that Jeanne was unimportant to Julien. The latter had begun to assume in Martine's mind the proportions of a future husband, while Jeanne had been conveniently relegated to the back of both their minds. The author chooses to introduce her on stage and remind everyone of her existence during the second tableau — that is, after the process of falling in love has been completed for Martine. Jeanne's arrival is announced to us at the very beginning of the tableau, [12] so that later on the significance of the stiffened attitude of Martine and Julien on hearing the doorbell is at once patent:

> On entend la clochette. [. . .] Tous deux s'immobilisent brusquement. Et puis Martine, sans parler, parce qu'elle n'en a pas la force, désigne la fenêtre du doigt. [13]

This is the first occasion in the play on which Bernard indicates that Martine is physically incapable of speech, and no doubt Julien's implicit rejection of her (on her failure to visualize the cornucopia) which directly precedes Jeanne's entrance is partly responsible. The timing of Jeanne's arrival is from the technical point of view excellent, in that it contributes decisively to the destruction of Martine's secret aspirations. She stands in paralysed silence, as yet unnoticed by Jeanne, as Julien and Jeanne hold hands and look at each other. She has more or less to be dragged out of the room by Madame Mervan,

---

[11] Tableau 1, p. 102.
[12] P. 115.
[13] Tableau 2, pp. 124-125.

anxious to leave Julien and Jeanne together alone. From this time forth, Martine's words will be numbered.

One may say that in this play the author uses the theatre as a laboratory: he is eager to test the dramatic possibilities of unspoken thought and sentiment, and, what is more, he treats the protagonist like the subject of an experiment. The play proceeds through a series of quasi-scientific experiments, during which we are invited to observe the effect of certain stimuli on a passive subject. Since Martine is not given to self-analysis and soliloquies, since she becomes in the play more and more of an introvert, our intimate acquaintance with her personality is derived from what others say about her, and from her own monosyllabic, incomplete or repetitive responses when others speak to her. In conjunction with observation, then, some measure of imaginative effort is required from the spectator or reader.

For instance, we can sense throughout the play that Martine would instinctively like to remain free from the atmosphere of boorishness which Alfred is meant to exude. But because this is on a non-reflective level, she never says so directly. Instead, her revolt at the idea of being submerged in the life from which she might just have escaped is conveyed through one repeated phrase:

> ALFRED. Faut qu'on vive ensemble tous les jours, dans la même maison.
> MARTINE. Tu vas te taire? ...
> ALFRED. Faut qu'on ait les mêmes meubles, les mêmes champs. Faut que tu prépares la soupe pour moi tous les soirs.
> MARTINE. Tu vas te taire? ...
> ALFRED. Faut que tu aies des enfants avec moi. Faut que tu les nourrisses près de moi. Faut qu'on soit tout un, toi et moi. Faut que tu sois la mère et moi le père.
> MARTINE. Tu vas te taire? ... Tu vas te taire? ...
> ALFRED. Dis-moi que ce sera comme ça.
> MARTINE. Non, non, non! [14]

Whether any man, peasant or not, would court a maiden in this fashion is of course debatable. Alfred displays here and elsewhere an unbelievably sad lack of sensitivity, and it is regrettable that such a

---

[14] Tableau 3, pp. 135-136.

highly sensitive being as Martine should eventually have to make do
with him. There is, however, little reason to believe that he realizes
to what extent his litany is distressing Martine. Allowing his impatience to get the better of him, keen to encourage Martine, he is
painting a picture of future domestic bliss which he innocently
imagines is as much of an enticement to her as it is to him. As he
is endowed by the author with no great insight, her repeated "Tu
vas te taire?" merely represents a shallow act of resistance which
time and effort will be sure to counter. But this repetition signifies
more than an inability to set forth her revolt categorically enough to
allow Alfred finally to begin to understand her. Rather it is an instinctive, desperate attempt to block completely from her own view
future life with Alfred and its concomitant atmosphere, to which she
appears doomed. By so doing, she manages to keep her 'revolt' in a
dormant state and to lessen the force of its reality. Needless to say,
this is not a conscious process. What she is conscious of is her responsibility to carry on the management of her parents' farm in their
old age, the impossibility of winning Julien, and the futility of any
aspirations to an alternative to Alfred. It appears in the end that the
elemental attitude of resignation has conquered the once nascent urge
to escape from Alfred and his aura. It is then we realize that this
internal struggle, which is so basic to the play and which is always
perceptible, has never once been mentioned.

The stimuli that evoke discernible reactions in Martine are largely
stimuli of pain administered through the words of others; the play
is made up, to a great extent, of sectional views of her suffering.
Living with Alfred, she is subjected to a number of painfully tactless
statements, which force her to contemplate, in spite of herself, her
life with him, and to measure the distance between this actual life
and the one of which she once dreamt. Such statements occur for
example when Jeanne invites Martine and Alfred to Paris:

> JEANNE.   Eh bien! c'est ça, Alfred, et plus tard, au prin-
> temps, ce sera le tour de Martine, n'est-ce pas?
> ALFRED.   C'est qu'au printemps ... y aura le gosse ...
> Et vous savez ce que c'est quand les enfants se mettent à
> venir dans une maison. D'abord faut les nourrir et, tandis
> qu'on nourrit le premier, y a le deuxième qu'est pas loin
> d'arriver. (*Il se met à rire.*) Hé! Hé! ce n'est pas nous qu'on
> renâclera à la besogne, pas, Martine? (*Il est allé vers elle et
> lui donne une petite bourrade sur l'épaule.*)

MARTINE. (*D'une voix étranglée.*) Laisse-moi donc...
JEANNE. (*Doucement.*) Ne craignez pas d'avoir des enfants, Martine. C'est le vrai bonheur...
ALFRED. (*Tassant sa pipe en marchant.*) Chez nous, on
était six. Ça donnait du mal à la mère, c'est vrai. A peine
levée, avant le jour, fallait qu'elle récure et qu'elle torche;
et puis c'était la soupe à faire pour tous, sans parler des
bêtes qu'on ne peut pas oublier parce qu'on a des gosses.
Mais elle n'aurait jamais de la vie changé contre une qu'en
n'avait point. [15]

Martine is seen here to be suffering through the words of a simple-
minded person. With another character we could safely have assumed
that the last remark was an indirect way of reproaching her. But the
author has throughout the play taken such pains to assure us of
Alfred's ignorance of her emotional make-up, to indicate the wide
gap between Martine and Alfred, who continually despairs by his
inability to attune himself to her, that such an assumption would
probably be false. Naturally, this does not help to make Alfred particularly convincing as a character.

The process of suffering begins for Martine as soon as Jeanne
appears and wins Julien's favour; Martine distinguishes herself by
the passivity with which she undergoes pain, and by her failure to
retaliate or defend herself verbally. Every character in the play contributes to her suffering, though (as in the case of Alfred) not always
with any intentional malice. With Alfred a plea of ignorance is acceptable. After all, Bernard does not furnish him with great powers
of perception, and since Martine never speaks of her unhappiness he
is not expected to have noticed it. The suffering which Julien and
Jeanne cause Martine cannot be explained on these grounds. They
are both highly sensitive and perceptive beings.

A curious relationship develops between Martine and Jeanne.
Julien's position as a journalist in Paris demands that he spend much
of his time away from Grandchin; during his absence the two women,
whom another author would perhaps have made *femmes rivales*, take
obvious delight in each other's company, deliberately seek each other
out, and invariably speak of Julien. There is a scene between them,
full of contained emotion, in which Bernard gives of his best, a scene
which ends with the woman who has reason to be bitter and resentful,

---

[15] Tableau 5, p. 181.

and the one who declines to adopt the arrogant stance of the victorious rival departing arm in arm.

Jeanne is aware that whatever took place, before her arrival, between Julien and Martine has had a far more lasting effect on Martine than on him. She is therefore hesitant at first to speak of him:

> JEANNE. Savez-vous... quand je vois vos cheveux et vos yeux... je pourrais être jalouse...
> MARTINE. (Dans un mouvement en arrière.) Ma... demoiselle...
> JEANNE. Allez! ne protestez pas... Je plaisantais, car je connais Julien... Et vous aussi, ma petite Martine, je vous connais bien. [16]

Jeanne then turns the conversation to Alfred, and, when she sees that the topic distresses Martine, she conveniently talks about the weather. A few moments later, she returns to Julien, only to be given by Martine herself encouragement to continue:

> JEANNE. Il n'y a que vous à Grandchin avec qui je puisse causer cinq minutes sans fatigue. Du moins en ce moment... Oh! car en temps normal, c'est différent... Mais ce voyage de Julien est si long...
> MARTINE. (Avec anxiété.) Est-ce que... monsieur Julien va revenir bientôt?
> JEANNE. Dans huit jours. Cela fait trois semaines d'absence... Trois longues semaines qui ne m'ont pas fait grâce d'un seul jour... Mais je vous ennuie... Parlons plutôt de vous...
> MARTINE. Non, non, ne parlons pas de moi... Vous disiez que... dans huit jours...
> JEANNE. Oui, nous sommes plus près de son retour que de son départ maintenant.
> MARTINE. (Vivement.) Oh! oui...
> JEANNE. (Lui serrant la main.) Vous êtes bien gentille... Quand on lui a proposé de faire une enquête en Allemagne pour le compte de son journal, je n'ai voulu voir que les avantages: les belles impressions qu'il allait rapporter de là-bas et sa situation au journal après cela... Je ne pensais pas manquer de courage. Car c'est ridicule; une semaine, ça va passer vite...
> MARTINE. Une semaine... ça... ce n'est plus rien...
> JEANNE. Oh! n'est-ce pas... Répétez-le-moi.

---

[16] Tableau 3, p. 140.

MARTINE. Oui, mademoiselle, il ne faut pas... (*Elle ne peut achever.*)

JEANNE. Allez! ce sera bon de le voir revenir... Nous illuminerons ce jour-là...

MARTINE. (*Convaincue.*) Oh! oui...

JEANNE. Vous serez du premier dîner chez grand'mère. Oh! ce premier dîner... Et puis le mariage dans la petite église de Grandchin... Ensuite nous serons tranquilles jusqu'à la rentrée des Chambres... A ce moment, il fera le voyage de Paris presque tous les jours... Mais les journées ne seront pas tristes, puisqu'il y aura du bonheur au bout... Seulement, c'est alors que mon amie Martine sera la bienvenue dans la maison... Vous viendrez souvent, j'espère...

MARTINE. Je viendrai, oui... souvent... très souvent, je vous le jure...

JEANNE. (*Rêveuse.*) Je sais bien qu'il vaudrait mieux que nous allions habiter Paris... Mais pour grand'mère... Et puis il y a la question matérielle — vous comprenez — au moins pour l'instant... Paris, ce sera pour plus tard... dans quelques mois, j'espère... Qu'est-ce qu'il y a?... Vous avez froid?...

MARTINE. Non, non...

JEANNE. (*Les yeux au loin, après un silence.*) Évidemment, ici, nous serons toujours un peu dans le provisoire... Le rêve, ce sera de créer un foyer nouveau... Des meubles à nous... Une table familiale... le père... la mère... les enfants... Mais vous frissonnez... Décidément vous mourez de froid. Il fait presque nuit. Nous allons partir.

MARTINE. (*Épouvantée.*) Oui, oui... (*Elles se lèvent toutes les deux.*)

JEANNE. (*La regarde avec surprise et puis l'attire à elle.*) Vous êtes triste... Ah! je parle de moi et je vous oublie... Vous avez quelque chose sur le cœur que vous allez me raconter. Est-ce que je vous ai fait de la peine tout à l'heure?

MARTINE. (*Vivement.*) Je n'ai rien, non, je n'ai rien, je n'ai rien.

JEANNE. Eh bien! vous me direz ce que vous voudrez. Voulez-vous rentrer par les petits chemins? Nous serons plus longtemps ensemble... Oui?... Non, vous préférez la route?

MARTINE. (*S'accrochant à son bras.*) Si, si... par les petits chemins... Et vous me parlerez de... de... puisque... ça vous fait du bien... (*Elles s'éloignent bras-dessus bras-dessous, les têtes presque jointes.*) [17]

---

[17] *Ibid.*, pp. 143-145.

We witness in Martine during this exchange two successive emotional processes, the clues for which are found primarily in Jeanne's words, and, by refraction, in Martine's briefer interjections. The first phase is one in which Martine so totally identifies herself with Jeanne that she becomes the silent echo, perceptible to an attentive audience, of Jeanne's sentiments. As much as, or perhaps even more than Jeanne, Martine misses Julien, is anxious to see him again, and is happy that he will soon be back. In the second phase, Martine is made to watch her own dreams which will never come true being dreamt aloud by the person for whom they are a preface to reality. She takes pleasure in picturing the happiness in which Julien will share, albeit without her; at the same time, she inevitably suffers on witnessing the enthusiastically sketched picture of the happiness which she would have liked for herself; but she is even more afflicted by the prospect that the last thread of contact with Julien may be broken if Julien and Jeanne do decide subsequently to leave for Paris. [18] Her expeditious denial — "Je n'ai rien, non, je n'ai rien, je n'ai rien" — is a patent avowal that something *is* the matter. Her reaction, then, is a mixture of pain and vicarious satisfaction, both conveyed through the nervous quivering which Jeanne appears at first to take for the effect of the cold.

Martine's brevity and Jeanne's reverie combine to make a monologue out of a dialogue. The monologue is broken only intermittently; its completion coincides with Jeanne's belated realization that her words are responsible for Martine's convulsive trembling. Jeanne pursues a train of thought in which she is soon so wrapped up that she becomes almost oblivious of the presence of Martine; the latter, for her part, does little to make her presence felt. And yet, it is obviously on Martine that our attention is meant to be focussed. This spotlight on self-effacement is, in effect, one of the main features of the play, and with it Bernard develops a totally unhackneyed way of producing pathos.

Jeanne's motives in seeking out Martine are not selfless. She does not attempt to conceal from Martine that it is only when Julien is away that, in preference to the company of the elderly Madame Mervan, she needs Martine's company. Such an admission — a sign

---

[18] It is significant that Jeanne first notices her trembling when she mentions this future plan to migrate.

of Jeanne's honesty — seems to leave Martine unaffected. Yet it would probably have hurt her feelings if she herself found pleasure in Jeanne's company for Jeanne's own sake. Since Jeanne senses that this is not the case, that particular admission is evidently not determined by an urge to wound. On the other hand, her admission of absolute confidence in Julien, the assurance she gives Martine that she does not even stand consideration as a rival — "Quand je vois vos cheveux et vos yeux... je pourrais être jalouse. [...] Je plaisantais, car je connais Julien" [19] — is tinged with a semi-conscious, uncontrollable desire to hurt Martine, to which Jeanne confesses in the lucid analysis of their relationship that she later makes:

> JEANNE. Je vois clair à présent. Nous ne saurons jamais ce qu'un flirt de quelques jours, qui n'a eu aucune importance pour toi, a pu laisser dans cette âme simple...
> JULIEN. C'est ridicule.
> JEANNE. Non. Il doit y avoir là un pauvre petit secret mal caché... Et je la laisse venir. Bien mieux: je lui cours après. Quand tu es loin, je ne peux me passer d'elle. Et je lui parle de toi. Et je lui fais mal. Et je ne peux pas faire autrement.
> JULIEN. Pourquoi lui parles-tu de moi?
> JEANNE. Je me promets chaque fois de ne plus recommencer. Mais tout dans son attitude m'y pousse. Et chaque fois je succombe à la tentation. Naturellement, ce qui m'attire, ce n'est pas de faire souffrir: c'est de sentir en cette petite l'inconscient désir de se raccrocher à cela... Je suis tout ce qui lui reste de toi.
> JULIEN. Si tu le sens, comment ne réagis-tu pas?
> JEANNE. J'essaye... Et c'est plus fort que moi. Car, comprends: moi aussi, je te retrouve en elle.
> JULIEN. Tu me retrouves... Par exemple!
> JEANNE. Oui, quand tu n'es pas là... Tu as mis en elle un peu de toi, comme dans un livre que tu aurais aimé ou dans un petit chien avec lequel tu aurais joué quelques jours... Je devrais plutôt être jalouse, n'est-ce pas?
> JULIEN. Il n'y a pas lieu...
> JEANNE. Non, pauvre petite, il n'y a pas lieu et elle doit bien le sentir... Mais le plus cruel, c'est qu'aussitôt que tu reviens, elle n'existe plus pour moi. Pour un peu sa présence m'agacerait. [20]

---

[19] Tableau 3, p. 140.
[20] Tableau 4, pp. 158-159.

Jeanne's "nous ne saurons jamais ce qu'un flirt de quelques jours, qui n'a eu aucune importance pour toi, a pu laisser dans cette âme simple" is reminiscent of the chorus's words in *On ne badine pas avec l'amour*:

> Hélas! la pauvre fille ne sait pas quel danger elle court, en écoutant les discours d'un jeune et galant seigneur. [21]

As might be expected, there are important differences of tone, structure and content in the two plays. After all, Rosette's rôle is relatively minor, and it is obvious to everyone, except to her, that Perdican's love for her is wholly spurious. True, it appears that both dramatists subscribe to the commonplace according to which the features of the peasant are ignorance and naivety. Yet Perdican is far more patronizing and authoritative than Julien, and Rosette possesses a credulity and a promptness to submit to the overlord that Martine is unable to match:

> PERDICAN. (*S'avançant.*) Descends vite, Rosette, et viens ici.
> ROSETTE. (*Entrant.*) Oui, monseigneur.
> PERDICAN. Tu me voyais de ta fenêtre, et tu ne venais pas, méchante fille? Donne-moi vite cette main-là, et ces joues-là, que je t'embrasse.
> ROSETTE. Oui, monseigneur. [22]

All the same, though Julien, unlike Perdican, does not drastically declare love and promise marriage to Martine, and though the effect of the 'adventure' on the latter will presumedly not be fatal, *On ne badine pas...* does easily suggest itself as a prototype for *Martine*. In retrospect, Julien can see that his innocent flirtation has not been innocuous. As Serge Radine puts it,

> Ce qui n'est pour [lui] qu'une idylle délicieuse, mais sans lendemain, sera pour Martine le grand amour de sa vie, et cet amour malheureux la rendra désormais incapable de connaître le bonheur. Par suite de [sa] légèreté [...] qui, pour

---

[21] Alfred de Musset, *On ne badine pas avec l'amour*, Act III, sc. 4, p. 62 in *Comédies et proverbes II*, Paris, Société Les Belles Lettres, 1952.
[22] Act I, sc. 4, p. 21.

être innocente n'en est pas moins cruelle, voici une destinée brisée. [23]

It is difficult to agree with May Daniels who says that "for an educated and intelligent man [Julien's] total incomprehension of the state of affairs he has brought about is disquieting," and who sees this as "an outstanding weakness in the play." [24] When Julien tells Jeanne: "Tu grossis tout cela, je t'assure," [25] he is attempting to convince *himself* that he has not done Martine any great harm; he proves thereby that he is not unable to understand, but, in effect, eager to shirk the responsibility for Martine's unhappiness.

Even so, Julien is not, in our view, convincingly delineated. Admitting the strong affinity between himself and Jeanne, which they both immediately recognize, we still find his cool treatment of Martine too instantaneous. With what looks like willed indifference, he 'forgets' to introduce her to Jeanne, who assumes that Martine is the maid; he summarily dismisses her as a nonentity to Jeanne — "Oh! C'est un flirt si vous voulez. Vous savez, à Grandchin...";[26] as from this moment on he has eyes only for Jeanne, Martine ceases to exist for him. We are left to imagine that he does not want to cause any deterioration in an already bad situation.

His behaviour towards Martine in the last tableau is therefore as inexcusable as it is inconsistent and difficult to explain. He seems suddenly infused with the egoism and arrogance of the man who assumes that his forsaken admirer will never be able to find happiness with anyone else, and who seeks a reassurance to his pride in an unambiguous acknowledgement of this. He seems driven by a sadistic urge to wrench from her her "pauvre petit secret mal caché." His tactless questions ("Est-ce que vous êtes heureuse avec Alfred? [...] Vous allez être maman, Martine. Êtes-vous contente? [...] Alfred est-il gentil avec vous? [...] Vous ne regrettez rien?") [27] help to reopen the wounds that time was probably beginning to heal partially, and effectively deny her the possibility of ignoring her unhappiness and

---

[23] Serge Radine, *Essais sur le théâtre* (1919-1939), pp. 123-124.
[24] May Daniels, *The French Drama of The Unspoken*, Edinburgh at the University Press, 1953, p. 188.
[25] Tableau 4, p. 159.
[26] Tableau 2, p. 127.
[27] Tableau 5, pp. 175, 177.

her regrets. And this when Julien himself, by his previous attitude, had suggested to us and to her that he would have wished her to forget painlessly.

The scene points to a real inconsistency in Julien's character, and one explanation for this weakness is that Martine was the only character who really interested the author, and to whom he paid scrupulous attention. We whole-heartedly endorse the view of Henry Bidou who says:

> Il a fait sa pièce de la suite des douleurs de Martine et de sa résignation: *au fond, l'ouvrage est un monodrame.* Martine séduite, Martine amicalement délaissée, Martine ramassant les miettes de son bonheur, Martine importune, Martine fidèle à sa douleur, Martine enfin consommant le sacrifice, perdant jusqu'à la liberté de sa souffrance et se laissant marier. [28]

Indeed there is a perilous tightrope exercise involved in writing a monodrama where the words of others illuminate the one reticent performer, and where these others are not supposed to form an invisible and undifferentiated chorus. The obvious unfortunate (and to some extent unavoidable) defect of Bernard's monodrama is the relative weakness of the surrounding characters: the portrait of Madame Mervan gives an over-all impression of sketchiness, and that of Alfred merely embodies the stereotype of the boor. Jeanne is a more carefully elaborated character, but Julien, in his uncalled for cross-examination of Martine, is given attitudes which we find inconsequent. The scene is gratuitous, and extracts from Martine a gratuitous ounce of pain. In fact, one feels that it is designed solely to present Martine during yet another moment of suffering. The sheer desire to show us Martine responding to another stimulating dose of pain appears here to override all other considerations on the part of the author.

Julien's interrogation has, *mutatis mutandis,* all the severity of 'third degree' questioning. So much so that Martine comes remarkably close to letting the suppressed fact be elicited explicitly. She is finally goaded into a hint of protest which, true to form, she does not develop:

---

[28] Henry Bidou, 'Chronique Dramatique,' *Journal des Débats,* 19 mai 1922, p. 841. My emphasis.

MARTINE. Mais je ne vous ai rien dit, monsieur Julien... Je croyais que vous vouliez que j'aie oublié... Alors qu'est-ce que vous voulez?
JULIEN. *(Incertain.)* Ce que je veux?... Mais... savoir que vous pensez encore à... à...
MARTINE. A quoi est-ce que ça sert, monsieur Julien?
JULIEN. ...A rien...
MARTINE. Si ça ne sert à rien, pourquoi me dire tout ça maintenant?... Ça ne vous suffit pas, ce que vous m'avez fait?
JULIEN. Ce que je vous ai fait?...
MARTINE. *(Effrayée de ses paroles.)* Enfin... j'ai mal dit... Vous comprenez... Enfin, je ne sais pas, moi. [29]

For all her simplicity, Martine must possess self-esteem, and her failure to amplify could be in this instance an automatic attempt to preserve some of her pride. Be that as it may, the spectator or reader, while feeling compassion for her, is entirely justified in experiencing, at the end of such a scene, a deep sense of frustration. The traditions of the psychological theatre condition us to expect that powerful emotion, if not at once stated, will eventually break through all existing barriers and receive fairly coherent expression. Our frustration is therefore in direct proportion to the sum of expectations that the conventional psychological drama has fathered in us; the more we anticipate development, elaboration and expansion, the greater our sense of disappointment. A further reversal of values lies in the prominence afforded to the seemingly unobtrusive, and to what is absent. As in the Martine-Jeanne scene discussed above, [30] the spotlight is on self-effacement, and meaning and emotion are derived more from what the protagonist fails to say than from what she says.

Nowhere, however, is the emotive power of her silent passivity more striking than in the fourth tableau:

JEANNE. Ce n'est pas seulement de l'impatience. Je suis nerveuse, très nerveuse... Je vais vous dire pourquoi, si vous me promettez de ne pas le répéter. *(Martine la regarde avec surprise.)* Depuis quelques jours... je suis à peu près sûre que je suis enceinte.
MARTINE. *(D'une voix blanche.)* Enceinte...

---

[29] Tableau 5, pp. 178-179.
[30] Pp. 82 ff.

JEANNE. Cela vous explique ma nervosité... Il n'y a
que Julien et grand'mère qui le sachent... et vous, maintenant. N'en parlez pas encore... (*La porte* [...] *s'ouvre en
coup de vent.*)
JULIEN. (*Entrant.*) Coucou!
JEANNE. Julien!... Je ne t'avais pas entendu...
JULIEN. Je suis venu avec la voiture de Mulin et je suis
descendu au bas du village... Bonjour, Martine...
JEANNE. Ah! Julien! (*Elle tombe dans ses bras en san-
glotant. Martine est remontée vers la fenêtre.*)
JULIEN. Eh bien! qu'est-ce que tu as, Jeanne? En voilà
une enfant!
JEANNE. (*Se redressant et le regardant.*) Je suis ridicule.
Je m'étais mis dans la tête que tu arriverais par le train de
neuf heures. Et, comme tu n'arrivais pas, il me venait des
idées folles... (*Elle se met à rire.*) Qu'est-ce que tu dois
penser de moi? Je suis honteuse.
JULIEN. Tu devrais pourtant savoir qu'il n'y a pas lieu
de t'inquiéter.
JEANNE. Je n'étais pas inquiète.
JULIEN. Alors?
JEANNE. Ça ne s'explique pas.
JULIEN. La séance d'hier a fini à minuit passé. Il y a
séance aujourd'hui, mais Mourron me remplace... Martine,
est-ce que je vous ai dit bonjour?
MARTINE. Oui, quand vous êtes entré...
JEANNE. Mourron te remplace. Est-ce qu'il ne pourrait
pas?...
JULIEN. Permuter avec moi... C'est justement... (*Il
regarde Martine. Jeanne la regarde également. Martine semble
rivée au sol. Julien baisse la voix.*) Il en a touché un mot
au directeur qui paraît favorable. Au lieu de la Chambre,
j'aurais le supplément littéraire: trois après-midi par semaine
au journal. Le reste du temps, travail ici.
JEANNE. Le rêve...
JULIEN. J'ai bon espoir, mais n'en parle pas. (*Regardant
Martine et élevant la voix.*) Mulin a été très complaisant...
Grand'mère n'est pas là?
JEANNE. Elle est sortie. Je crois bien qu'elle mijote
quelque chose... (*Elle hésite et baisse la voix.*) pour Noël...
Entre nous...
JULIEN. Enfin, nous sommes tranquilles jusqu'à lundi.
Moi, je ne veux plus penser à Paris. Je suis ici, c'est l'essen-
tiel. (*Il s'assied. Silence. Tous deux regardent Martine à la
dérobée.*)
JEANNE. (*Embarrassée.*) Tu n'as pas besoin... de te re-
poser?...

JULIEN. Oh! non. Je n'ai besoin que ... de bavarder un peu avec toi ... (*Silence.*) Tout le monde va bien chez vous, Martine? ...

MARTINE. Oui, monsieur Julien.

JULIEN. Ah! ... tant mieux ... Jeanne, il n'y avait pas de lettres pour moi?

JEANNE. Non, pas ce matin ... (*Silence.*)

JULIEN. J'ai vu tes parents ... Ils comptent venir la semaine prochaine ...

JEANNE. Papa n'est pas trop fatigué?

JULIEN. Non ... (*Il regarde Martine, puis se lève.*)

JEANNE. Veux-tu que nous montions? ... Mais non, j'y pense, Simone fait la chambre.

JULIEN. Eh bien! restons ici ... (*Il tapote sur la cheminée.*)

JEANNE. (*Avec effort.*) Tu as ... tu as ... quelque chose à me dire?

JULIEN. (*Geste vague.*) Oh! ... Je suis content de te voir ... (*Silence.*)

JEANNE. (*De plus en plus péniblement.*) Nous parlions de toi, Martine et moi, avant ton arrivée ... Martine avait été assez gentille pour ... pour ... interrompre son travail ... un instant ...

JULIEN. Surtout, Martine, si ... vous avez à faire ... Avec nous ... ça n'a pas d'importance ... (*Pendant qu'ils parlaient, Martine les regardait fixement, sans bouger. Elle avait bien conscience de sa situation fausse, mais partir était au-dessus de ses forces ... Quand Julien se tait, elle essaye de parler, mais vainement. Et tout à coup, sans un mot, elle sort.*) [31]

The same material that is used in this scene could have been used for purposes of comedy. In a sense, what we witness is an attempt to get rid of someone who is *de trop*. The laws of discretion require a quick retreat from Martine after an exchange of greetings with Julien, and a cursory enquiry about his general welfare; the laws of hospitality forbid the couple to call upon her to leave. The scene, constructed between Martine's apparent reluctance to abide by the first laws and the couple's awareness of the second, provides a seesaw movement that Tristan Bernard — Jean-Jacques' father — would probably have been delighted to exploit. And yet the laughter

---

[31] Tableau 4, pp. 153-157.

which this scene threatens to provoke could hardly be Homeric, if only because of Martine's silent, unsettling presence.

Her silence during this scene is part of what Bernard understood by the 'unexpressed':

> Ce dialogue sous-jacent qui court sous les répliques, les sentiments que les personnages ne peuvent ou ne veulent exprimer ou dont ils n'ont pas conscience, ou, *pendant un dialogue, ceux d'un tiers qui l'écoute.* [32]

This silence of the third person is not uncommon, and has been employed to convey a variety of reactions. There are two obvious examples of it in Act II of *Le Tartuffe*: in the second scene Mariane's silence is one of fear, anxiety and amusement as she listens to Dorine getting the better of Orgon in the argument about the latter's choice of Tartuffe for his son-in-law; then, in the fourth scene, it is Dorine's turn to be silent with the silence of amusement — an amusement which she shares with the audience — as she listens to the would-be angry dispute between Mariane and Valère. Further back in time, we notice the effective use that Sophocles made of such silence in *Œdipus Rex*; Jocasta listens speechlessly, with growing horror, as the Messenger explains to Œdipus how the latter, with his feet pierced and bound, was entrusted to him by one of Laius' servants; when she makes her exit, it is to go and hang herself.

Martine's exit (which, unlike Jocasta's, is silent) has no such fearful consequence; fortunately too, for in this play it would have served to add an unnecessary touch of melodrama, similar to that which characterizes the last lines of *On ne badine pas....* The revelation which occasions Martine's silence is, all things considered, of no great moment. It is not easy to determine exactly what her reaction is to the news of Jeanne's pregnancy. While it is clearly visible that she does not welcome the announcement with rapturous enthusiasm, it is difficult to see how she could be disappointed, astonished, grieved or angry. The stage directions do not help to resolve the conundrum, for Martine is meant to echo the word *enceinte* in a *toneless* voice. We are therefore obliged to platitudinize that different things affect different people differently, and that the news of Jeanne's pregnancy

---

[32] Bernard, 'Le Théâtre de Demain,' *La Revue Mondiale*, 1er mars 1923, p. 9. My emphasis.

has affected Martine most gravely. But once we have accepted that the emotion is vague, there is no denying that it is powerful. It physically paralyses Martine and nails her to the ground so that she is unable to take various cues to depart; just before her eventual departure, it chokes her and prevents her from speaking, though she makes the necessary effort. The effect is potentially excruciating for the spectator.

For us, the most interesting aspect of the scene remains the competitive movement between silence and dialogue. In this respect, the author's arrangement of pauses is nothing short of masterly. Julien and Jeanne soon exhaust what they can say in front of Martine without feeling too ill at ease. But beyond lies silence, to which Martine is stubbornly adhering, and which already causes them discomfort. It threatens to overrun them and add even more to their discomfort. Hence the frequency of empty remarks which keep a superficial conversation going, and which, by covering up the invading silence, betray a fear of it:

> Grand'mère n'est pas là? [...] Tout le monde va bien chez vous, Martine? [...] J'ai vu tes parents... Ils comptent venir la semaine prochaine.

Long before the era of Beckett and Pinter, Jean-Jacques Bernard was using dialogue in defiance of the fearful void of silence. But we shall return to this later. [33]

Martine invites us to enter the realm of intuition. It is a song in praise of the virtues of unmediated perception. In the second tableau Julien makes a statement which, on consideration, is seen to apply to this play as a whole, and to Bernard's other plays of the same type:

> Je parlais une langue étrangère et je retrouve un parler familier, une façon directe de comprendre les choses... sans explications. Le langage de ce qui ne s'exprime pas. [...] Il y a tant de choses qui ne s'expriment pas et qu'il faut comprendre. [34]

---

[33] See below, pp. 208-209, 212 ff.
[34] Tableau 2, pp. 129-130.

Of all the characters in the play, Alfred is the only one who appears totally wanting in clairvoyance; the result is that for him Martine's suffering has no reality. In like manner, for the spectator or reader who does not accept the direct intuitive association which the play proffers, the reality of Martine's suffering is substantially diminished.

Though he was not concerned with crudely dragging the spectator on to the stage and duly embarrassing him, it is true to say that before 'audience participation' had become a rallying cry, Bernard was demanding a vital creative contribution from his audience. For *Martine* is a play that defies passive digestive attitudes. The fact that the play invites intuition does not mean that the mind is left fallow. Bernard assumes in his spectator the will to participate imaginatively and emotionally, and in the final analysis, the spectator harvests as much as he has sown. Bidou's remarks that with this play the spectator becomes the principal collaborator are well-grounded:

> [La pièce] émeut par ce qu'elle ne dit pas, bien plus que par ce qu'elle dit, et, au fond, c'est le spectateur qui fait la pièce. L'auteur ne lui donne qu'un prétexte à rêver, à imaginer des sentiments, à s'attendrir sur la grande pitié de la souffrance humaine. [35]

There remains, however, a grave danger: the play is wholly about Martine, and Martine exists as a character through her suffering and for her suffering; hence the protagonist and the play are simultaneously threatened with non-existence once this suffering begins to grow pallid, once its reality is diminished. Bernard attempts to avoid this by seeking the immediacy of the image. The play is to a tragic discourse on love's suffering as a Mantegna *St. Sebastian* is to D'Annunzio's *Le Martyre de Saint Sébastien*. [36] Whereas D'Annunzio's grandiose theatrical fresco is made diffuse by a delirious orgy of verbal colour, Mantegna had at his command the pictorial image, which enabled him to create economically a vivid and convincing presence of St. Sebastian.

---

[35] Henry Bidou, 'Chronique Dramatique,' *Journal des Débats*, 19 mai 1922, p. 840.
[36] First performed 22 May 1911 at the *Théâtre du Châtelet*.

Martine is a succession of concrete images of Martine's agony;[37] instead of letting us hear the rhetoric of anguish, Bernard makes us stare at the graphic picture of torment. The recognizable cause of Martine's torment is her thwarted love and overpowering frustration, conjoined with the thoughtlessness of others. But it is more difficult to account for the degree of torment visible in every portrait of her suffering. [38] Her suffering *is*, and the image justifies itself by its existence as a projected illustration of it.

The play, depending for its life on the creation of image, rather than the arrangement of impressive event, is characterized by a certain lack of mobility. There are various occasions on which physical motion on the stage is completely frozen. Martine, for her part, is often photographed as it were during moments of paralysis:

> Martine semble ne pas pouvoir bouger. [39]
> Martine semble rivée au sol. [40]
> Martine les regardait fixement, sans bouger. [...]
> Partir était au-dessus de ses forces. [41]
> Martine reste immobile. [42]

Furthermore, her love and suffering are so well tempered by her forbearance that they are denied their dramatic content; they are refused an outlet in positive action as well as in words; they prelude no decision on her part, they produce no event. Action is here kept in abeyance, for we are in the domain of static drama. And when the play ends, we are enveloped in a mood of chair-borne quiescence incarnated by Alfred and Martine:

> *(On entend les grelots de la voiture qui s'éloigne.)*
> ALFRED. Les v'là partis... *(Ils se taisent jusqu'au moment où l'on n'entend plus la voiture.)* [...] T'ai-je t'y dit qu'ils l'avaient vendue, la maison?...
> MARTINE. *(Sans comprendre.)* ...Vendue?...

---

[37] In this regard, the division of the play into tableaux instead of acts is a coincidence, to which it would be unwise to attach too much importance here.

[38] See above, pp. 92-93.

[39] Tableau 2, p. 126.

[40] Tableau 4, p. 155.

[41] *Ibid.*, p. 157.

[42] Tableau 5, p. 183.

ALFRED.   Oui, ce matin . . . Au nouveau gendre des Du-
boyer . . . Paraît qu'il va faire des changements. Il veut cons-
truire une aile et, rapport à la mauvaise exposition, fermer
les fenêtres de ce côté . . . (Il allume la lampe au-dessus de
la table. Martine s'est assise. Il s'assied en face d'elle. On
n'entend plus que l'horloge . . . Le rideau tombe lentement.) [43]

The vein is reminiscent of the last moments of The Cherry
Orchard: the stage is vacant, and the off-stage noises (of doors being
locked and carriages departing) gradually give place to a silence that
is interrupted only by the sound of a chopping axe. Firs appears
alone, talks to himself, and is eventually embraced by this silence:

A distant sound is heard, which seems to come from the
sky, the sound of a breaking string, slowly dying away, melancholy. It is followed by silence, broken only by the sound
of an axe striking a tree far away in the orchard.
Curtain. [44]

In Martine, the long silence, punctuated by the ticking clock and
preceding the final curtain, has, as in Chekhov's play, great dramatic
potential. But it is self-evident that this sort of pure silence was only
a part of Bernard's design, and that there is considerably more in
his play than an illustration of "the dramatic possibilities inherent in
the gaps between bits of dialogue." [45] Martine is not the main performer in a dumb-show. Her behaviour is dictated by the interaction
of instinct, common sense, self-respect, stubbornness and timidity. To
this is added a physical inability to formulate coherent phrases when
emotion is too great. Doubtless, there are people who in similar
circumstances pour out their hearts. Doubtless too, there are people
like Martine — and not only in the idyllically untutored provinces.
Yet the fact that Martines are so seldom the protagonists of plays
(as opposed to novels) is no little testimony to the formidable nature
of the problem posed to the dramatist by such a character.

With Martine, then, the author had proved to himself that he
could dramatize the sentiments of a main character that were not

---

[43] Ibid., pp. 183-184.
[44] Anton Chekhov, The Cherry Orchard, Act IV, p. 244 in Four Plays
(Translated by David Magarshack), London, Allen and Unwin, 1970.
[45] Bamber Gascoigne, Twentieth-century Drama, London, Hutchinson
University Library, 1963, p. 13.

externalized verbally. But this, for him, represented only a first step. "Les sentiments de Martine," he said, "sont simples. De l'espoir à la résignation, sa souffrance suit une ligne droite. N'était-il pas intéressant de chercher à traduire des passions moins unies? Une cristallisation — on sait que le mot est de Stendhal — comme dans *L'Invitation au voyage,* une passion refoulée comme dans *Le Printemps des autres?*" [46]

---

[46] Bernard, 'Quelques précisions, après deux récentes expériences,' *Comœdia,* 7 avril 1924, p. 1.

CHAPTER THREE

LE PRINTEMPS DES AUTRES

Martine BORE WITNESS to the author's recognition of silence as a forcible means of expression on the stage, and showed signs of his general inclination towards direct non-verbal presentation of the dramatic crisis. Bernard's method, however, involved not only muting words when he sensed that silence would be equally, or more, eloquent, but also exploiting situations where words relating to the central emotional event would be impossible. This tendency is strongly marked in *Le Printemps des autres,*[1] a play which centres on what is unexpressed because incommunicable, and incommunicable because unknown, a play with which Bernard moved consciously into the field of the unconscious.

Even more than *Martine* and *L'Invitation, Printemps* demands the consistent attention of the spectator. The play is strewn with a certain amount of unimposing detail which he may ignore at his own peril. If he has not been watchful, he is likely to be extremely perplexed at the end. But even if he is vigilant throughout, he will perhaps not know, at times, in which direction he is going. For we are at a far remove from plays in which the author states the 'problem' early; here it is made known towards the end. The over-all effect is that of a mosaic, and we can discuss the play coherently only by proceeding from the completed picture. *Printemps,* in Bernard's words, is about "une mère secrètement éprise de son gendre et qui, poussée par tous les démons du subconscient, travaillait malgré elle à ruiner le bonheur de sa fille."[2] The mother is Clarisse, a widow, the daughter is Gilberte, the son-in-law is Maurice.

---

[1] First performed 19 March 1924 at the *Théâtre Fémina.*
[2] Bernard, *Mon père Tristan Bernard,* Paris, Albin Michel, 1955, p. 190.

The author's postulate is that Clarisse fell in love with Maurice on first meeting him in Act I, and that her love was instinctively smothered when she discovered that he was her daughter's suitor, at the end of the act. The fact that the entire first act is devoted to the mechanism of love at first sight invites a few reflections on the way dramatists have dealt with the matter of love. There are a number of plays where the operation of falling in love is completed before the rise of the curtain. *Antony and Cleopatra* is a typical example, the very first words — "Nay, but this dotage of our general's / O'erflows the measure" — referring to the end-product. Similarly, we find that there are many parallels to Phèdre's "Je le vis, je rougis, je pâlis à sa vue" [3] or to Juliet's "My only love sprung from my only hate! / Too early seen unknown, and known too late!" [4] But what we encounter less frequently are plays where the process of falling in love at first sight is shown as it is happening, without commentary by the person involved or by anyone else, either during the process or subsequent to it. Once again Bernard appears to be answering a challenge; the emotional event on which the whole play depends is presented in a stealthy, unemphatic fashion, and then is shrouded in secrecy.

Clarisse, on holiday in Stresa with her daughter, is trying to forget a recent disappointment in love, and has reached the stage in her life when she is starting to doubt whether she still appeals to the other sex. It is at this moment that she is brought into contact with Maurice. He approaches her and begins to tell her diffidently that he has long been watching her from a distance, trying to summon up the courage to talk to her. He does not reveal to her his close friendship with her daughter; his manner indicates an interest in Clarisse, which she assumes to be amorous; understandably she is flattered. Soon she finds herself confiding in him as if he were an old friend.

But at this juncture Gilberte enters, and Clarisse realizes immediately that her daughter and Maurice are acquainted. As Gilberte confesses that Maurice is her suitor and that they had both been too timid to announce their relationship to Clarisse, the latter digests the news in silence, obviously deeply affected by this revelation. The

---

[3] Racine, *Phèdre* (ed. Jean Salles), Paris, Bordas, 1970, Act I, sc. 3, l. 273.

[4] *Romeo and Juliet*, Act I, sc. 5, ll. 142-143. The line numbering is that of Shakespeare, *Complete Works* (ed. W. J. Craig), London, Oxford University Press, 1971.

play has been set in motion by an engineered misunderstanding. Clarisse had been led to envisage herself as the lucky object of Maurice's intentions, and her nascent hopes have now been shattered. Pride and tact, however, are sufficient to discourage her from disclosing any of this to her daughter. After Gilberte's confession all Clarisse can find to say is: "Gilberte... Gilberte... C'est vrai... c'est vrai que tu es belle."[5] She had hitherto not considered Gilberte (who is eighteen) to be more than a child. Now she sees her as a beautiful woman who has taken precedence over her. Clarisse has in a sense been rejected, cheated, supplanted, and at the end of Act I it is clear that her self-confidence, which was being fortified during her conversation with Maurice, has again been shaken. Her gesture has a compelling eloquence:

> Doucement, Clarisse tend le bras vers la table, prend sa glace [...], l'approche d'elle machinalement et se regarde sans bouger.[6]

An open contest between mother and daughter has no place in Bernard's scheme. "Imaginez," Jean des Vallières says, "ce qu'eût fait de ce thème tel ou tel dramaturge que nous savons, y poussant les sentiments à l'extrême, faisant de Clarisse une sorte de furie, plus déchaînée contre les siens que Phèdre même. [...] On peut être une mère consciente de ses devoirs, et en même temps subir, non sans y laisser quelques plumes, les plus douloureuses tentations."[7] On the surface, then, Clarisse accepts her dutiful rôle as mother-in-law. No sooner born, her love for Maurice, her resentment and jealousy of her young, beautiful daughter are forced out of her consciousness. Nevertheless, these sentiments are not disabled by this spontaneous repression; they prove that their power is in no way reduced by effectively controlling Clarisse's actions. The burden of the drama has shifted from emotion which, while being undeclared, is clearly visible to the protagonist and surrounding characters,[8] to undeclared, invisible emotion. The dramatic contest goes underground.

---

[5] Act I, p. 208 in *Théâtre I,* Paris, Albin Michel, 1925.
[6] *Ibid.,* p. 209.
[7] Quoted by Robert de Beauplan, '*Le Printemps des autres* au Théâtre Fémina,' *La Petite Illustration,* 2 août 1924, page not numbered.
[8] As with Martine's love.

Contradiction is the leading characteristic of this play, in which Clarisse vacillates incessantly between conflicting impulses. On the one hand we witness the actions determined by the unconscious urges; on the other hand there are the attitudes that correspond to her idea of maternal duty. We have here an example of multiple personality, and it would be wrong to see in Clarisse the deliberate pretence which characterizes the hypocrite. After the couple have been married for a few months, Gilberte begins to show concern about a certain Madame Desgrées, with whom Maurice often goes riding:

> GILBERTE. Cette femme l'attire, c'est visible.
>
> CLARISSE. Ma pauvre fille, si tu te montes la tête chaque fois que ton mari regardera une autre femme, tu te prépares une jolie existence!
>
> GILBERTE. Je ne suis pas assez sotte pour l'empêcher de regarder d'autres femmes. Mais celle-là m'effraye. C'est une femme dangereuse.
>
> CLARISSE. Qui t'a dit cela?
>
> GILBERTE. Mais toi, maman...
>
> CLARISSE. Je t'ai dit cela?...
>
> GILBERTE. Oui, oui, cet hiver. Tu ne t'en souviens pas?
>
> CLARISSE. Tu sais, on répète ce qu'on entend. [9]

Clarisse's present note of reasoned reassurance clashes with her former notes of caution; we also learn that she is always keen to invite the "dangerous woman" when the couple are present. Confronted with her contradictions by Gilberte, she nevertheless appears genuinely disturbed, and we see her trying to convince herself of her good intentions, and ward off the incitements to mischief, when she pleads: "Est-ce que j'ai d'autre souci que de te faire plaisir, ma chérie? Est-ce que j'ai d'autre but, d'autre joie?" [10]

By initially professing that Madame Desgrées represented a danger, Clarisse was sowing the seeds of uneasiness and mistrust. She did this because a part of her is commanded by her repressed grudge against her daughter. The situation is further complicated by the fact that Clarisse is also jealous of Madame Desgrées; this jealousy is conveyed indirectly, in an extremely instructive interview:

---

[9] Act II, pp. 225-226.
[10] *Ibid.*, p. 226.

CLARISSE. Vous avez beaucoup de plaisir à voir madame Desgrées?

MAURICE. *(Dans un mouvement de recul.)* Quoi?

CLARISSE. Tiens, ce nom vous fait quelque chose!

MAURICE. Mais vous êtes folle... Enfin, je vous demande pardon... Vous vous trompez...

CLARISSE. Est-ce que vous protesteriez si fort, est-ce que vous auriez ce visage si je n'avais touché une corde sensible?...

MAURICE. *(Se levant irrité.)* Mais, madame, comment vous prouver le contraire?

CLARISSE. *(Le regardant.)* Madame?... C'est 'madame' que vous m'appelez... quand vous ne vous forcez plus...

MAURICE. Clarisse, si vous voulez. Quelle importance?... Je veux savoir ce qui vous a donné cette idée. Est-ce Gilberte qui vous a dit quelque chose?

CLARISSE. Non, non, Gilberte ne m'a rien dit. Ce n'est pas Gilberte, c'est moi qui vous parle.

MAURICE. J'aime mieux cela... Mais, Clarisse, votre crainte est saugrenue, passez-moi le terme. Je me moque de cette madame Desgrées... *(Avec un rire forcé.)* Je vous assure qu'elle ne me fait pas plus d'effet que... enfin, je ne sais pas... que moi à vous, par exemple... *(Il rit.)*

CLARISSE. *(Grave, après un silence.)*... Ne plaisantez pas. Vous vous en défendez trop pour qu'il n'y ait pas en vous... au moins un peu d'émotion...

MAURICE. *(Changeant de ton.)* Eh bien, et après? Est-ce que cela n'arrive pas à tous les hommes? Il se peut que j'aie du plaisir à rencontrer madame Desgrées. Elle est plutôt agréable. Vous le reconnaissez vous-même, puisque vous l'invitez... *(Vivement.)* Vous n'allez pas monter la tête à Gilberte...

CLARISSE. Pour qui me prenez-vous? S'il y a quelqu'un que je veux mettre en garde, c'est vous...

MAURICE. Mais vous me croyez donc bien naïf?

CLARISSE. Peut-être... Ne serait-ce que la facilité avec laquelle vous trahissez vos émotions. Gilberte est bien jeune pour ne s'être aperçue de rien.

MAURICE. Croyez-vous possible?...

CLARISSE. Ah! votre inquiétude est un aveu. Je n'avais d'ailleurs pas besoin de cela. Est-ce que vous ne saisissez pas toutes les occasions de la rencontrer? Et, quand elle est ici, n'avez-vous pas un air désolé chaque fois qu'elle fait mine de partir? Et elle joue de cela! Ah! si vous pouviez vous voir tous les deux!... Est-ce que les plus belles roses du jardin ne sont pas pour elle? Et l'autre jour, quand nous

avons fait cette stupide partie de loto, est-ce que vous n'avez
pas triché pour la faire gagner?
    MAURICE. Mais, Clarisse ... comment avez-vous remar-
qué tout cela? [11]

This exchange, like so many others in the play, is full of general
truths about the verbal manœuvres in which people engage (at times
without conscious planning), and about the mental operations with
which these manœuvres keep pace. Clarisse is deceitful and most
sincere in the same breath: "Gilberte ne m'a rien dit. [...] c'est moi
qui vous parle." But the full sincerity of this is hidden from Maurice.
The statement is meant to impress on him, and on Clarisse herself,
that the person speaking is the impartial, benevolent mother-in-law,
eager to keep intact the happiness of the young couple; in fact the
cross-examination is being undertaken by the jealous person. This,
however, is one of the moments in the play when we are justified
in doubting whether Clarisse's ignorance of her feelings towards
Maurice could be total; especially when she says in a broken voice,
in reply to his last question:

> Mais j'adore Gilberte. Mais je vois cette petite enceinte,
> lasse, inquiète. Si elle ne sent pas ces choses, je vous jure
> que je ne les sens que trop pour elle. [...] Ah! vous êtes
> un enfant, vous êtes un enfant. Vous ne savez pas quelles
> souffrances provoque un geste maladroit. Vous ne savez pas
> ce qu'un regard de vous mal dirigé peut blesser un cœur qui
> vous aime. Enfant, enfant, vous faites mal, vous faites mal ...
> Vous ne devez pas faire tant de mal. [12]

Having already digested the substance of the warning: "Ce n'est pas
Gilberte, c'est moi qui vous parle," we can see the declaration of
love contained in Clarisse's plea: "Vous ne savez pas ce qu'un regard ...," and the real significance of her ostensibly disinterested
vigilance. We begin to wonder whether the inner echo of her words
does not momentarily make her aware.

    It may be that Clarisse is *less unconscious* here than at other places
(the point being that the several layers of perception are best defined
in relation to one another). The unconscious does not always form

---

[11] *Ibid.*, pp. 233-235.
[12] *Ibid.*, pp. 235-236.

a monolithic block; moments of lucidity can alternate with moments of imperfect realization. Such an alternation in Clarisse would be a natural consequence of the constant, complex internal tension between the urging forces and the forces of inhibition. It may also be argued, on the other hand, that when "you are causing me suffering" becomes "you are causing Gilberte suffering," what we have is a textbook example of Freudian 'projection'; normally this is an operation resembling ordinary dishonesty, but remaining distinct in that it is not deliberate.

One might have imagined, whether or not Clarisse is aware of her jealousy, that the jealous impulse would have led her to try to discourage Maurice from seeing Madame Desgrées. On the contrary, she seems to be advising him to be more careful and dissembling. She virtually exhorts him to continue seeing the woman:

> MAURICE. Je suis prêt à ne plus revoir madame Desgrées. (Il la regarde. Il attend.)
> CLARISSE. (D'une voix blanche.) Je ne vous ai pas dit cela...
> MAURICE. Si Gilberte doit souffrir...
> CLARISSE. (Incertaine.) Je ne sais pas, moi... Je vous ai mis en garde... Mais il ne faut rien... exagérer. [13]

Clarisse makes an omission which again illustrates the way she is uncontrollably torn by conflicting impulses; she had promised Gilberte to dissuade Maurice from going riding with Madame Desgrées, and while being aware of the promise, something prevents her from fulfilling it. When Maurice gets up to leave she appears anxious to delay him, and we see her suffering from the sort of momentary incapacity of speech that was frequent in *Martine*:

> (Clarisse veut parler, mais il semble qu'une force l'en empêche. Maurice secoue la tête et va vers la porte.)
> MAURICE. Ah! tenez, je vais me changer les idées. Et je connais un bon moyen.
> CLARISSE. Où allez-vous?
> MAURICE. M'habiller pour monter à cheval. (A ces mots, elle le regarde avec effroi. Elle veut parler, mais il est déjà sorti. Elle reste un moment comme pétrifiée. Et puis, avec un effort, elle arrive à l'appeler d'une voix faible.) [14]

13 Ibid., p. 237.
14 Ibid., pp. 239-240.

A few moments later she says to Gilberte that she had forgotten the promise.

'Forgetfulness' becomes a habit in the play. We saw where Clarisse could not remember warning Gilberte that Madame Desgrées was a dangerous woman. Elsewhere, mother and daughter discharge certain items from their respective memories:

> GILBERTE. Tu attires [madame Desgrées] à plaisir.
> CLARISSE. Moi?
> GILBERTE. Aujourd'hui encore tu l'attendais à goûter. Dieu merci, j'ai oublié ta commission.
> CLARISSE. (Souriant.) On n'oublie que ce qu'on veut bien...
> GILBERTE. (Agacée.) On n'oublie que ce qu'on veut bien! Alors, pourquoi as-tu oublié, toi, en l'invitant pour avant-hier, que j'avais souhaité passer la soirée à nous trois?
> CLARISSE. (Troublée.) Avant-hier... Je te jure, Gilberte, que ce que tu m'avais dit m'était sorti de la tête. [15]

Clarisse's words have a boomerang effect here; she displays that human characteristic which often makes us discover ourselves by first attributing to others our own secret motivations.

Such 'forgetfulness' is manifestly the result of an initial reluctance to perform a given act, and she has obviously not really forgotten to dissuade Maurice from going riding. She certainly does not seize her second opportunity to discourage him:

> GILBERTE. (Allant à lui et d'une voix tremblante.) Oh! Maurice, ne monte pas à cheval ce soir. (Clarisse fait un mouvement.)
> MAURICE. Qu'est-ce que tu as? Bien sûr, si cela t'est désagréable... Mais pourquoi?...
> CLARISSE. (Comme malgré elle.) Gilberte, enfin, c'est ridicule, si ça l'amuse...
> GILBERTE. (Se retournant.) Maman! (Elle regarde sa mère avec stupéfaction.) [16]

Clarisse realizes that she did not forget her promise to Gilberte; but we are left to ponder whether she grasps clearly what lies behind her unwillingness. The fact is that conjoined with the conflict between

---

[15] *Ibid.*, p. 226.
[16] *Ibid.*, p. 241.

her attitude of the neutral, benevolent mother-figure and her subterranean urges, there is conflict between these urges themselves. Her
jealousy of her daughter counteracts her jealousy of Madame Desgrées; by not impeding contact between the latter and Maurice, she
is, without definite design, preparing the destruction of her daughter's
happiness.

We encounter here the mechanism which in Freudian psychology
is described as 'reaction formation': [17] Clarisse's love for Maurice,
once repressed, is replaced on the surface by dislike; [18] so much so
that the couple positively feel that she bears him malice. At the same
time, her malevolence towards her daughter disguises itself as un-
stinted devotion. The crucial moment of the play arrives when a dis-
tressed Gilberte flies to her mother, convinced that Maurice, who did
not return home the night before, has left her. Gilberte's distress is
clearly based on a mere supposition; we imagine that in a similar
situation, a well-meaning mother would have tried to put her daughter's mind at rest by advising her against such hasty conclusions;
even if the worst was certain, some attempt would probably have
been made to pave the way for a future reconciliation. Yet Clarisse
receives the news of Maurice's presumed flight as if it had long been
a foregone conclusion, declaring to Gilberte that she had been expecting it. Maurice, she says maliciously, is the type of man who
sooner or later would have betrayed Gilberte. She seems immensely
pleased to regain possession of the dear little one that had been stolen
by the evil man: "C'est un bonheur de pouvoir me consacrer toute
à ma petite fille. [...] Laisse ta maman te guérir." [19] But this joy to
have her darling daughter back is no more than the overdress of a
greater delight, now that her secret and unconscious wish to destroy
her daughter's happiness is within an ace of fulfilment; simultaneously, the wish emerges from her unconscious, and it will soon be
perceived by her daughter.

Clarisse quickly suggests that the two of them go away and forget
Maurice; she is already making plans for the journey. Gilberte lets
herself be allured, worried at the idea of being all alone when her
child is born, clinging tenaciously to her mother. The *coup de théâtre*

---

17 Cf. below, p. 125.
18 Phèdre performs a similar operation with regard to Hippolyte.
19 Act III, p. 252.

comes in the form of a telephone call from Maurice. Clarisse hurriedly replaces the receiver, claiming that Gilberte is not there. This determination to prevent husband and wife from even conversing makes it plain to us that she wants the wedge between them to stand firm. Gilberte now suspects this, and her suspicions are confirmed when Clarisse tries to prevent her from going back to Maurice. The moment of full self-discovery for Clarisse coincides with the moment of Gilberte's realization that her mother has been wishing her unhappiness and has been secretly in love with Maurice. When the latter enters shortly afterwards, Gilberte begs him to take her away, and the play ends.

Bernard, by devoting all of the first act to the process of falling in love at first sight, started by dramatizing what other dramatists usually take as a *fait accompli*. Now he ends where most begin. On examining other plays that are governed by an illicit sentiment, one finds that the disclosure of the sentiment is the event that sets the play in motion. In *'Tis Pity She's a Whore* Giovanni has long recognized his love for his sister, and has been able to hide it from the view of all. Yet once the play begins, he reveals it explicitly, first to the Friar, and then to Annabella. It is the traditional case of powerful emotion eventually overcoming all impediments:

> Or I must speak, or burst.
> ... ...
> I have too long suppress'd the hidden flames
> That almost have consum'd me; I have spent
> Many a silent night in sighs and groans. [20]

As for Annabella, we learn that she herself has been aware of her love for her brother. But, in a more conscious version of Clarisse's exercise, she has driven away thoughts of her love:

> For every sigh that thou hast spent for me
> I have sigh'd ten; for every tear shed twenty;
> And not so much for that I lov'd, as that
> I durst not say I lov'd, nor scarcely think it. [21]

---

[20] John Ford, *'Tis Pity She's a Whore* (ed. N. W. Bawcutt), London, Edward Arnold, 1966, Act I, sc. 2, l. 153; ll. 218-220.
[21] *Ibid.*, ll. 244-247.

Without Giovanni's confession, Annabella would probably never have made hers. But without Giovanni's confession, there would also have been no *'Tis Pity*. Similar remarks apply to *Phèdre*. There the heroine's "sighs and groans," her masking of her love with a veneer of hatred precede the beginning of the play. But soon the author contrives to make her believe that there is no longer any reason to keep the passion secret, and it is declared. The drama unfolds from this point. Bernard, on the other hand, advances to the juncture where the repressed passion is revealed in silence to two of the characters, and having done this ends the play. "Le drame," Serge Radine says, "à peine entrevu, sera promptement étouffé." [22] Again, then, Bernard husbands his strength; again, reluctant to appear too robust, he is sparing of his dramatic effects, and declines to use strong methods to sustain the vigour of a powerful situation; again, not a few spectators might take exception to this reversal of traditional dramatic procedure.

Bernard was closely tied to the doctrine of internal necessity, and with his plays we have not yet reached the point in the history of modern drama where characters enter (like Le Pompier in *La Cantatrice chauve*) for no apparent purpose. But in *Printemps* the divorce between real purpose and apparent purpose is such that the spectator (seeing the play for the first time) could easily be led astray. There was not, we believe, a wilful attempt to mislead on the part of the author. Whatever 'false trails' there may be are a necessary part of Bernard's dramatic design, are a necessary result of his preference for characters who do not spontaneously and explicitly give guide-lines to the audience.

Maurice, we recall, found himself unable to tell Clarisse from the first that he desired her daughter's hand, even though he had numerous opportunities to do so. The author tried to impress on us Maurice's hesitant, tremulous nature, and an apology accompanied almost every remark:

> Je m'excuse de me permettre [...] Si j'ose venir à vous [...]
> Vous excuserez le sans-gêne avec lequel [...] Si je me suis

---

[22] Serge Radine, *Essais sur le théâtre* (1919-1939), Genève-Annemasse, Éditions du Mont-Blanc, S. A., 1944, p. 122.

permis de dire [...] Vous devez trouver que j'ai eu beaucoup d'audace! [23]

When asked directly what he was doing in Stresa, he gave a vague
reply, obviously concealing the truth; Clarisse deduced, from what
he had said before, that he was there on her account. But on Gilberte's
entrance Maurice, who happens to be a lawyer, displayed an inarticulate confusion worthy of Martine:

> CLARISSE. Mais vous vous connaissez!
> MAURICE. C'est-à-dire ... je voulais vous ... (Il ne peut
> achever.)
> GILBERTE. (Qui se remet peu à peu.) ... Maman, nous
> nous sommes rencontrés ... oui ... (Clarisse les regarde.)
> MAURICE. (Péniblement.) Permettez-moi ... Enfin, main-
> tenant, je vais vous laisser ... Mais sans doute vous reverrai-
> je ... ce soir ... peut-être ... au dîner ... n'est-ce pas, ma-
> dame? (Clarisse ne répond pas.) N'est-ce pas, mademoiselle?
> GILBERTE. (D'une voix encore tremblante.) Oh! oui ...
> Oh! sûrement, monsieur Gardier ... (Maurice s'incline gau-
> chement et sort.) [24]

It is then that Clarisse learnt through Gilberte what Maurice's
purpose was: "Il voulait te parler, mais il n'osait pas. [...] C'est
pour moi qu'il est venu à Stresa." [25] This also is the stage at which
the audience learns that Maurice did not at all mean to say what he
said implicitly to Clarisse. The spectator's interest in what looked
like a budding love affair between Maurice and Clarisse is destroyed.
At this late hour, after about twenty-five minutes of this 'exposition'
act, the spectator is virtually back where he began, and is obliged to
form a new theory about what is happening. He is led to wonder
what was gained by this suppression, this delayed revelation, of essential information.

The achievement is threefold: Bernard has created the misunderstanding in Clarisse's mind, the event from which the rest of the
play proceeds; at the same time, he has forced the spectator to participate in (rather than witness) her misunderstanding, and thereby

---

[23] Act I, pp. 187-189.
[24] Ibid., pp. 206-207.
[25] Ibid., p. 207.

truly identify himself with it; [26] indirectly, he has given the spectator
a warning, and a guide to looking at the play: the spectator is not
to take for granted the truth of the obvious and the apparent, and
he is to remember that the essential might, for a variety of reasons,
be left unsaid.

Uncertainty is therefore the spectator's chief companion throughout
his first encounter with the play. At the beginning of the second act
he knows little, except that the misapprehension has occurred. The
first part of the act does not promptly advance his knowledge; he
discovers a tranquil scene of domestic life, in which nothing of moment
is under discussion, nothing appears to be happening, no dramatic
crisis seems to be lurking anywhere. But all this while, Bernard is
transporting the audience from almost complete ignorance to relative
enlightenment.

The author is concerned with sentiments that are unknown to
Clarisse, unknown to the other characters, and of which, consequently,
no one can talk. To make the spectator aware of them, he shows
their effects, but because the spectator does not yet know about them,
he does not know that the effects are effects. *Printemps* is in fact
the Bernard play that most depends on the audience's retrospection.
Remarks, gestures and actions that do not at first appear particularly
important are illuminated *in extremis* as it were. This, obviously, is
not an unusual proceduce in the novel (especially the detective novel)
and in the drama. A certain attention to details, and to the order
in which they are presented, is always required from the theatrical
public. But it is well to bear in mind the extent to which the method
is used in *Printemps,* and the resultant demands on the spectator's
patience, goodwill and vigilance.

The desire to know will encourage the willing spectator to notice,
though he may not immediately grasp the significance of what he
notices. Bernard gives him ample scope for forming interpretations,
though they may turn out to be incorrect. There is, for instance,
Clarisse's silence as the couple talk about a planned trip to Milan:

> MAURICE.   La santé de cette petite fille m'est au moins
> aussi précieuse qu'à vous.

---

[26] Needless to say, this identification is only possible once; the next time
one can only stand back and reflect on the effectiveness of an identification
that was.

CLARISSE. (*Un peu crispée.*) Ai-je donc paru en douter? (*Pendant le dialogue suivant, elle demeure silencieuse, les regardant.*)

GILBERTE. Pour ma part, je serais désolée de renoncer à ce voyage.

MAURICE. Parbleu!

GILBERTE. Tu sais que je compte bien rapporter de là-bas des meubles pour notre salon.

MAURICE. Ah! tu peux être sûre que les antiquaires de Milan nous verront souvent. Mais, à mon avis, le plus urgent sera de chercher un buffet pour la salle à manger.

GILBERTE. Ce n'est pas en Italie que nous trouverons cela . . . Non, Maurice, à quoi pensons-nous? Le plus urgent, c'est la chambre du petit.

MAURICE. Tu as donc bien peur d'être prise de court? Tu as tout le temps.

GILBERTE. On ne sait jamais. Plus tard, je peux être moins valide. Crois-tu qu'il serait ridicule de choisir un moïse tout de suite? Tu ne viendrais pas avec moi après-demain?

MAURICE. Tu sais bien que ces choses-là ne m'ennuient pas.

GILBERTE. Dès notre retour, j'arrangerai aussi ton cabinet de travail. Je veux que tu aies un bon petit bureau bien confortable.

MAURICE. (*Souriant.*) Beaucoup de livres et beaucoup de fleurs.

GILBERTE. Et de bons coussins pour que je puisse m'asseoir à tes pieds pendant que tu écriras.

MAURICE. Je suis tranquille. Si tu t'occupes de cela, ce sera bien. (*Clarisse se met à ranger les tasses sur le plateau, un peu nerveusement.*)

GILBERTE. Veux-tu que je fasse enlever ce plateau?

CLARISSE. Non, laisse. [27]

The lingering rhythm is characteristic of the play. The dialogue is noteworthy because it forms a counterpoint to Clarisse's silence. This is another example of Bernard's silence of the third person, and, unlike that of Marie-Louise at the beginning of *L'Invitation*, Clarisse's silence attracts attention. [28] She has up to this moment been taking an active part in the conversation, and has just made known her opposition to the couple's plan to visit Milan — ostensibly because of

[27] Act II, pp. 216-217.
[28] See below, p. 122.

Gilberte's health. Her silence, one imagines, is a sullen silence, inasmuch as the couple have overridden her objections. It could also involve a sense of exclusion combined with a sense of sadness, as she is made to envisage the days of lonely widowhood ahead with Gilberte and Maurice entirely independent of her. The point is that it is difficult to see at this stage the most powerful emotion behind her silence. May Daniels observes that "while the young couple talk and plan their ménage, [Clarisse's] eyes are fixed on them and in that steady gaze is revealed her unconscious jealousy." [29] In effect, this jealousy is not revealed in her gaze; it will, however, later be seen to have been present in the gaze.

Through his manipulation of detail and his arrangement of thematic patterns, through his use of repetition and emphasis, Bernard succeeds in making certain cardinal points stand out in the mind of the audience. What could not have failed to 'register' is the way Clarisse fostered the relationship between Madame Desgrées and Maurice, and her joy at the prospect that he had abandoned Gilberte. When Clarisse suggests that she was the passive, unwilling recipient of vague premonitions, the spectator at once discerns that she has been desiring rather than simply expecting the breach:

> CLARISSE. Il y a beau jour que je sentais venir la catastrophe.
> ... ...
> Je m'attendais bien, un jour ou l'autre, à jouer ce rôle, va. J'ai pu m'y préparer.
> GILBERTE. (Après un silence.) ... Tu t'y attendais?
> CLARISSE. (Rêveuse.) Malgré moi, parfois, une pensée ... une crainte fugitive m'effleurait: 'Elle me reviendra et il faudra que je lui donne tout.' Peut-être, sans m'en douter, vivais-je pour cet instant... (Vivement.) cet instant cruel. [30]

Together with Gilberte, the spectator soon senses that it is not because of her possessiveness towards her daughter and her dislike of Maurice that Clarisse has been desiring the rupture; the audience progresses with Gilberte towards the realization that Clarisse's dis-

---

[29] May Daniels, The French Drama of The Unspoken, Edinburgh at the University Press, 1953, p. 197.
[30] Act III, pp. 249, 251-252.

like of Maurice has been a façade and that she envies her daughter's happiness.

As soon as we recognize this we are flooded with recollections of incidents, statements and attitudes. The oddities with which the play is interspersed (Clarisse's self-contradictions, her 'lapses of memory,' her involuntary cry when she sees the couple embracing) assume the importance which they have always had, but which was not manifest earlier. The pattern of the hidden drama begins to fall into place.

The advantage we have over Maurice (who is baffled at the close) is our knowledge that Clarisse initially mistook his intentions. Her misapprehension is used by Bernard to create the sort of irony that he favours, where the instigator remains ignorant of his rôle. [31] Maurice still takes for granted the truth of the obvious, and, as a result, he believes to the end in Clarisse's *apparent* dislike for him, a dislike he attributes to maternal jealousy. Hence his inability to see the confession of Clarisse's love concealed in:

> Ah! vous êtes un enfant, vous êtes un enfant. Vous ne savez pas quelles souffrances provoque un geste maladroit. Vous ne savez pas ce qu'un regard de vous mal dirigé peut blesser un cœur qui vous aime. Enfant, enfant, vous faites mal, vous faites mal ... Vous ne devez pas faire tant de mal. [32]

We do not suspect in him a will not to understand as in Hippolyte's evasive

> Je vois de votre amour l'effet prodigieux.
> Tout mort qu'il est, Thésée est présent à vos yeux. [33]

Maurice is wholly convinced of the genuinenesss of Clarisse's good intentions towards her daughter, of her aversion towards him, and, in addition, he is excluded from the scene of revelation between mother and daughter. His perplexity when he learns that Clarisse has suddenly decided to leave for Spain is a logical conclusion:

---

[31] Maurice resembles in this respect the invisible Philippe in *L'Invitation*; in addition, the Madame Desgrées of whom we hear so much is never seen. Cf. below, p. 137.

[32] Act II, p. 236.

[33] *Phèdre*, Act II, sc. 5, ll. 631-632.

> MAURICE. *(Regarde les deux femmes et brusquement.)*
> Que s'est-il passé?
> CLARISSE. [...] Il ne s'est rien passé. [...]
> MAURICE. Je pense que Gilberte m'expliquera...
> CLARISSE. *(Qui regarde fixement Gilberte.)* Il n'y a rien
> à expliquer...
> GILBERTE. ... Mais non, Maurice.
> MAURICE. Quand reviendrez-vous?
> CLARISSE. Quand je m'ennuierai...
> MAURICE. Décidément, vous serez toujours un mystère
> pour moi.
> CLARISSE. Eh bien, je serai toujours un mystère pour
> vous. [34]

In these closing moments of the play, Bernard ingeniously embeds
remarks about the play in the dialogue: "Il ne s'est rien passé [...]
Il n'y a rien à expliquer [...] Vous serez toujours un mystère pour
moi." Because interest has been concentrated on invisible, unknown
sentiments, nothing has *appeared* to happen. Because of the nature
of the revelation between mother and daughter, the Bernardian taboo
prevents it from being clothed in words; the author addresses the
remark "Il n'y a rien à expliquer" to the spectator who is still awaiting
the display of declamation. The term 'mystery' has an obvious application to *Printemps,* and Maurice's resigned conclusion leads us
back to what he once said to Clarisse:

> Il vous arrive d'être poussée par des sentiments contradic-
> toires que vous avez souvent l'air de ne pas comprendre vous-
> même. [...] Est-ce que personne est jamais sûr de se com-
> prendre? [35]

For during the major part of the play, Clarisse is not only a puzzle
to Maurice and Gilberte, but also one to herself. We have indeed
come a long way from the heroine who knows herself so completely
that she can deliberate at great length on the meaning of her actions,
and ponder on her vague presentiments of hidden motivations.

The idea that the motors of action are in essence indefinable and
human personality never entirely comprehensible floats over the play.
Bernard denies us the comfortable feeling of certainty that many

---

[34] Act III, pp. 261-262.
[35] Act II, p. 215.

plays afford. The *suppressio veri* in the first act had the precise effect of undermining any sense of infallibility we might have had. Furthermore, the protagonist is such a complex figure that we cannot boast to have understood her completely or to be able to enclose her in a formula (though with her Bernard does not propose as impenetrable a riddle as Pirandello does with Signora Ponza in *Right You Are! (If You Think So)*). Having been obliged to collate the evidence ourselves and form our general conclusions about the forces to which she has been responding, we find that it is not always easy to follow her oscillation between contradictory forces, and that there can be little certainty about the degree to which she has been aware of these forces.

James Agate remarks about the protagonist that "she is to be tormented by she knows not what, to respond to incitements without knowing that they exist, to feel pangs without realising that they are those of jealousy. [...] Bernard demands that Clarisse should be presented like a signpost which should know nothing of the directions written on it." [36] Such a person is possible in the absolute world of the psychoanalyst, but is perhaps not entirely credible within the context of the play. The best indication that Clarisse is moved by forces invisible and unknown to her is her tendency to contradict herself in word and action, without appearing to be conscious of her contradictions. But we have seen that Maurice draws them to her attention. It is therefore reasonable to imagine that Clarisse, once aware of some of her inconsistencies, is aware, at least at random moments, of their significance. And yet, to go to the extreme of assuming that Clarisse completely understands herself throughout the play is to give her a capacity for calculation that does not at all correspond to the total impression we receive. Once again, as is so common with Bernard, we have to depend largely on impressions to form judgements about immeasurable entities.

In effect, the play raises questions about Clarisse's consciousness — How far does her lack of awareness go? How much of it is real, and how much apparent? How and where can one draw the line between the real and the apparent? — to which it is impossible to give categorical replies. It is to be noticed that similar questions are posed

---

[36] James Agate, *The Contemporary Theatre: 1926*, London, Chapman & Hall, 1927, p. 95.

by Camus' *L'Étranger*: whether Meursault is an unconscious illustration of the condition of absurdity, well and truly unaware at the beginning of the narrative, or whether this lack of consciousness is only apparent. The fact that no unequivocal statement about the awakening to the absurd is made by the narrator is used by a few to support the argument that his unawareness is unimpaired. Our view is that such reasoning betrays a bias (common to many novelists, dramatists and critics) according to which declaration *must* accompany realization. But as John Cruickshank points out, "Camus is concerned to convey the experience of absurdism rather than to expound it rationally." [37] Explanations, whether about attitudes to life or about emotional states, are relegated to humble rank when direct presentation becomes a priority.

Direct presentation was of course a priority for Bernard, who was already disinclined to portray characters who expatiated, and who, in any event, could not make them expound that of which they were not conscious. When the hour of complete realization comes for Clarisse, a thick veil of discretion surrounds and gags her daughter and herself, and the declaration remains absent:

> CLARISSE. (*Toute désorientée, la retenant par le bras.*) Tu... plaisantes... Tu n'y vas pas... Tu...
> GILBERTE. S'il revient, c'est qu'il m'aime encore. (*Se débattant.*) Maman, laisse-moi partir.
> CLARISSE. Mais c'est ta perte.
> GILBERTE. Tu ne veux donc pas mon bonheur?
> CLARISSE. Je ne pense qu'à cela...
> GILBERTE. (*Rageuse.*) Ce n'est pas vrai. (*Clarisse la lâche, effrayée.*) Mais oui, pourquoi as-tu répondu que je n'étais pas là? Et tout ce que tu m'as dit sur lui! Non, tu ne veux pas notre bonheur. Je connais bien tes sentiments maintenant...
> CLARISSE. (*Balbutiant.*) Qu'est-ce que tu dis?
> GILBERTE. Tu le hais...
> CLARISSE. Ce n'est pas vrai!
> GILBERTE. Alors? alors? alors?... (*Elles se tiennent un instant l'une devant l'autre, comme deux ennemies. Et soudain Clarisse recule, terrifiée.*) Maman?

---

[37] John Cruickshank, *Albert Camus and the Literature of Revolt*, London, Oxford University Press, 1959, p. 153.

CLARISSE. (*Qui prend conscience pour la première fois de toute la réalité.*) Tais-toi ... tais-toi ... (*Brusquement.*) Va-t'en ... (*Gilberte recule vers la porte. Clarisse a un mouvement comme pour la retenir, mais elle se contient et cache sa figure.*) [38]

The two women recoil in silent horror at the thought of rivalry and at the ghost of an incestuous passion. Henry Bidou remarks:

> Par une sorte de gageure, qui est d'ailleurs fort belle, cette passion contrainte et surveillée gouverne toute l'action. Filandière invisible, c'est elle qui fait la trame de l'ouvrage; sa main se reconnaît à des irrégularités, à des trous, à des fils noués. Mais, dès qu'on l'a reconnue, le scandale de sa présence est aussitôt étouffé. [39]

The silent look accompanying the revelation is duplicated when they part company at the end of the play: "Très long regard muet, regard d'intelligence de femme à femme." [40] John Palmer has aptly described the effect and appropriateness of these silent looks:

> There is no need of comment, explanation or any further word between mother and daughter. The whole play is summed up and illumined by the sudden realization of the two persons concerned of the secret motive which has been implicit in every line of the play. [...] Anything which the two women might have explicitly said to one another at the close of the play must necessarily have strained and falsified the truth conveyed implicitly by the whole progress of events up to that particular moment. They must inevitably have said too much. The position, containing within itself all that has gone before, speaks for itself so completely that nothing further remains to be said. [41]

Bernard has commented extensively on his techniques, and, at times, he has made remarks which are more ill-advised than others, which might betray lazy reasoning, which might be used in evidence

---

[38] Act III, pp. 257-258.
[39] Quoted by Robert de Beauplan, 'Le Printemps des autres au Théâtre Fémina,' *La Petite Illustration*, 2 août 1924, page not numbered.
[40] Act III, p. 262.
[41] John Palmer, *Studies in the Contemporary Theatre*, London, Martin Secker, 1927, pp. 103-104.

against him, but which none the less contain a solid element of good sense. One such remark is: "Un sentiment commenté perd de sa force. La logique du théâtre n'admet pas les sentiments que la situation n'impose pas. Et si la situation les impose il n'est pas besoin de les exprimer." [42] The argument against overstatement is well worth making, and the closing scene between Clarisse and Gilberte is, as Palmer suggests, a fine example of redundancy avoided. In this regard, we notice an interesting point of correspondence between *Printemps* and *Mourning Becomes Electra*, though the latter can in no way be described as an 'unexpressed' play. There is of course the slight parallel of rivalry (an unconcealed antagonism in O'Neill's play) between mother and daughter: Christine accuses Lavinia not only of trying to become the wife of her father and the mother of Orin, but of wanting Brant for herself. [43] More important, however, is the similarity in technique in the scene where Lavinia, certain that her mother poisoned Erza, communicates this to Christine without pronouncing a single word:

> (*Christine comes out, [...] and walks to the head of the steps. For a moment mother and daughter stare into each other's eyes. Then Christine begins haltingly in a tone she vainly tries to make kindly and persuasive.*)
> Vinnie, I — I must speak with you a moment — now Orin is here. I appreciate your grief has made you — not quite normal — and I make allowances. But I cannot understand your attitude towards me. Why do you keep following me everywhere — and stare at me like that? I had been a good wife to him for twenty-three years — until I met Adam. I was guilty then, I admit. But I repented and put him out of my life. I would have been a good wife again as long as your father had lived. After all, Vinnie, I am your mother. I brought you into the world. You ought to have some feeling for me. (*She pauses, waiting for some response, but Lavinia simply stares at her, frozen and silent. Fear creeps into Christine's tone.*) Don't stare like that! What are you thinking? Surely you can't still have that insane suspicion — that I — (*Then guiltily.*) What did you do that night after I fainted? I — I've missed something — some medicine I take

---

[42] Bernard, 'Le silence au théâtre,' *La Chimère. Bulletin d'Art Dramatique,* mai (2) 1922, p. 67.

[43] Eugene O'Neill, *Mourning Becomes Electra,* London, Jonathan Cape, 1932, Part I, Act II, p. 59.

to put me to sleep — (*Something like a grim smile of satis-faction forms on Lavinia's lips. Christine exclaims, frigh-tened:*) Oh, you did — you found — and I suppose you connect that — but don't you see how insane — to suspect — when Doctor Blake knows he died of! — [44]

As might be expected from two dramatists with unlike conceptions of drama, there is a fundamental difference in function and effect between Lavinia's silence and the silence which embraces mother and daughter in *Printemps*. The latter is an attempt to slur over the implications of the revelation, and a back-to-back flight from battle. At the moment when the intrapersonal conflict surfaces and threatens to become interpersonal, silence intervenes as pacifier. Lavinia's silence, on the other hand, is another active weapon against Christine, in a play that places interpersonal conflict in the forefront.

The menace hovering behind the daughter's contemptuous refusal to speak has a destructively unnerving effect on Christine that could not easily be achieved by a violent diatribe. With silence Lavinia elicits from her mother a confession of murder which does not need to be voiced. In effect, what the scene shows is that O'Neill accepted the axiom (habitually underlined by Bernard) which is apparently not always remembered by dramatists in the strongly verbal tradition: there are moments when words are superfluous and when the unut-tered has greater potency.

In *Printemps* the emphasis is on the unpremeditated; the in-voluntary cry is the echo of the unheard explosive outburst; the slight impulsive gesture is the signal of inner commotion. The play makes demands on the spectator not unlike those made on the reader of detective stories. The clues we are given encourage us to conduct our own investigation and discover what lies beneath the veils. The 'mystery' is not extraordinary; Clarisse's jealousy of one who had become a sort of little sister is neither incomprehensible nor ex-ceptional; the mechanism of repression and the process of reaction formation are not uncommon. Part of the fascination of *Printemps* derives from Bernard's ability to charge the ordinary with dramatic significance, and to suggest the untold mysteries of day-to-day life. Surrounding his protagonist with a halo of ambiguity (which a few

[44] *Ibid.*, Part II, Act I, pp. 129-130.

could conceivably find disorientating), he indirectly makes a statement about the general unknowable essence of human personality. Clarisse may be more talkative than Martine; but she is far less transparent. To move from *Martine* to *Printemps* is to leave a world of relative simplicity, certainty and awareness for one governed from an imperfectly defined subterranean complex. But in both plays we were still in the presence of concrete emotions. From the love and suffering of Martine, from the repressed passion of Clarisse, Bernard was to turn to an altogether more rarefied area of emotional activity in his next play: *L'Invitation au voyage*.

CHAPTER FOUR

L'INVITATION AU VOYAGE

THERE EXIST TWO VERSIONS of *L'Invitation au voyage*. The original version was first performed in February 1924; [1] the revised and more condensed version was first performed in October 1926. [2] Unless otherwise stated, our comments refer to the original version.

Marie-Louise, the daughter of a nail-manufacturer, has been married for the past eight years to Olivier, who, with her father, is in charge of the nail-factory. Philippe (the son of a nail-merchant) is at the beginning of the play on an inspection tour of the factory, and appears to find little favour with Marie-Louise. However, his departure for Argentina causes her to entertain exotic dreams, which are nurtured by her reading of a book of Baudelaire poems — one of Philippe's gifts. On his return to France, she convinces herself that he has come back on her behalf, and rushes off to see him in Épinal; she returns the following day, realizing that she means nothing to Philippe, and that he talks only of nails, having become a nail-merchant like his father.

The play presented Bernard with a problem of exposition which he was unable to tackle successfully. He wanted to make the spectator sense, from the outset, the annoyance and spiritual seclusion of a being with a propensity to dream and an artistic and musical temperament, who is surrounded by persons whose interests never seem

---

[1] At the *Odéon*; published in *Théâtre I*, Paris, Albin Michel, 1925. *L'Invitation*, though staged before *Printemps*, was written after it; the two were playing simultaneously in Paris in March 1924.

[2] In Geneva, by the *Studio des Champs-Élysées* Company; published in *Masques. Cahiers d'Art Dramatique*, huitième cahier, 1928.

to go beyond uninspiring and uncompromisingly practical activities. Somewhat adventurously, he began the play with the third-person silence, which, as we have seen, is part of what he understood by the 'unexpressed.' [3] He therefore has Marie-Louise sitting in silent irritation as her father, Landreau, shows a visitor round. The scene is plainly introductory, and is useful for the essential information which it provides. But the spectator is likely to miss completely its main point by ignoring Marie-Louise's silence, at least on his first encounter with the play; rather in the way that we often miss unobtrusive clues in a detective novel. The full significance of the scene becomes obvious only in retrospect, when Marie-Louise is conversing with her sister Jacqueline.

In the opening section, then, (as so often in *Martine*) we are intended to project our gaze on the person who does nothing to arrest our attention. But here, as it is an exposition scene, and as we know nothing of anyone, we are tempted to do the opposite. Thus we hear Landreau describing the layout of his domain and talking about his nail industry, we hear Galais' courteous interruptions; but we do not notice the minute signs of Marie-Louise's irritation, which demand as much from the actress's control as from the spectator's ability to see all things.

There is a tribute of praise to be paid to Bernard's efforts to transfer to the stage a technique which traditionally belongs to the detective-type novel. Besides, even in a play, this sort of *a posteriori* illumination and shifting of emphasis by a following scene can be aesthetically rewarding — though, admittedly, more often for the reader than for the spectator. But Bernard's attempt, at the very beginning of *L'Invitation*, to fill with significance the silence of one about whom we as yet know nothing is a gamble which he loses, and suggests in him an initial over-estimation of the evocative power of the unexpressed. [4]

The play is also challenging for the author because it depends so heavily on the incorporeal. We are here in the province of extremely subjective impressions, which, within Bernard's scheme, are to be indirectly conveyed; either because of the character's reluctance to formulate that which, once formulated, has a more menacing reality,

---

[3] See above, pp. 92, 111.
[4] On revising the play Bernard decided to cut the opening scene.

or because the impressions, by their insubstantiality, make direct expression difficult. The *décor* has in this respect an indispensable rôle in *L'Invitation*, since it is one of the agents through which the protagonist's mood is transmitted to us. A fir-forest, a photograph, a fan, a volume of Baudelaire, and a chair are all active objects in the play.

The author suggests from the beginning a cloistered atmosphere. The house in which Marie-Louise lives is itself physically isolated in the Vosges, both the nail-factory and its workers being kept well away from it. All the action takes place in a round room, designed to look like a glass cage — "une pièce arrondie, presque entièrement vitrée" [5] — and surrounded by a fir-forest. "L'atmosphère," we are told, "est moins donnée par l'arrangement de la pièce que par la forêt de sapins, profonde, écrasante." [6] In fact, the house could appear to be a prison, depending on one's vision. Bernard intimates that Marie-Louise's response to her environment is purely individual and subjective. She may find the business of nail-making humdrum, but her husband and father find it specially absorbing. Similarly, while the firs appear to leave the others unmoved, they definitely increase Marie-Louise's feeling that she is physically fenced in; to this feeling is added that sense of isolation caused by her different vision.

We saw earlier that by denying Martine the convenience of protracted soliloquy and the company of a confidante, Bernard ensured that we never heard her declarations of love and suffering. With Marie-Louise, however, he was dealing with subjective impressions and unconscious mental processes of a far more complex nature than Martine's smothered passion and silent grief; this is probably why he chose to introduce in *L'Invitation* the figure of the confidante in the person of Jacqueline. It is when Jacqueline and Marie-Louise are in conversation that we first grasp the significance for the latter of the firs, and learn of her sense of imprisonment:

> MARIE-LOUISE. Ne t'es-tu jamais dit qu'au lieu de ces arbres, qui ne changent jamais, nous pourrions en avoir d'autres qui perdraient leurs feuilles et en pousseraient de nouvelles chaque printemps?

---

[5] Act I, p. 265 in *Théâtre I*.
[6] *Ibid.*

> JACQUELINE. Si on nous donnait d'autres arbres, tu
> serais capable de regretter ceux-là.
> MARIE-LOUISE. C'est possible... Tout à l'heure, papa
> disait à ce monsieur: 'Vous pouvez marcher une heure et
> demie dans tous les sens, vous ne verrez que des sapins, des
> sapins, des sapins... (Comme à elle-même.) des sapins...
> des sapins...
> JACQUELINE. Pourquoi me dis-tu cela?
> MARIE-LOUISE. Je ne sais pas. Pour rien. [7]

Bernard makes her project to the fir-forest her sense of monotony,
and her dissatisfaction with everything that surrounds her, and this
indirect statement of ennui is in its own way just as forcible as Emma
Bovary's "J'ai tout lu." [8]

Both Marie-Louise and Emma are able to feel overwhelmed by
boredom and dissatisfaction where others who are less imaginative
and demanding would perhaps have found bliss. But the phenomenon
of bovarysme is more a primum mobile than a final result. Charles's
habit of licking his teeth after eating, and of making a gobbling sound
on swallowing his soup, his inability to swim, shoot, or explain
equestrian terms, are pretexts for Emma's irritation rather than its
causes. Bernard, for his part, does not suggest any such 'failing' in
Olivier, but it is irrelevant for one to argue like Jacqueline:

> Tu as tout ce qu'il faut pour être heureuse: un bon mari,
> un bel enfant. Je ne vois pas de quoi tu te plaindrais. [9]

Marie-Louise's dissatisfaction (like Emma's) lies primarily within
herself. The fir-forest does not give her a feeling of imprisonment;
it is the material representation of a feeling that is already there.

Marie-Louise's attitude to Philippe does not at the beginning appear particularly amiable. She describes him to Jacqueline with an
obvious attempt at derision:

> Il sent sa ferraille à vingt mètres. [...] Il a une façon de
> taper sur les balles qui rappelle tout à fait le mouvement de
> la machine à écraser les têtes de clous. [...] Et quand il dit

---

[7] Act I, tableau I, p. 275.
[8] Gustave Flaubert, Madame Bovary, Paris, Garnier Frères, 1951, p. 59.
[9] Act I, tableau I, p. 274.

des vers! Je ne peux pas m'empecher d'entendre le ronronne-
ment de la scierie. [10]

She does not show great appreciation for his presents either. She
finds the design on a fan he gave her tasteless, and she points out to
Jacqueline that he blundered by giving her a volume of Baudelaire, a
poet she finds too abstruse.

We note, therefore, with considerable interest her reaction to the
news that Philippe is going to Argentina:

> OLIVIER. Il s'en va après-demain.
> JACQUELINE. Philippe?
> MARIE-LOUISE. Bon voyage!
> JACQUELINE. C'est tout nouveau, alors? Il ne m'a rien
> dit.
> OLIVIER. [...] Il faut qu'il s'embarque mercredi pour
> l'Amérique...
> MARIE-LOUISE. (Surprise.) L'Amérique...
> OLIVIER. Oui, [...] en Argentine.
> MARIE-LOUISE. (D'une voix toute changée.) En Argen-
> tine?
> OLIVIER. Oui, en Argentine. [...]
> MARIE-LOUISE. Mais... pour longtemps?
> OLIVIER. Comment, pour longtemps?
> MARIE-LOUISE. C'est une affaire pour rester... là-bas?
> OLIVIER. Naturellement.
> MARIE-LOUISE. Mais combien de temps?
> OLIVIER. On ne sait jamais. Peut-être toute sa vie...
> si ça marche. [11]

Suddenly Marie-Louise's former attitude towards Philippe begins to
look like a pretence, and at this stage we are justified in wondering
whether there is not an illicit relationship between the two which
she was earlier trying to conceal. In effect, we are confronted with
a case of the 'reaction-formation' process to which we drew attention
on discussing Printemps: [12] Marie-Louise's attraction towards Philippe
is excluded from her consciousness by that which on the surface
looks like repulsion. As Frank Chandler puts it, the fan and the
volume of Baudelaire are "things she professes to scorn, thus screen-

---

[10] Act I, tableau I, p. 277.
[11] Act I, tableau I, pp. 281-282.
[12] See above, p. 106.

ing from herself her real liking for the donor." [13] This attraction is forced further towards her consciousness by the unexpected news of Philippe's impending departure for Argentina.

The operative word here is Argentina. "L'Argentine...," she muses in the presence of Jacqueline, "Oui, c'est drôle de se dire cela quand on est enfermé quelque part." [14] Marie-Louise's sense of restriction and monotony leads logically to a thirst for freedom and exciting new vistas. She probably feels, like her spiritual ancestor Madame Bovary, that "certains lieux sur la terre devaient produire du bonheur, comme une plante particulière au sol et qui pousse mal toute autre part." [15] For Marie-Louise Argentina becomes one of those places, and when Philippe bids farewell, she herself takes flight by proxy. At the same time, the part of her that remains in her house in the Vosges takes refuge in day-dreams. She therefore performs doubly the rite of romantic *dépaysement*.

Subsequent to the process of reaction formation, then, there begins another unconscious process. Henry Bidou sees her reverie as being obscure, indeterminate and fluid at the start:

> Pour [que sa rêverie] se solidifie, il ne faut qu'un choc. Le départ de ce jeune homme sera le fait initial; un peu d'émotion, un peu de regret, il n'en faut pas plus pour former le premier cristal. Et bientôt l'âme cristallisera tout entière autour de lui. Qui se défendrait d'un absent, qu'on ne reverra plus? Le pays où il est devient le pays des chimères. [16]

By coincidence or by design, on the same day that Bidou's article appeared, Bernard was, in another article, using the term *cristallisation* in reference to *L'Invitation*. [17] It is a term which has the advantage of being neat, but the disadvantage of being misleading if we apply it to Marie-Louise without certain reservations. According to Stendhal, 'crystallization' occurred in two stages, the primary stage — separated from the secondary stage by 'doubt' — following close upon the birth

---

13 Frank W. Chandler, *Modern Continental Playwrights*, New York-London, Harper and Brothers, 1931, p. 250.

14 Act I, tableau 1, p. 283.

15 *Op. cit.*, p. 38.

16 Henry Bidou, 'La Semaine Dramatique,' *Journal des Débats*, 7 avril 1924, p. 3.

17 Bernard, 'Quelques précisions, après deux récentes expériences,' *Comœdia*, 7 avril 1924, p. 1.

of love. In fact, crystallization designated for him "le principal phé-
nomène de cette folie nommée amour." [18] Now not only does Marie-
Louise not live through the seven phases of Stendhalian passion, but
it is uncertain whether her feelings for Philippe can be described as
love. At most they represent a half-formed passion, a love in embryo.

Nevertheless, once we bear in mind that Philippe is not irrefutably
the *objet aimé*, we can see how the term, as Stendhal defines it, has
reference to Marie-Louise:

> Ce que j'appelle cristallisation, c'est l'opération de l'esprit,
> qui tire de tout ce qui se présente la découverte que l'objet
> aimé a de nouvelles perfections. [...] Une certaine fièvre
> d'imagination, laquelle rend méconnaissable un objet le plus
> souvent assez ordinaire, et en fait un être à part. [19]

We observe such a mental operation when Marie-Louise idealizes the
image of the absent Philippe. Here, as with the firs, a material object
intervenes prominently, and provokes a reaction from Marie-Louise;
in this way, Bernard is able to present economically the type of mental
process which was once considered to be within the province of the
novelist alone, and on which the character involved can seldom be
expansive. Olivier, Jacqueline and Marie-Louise are looking at a
photograph of Philippe:

> JACQUELINE.   Vous ne trouvez pas qu'il a une bonne tête
> là-dessus?
> OLIVIER.   Il est assez ressemblant.
> JACQUELINE.   Tout à fait ressemblant.
> MARIE-LOUISE.   Je ne trouve pas du tout.
> OLIVIER.   Pourtant, on le reconnaît bien.
> JACQUELINE.   C'est absolument lui.
> MARIE-LOUISE.   A peine! Cette photo n'est pas bonne.
> OLIVIER.   Mais si, très bonne, je t'assure.
> JACQUELINE.   On ne peut pas dire le contraire.
> MARIE-LOUISE. (*Rêveuse, devant la photo.*)   C'est com-
> me vous voudrez...
> OLIVIER.   Voyez comme c'est curieux. Voilà un homme
> qui n'est pas parti depuis deux mois et nous ne sommes

---

[18] Stendhal, *De l'Amour*, Paris, Éditions de Cluny, 1938, p. 48.
[19] *Ibid.*, pp. 43, 69.

déjà plus d'accord sur la ressemblance d'une photo. Il y a
au moins l'un de nous trois qui a trop d'imagination.
MARIE-LOUISE. *(S'écartant, avec un peu d'humeur.)* Eh
bien, mettons que ce soit moi et n'en parlons plus. [20]

Bernard outlines once more the spiritual solitude of Marie-Louise,
from whom the photograph, like the fir-forest, obtains a response that
is peculiar to her. But if she stands alone, it is because she has too
active an imagination. This industrious imagination of hers has been
exerting itself since Philippe's departure, and she has constructed an
image of him from which all defects have vanished; because it is an
ideal image, it must necessarily be superior, more satisfactory, more
real even, than his mere photograph. Bernard succeeds in showing us
this semi-conscious process of idealization by muting the actual words
of idealization, and letting us hear instead her lack of applause for
the photograph — the representation of the non-ideal. Her destruction
of the picture at the end of the scene serves to reaffirm her neutraliza-
tion of this non-ideal.

Once she has begun her imaginative exercise, Marie-Louise not
only transfigures the form of one she can no longer see, but also
transfigures a country that she has never seen. In a geography lesson
to her young son Gérard, South America becomes a wonderland:

C'est loin, tu sais, très loin d'ici... aussi loin... qu'un
conte de fées. [...] J'ai lu quelque part que tout ce qui est
là-bas est beaucoup plus extraordinaire que partout ailleurs.
Les plantes, les fleurs sont fantastiques, dix fois plus grandes
que les nôtres. [...] Les arbres sont si épais qu'à plusieurs
on ne peut pas les entourer. Et les animaux! Il y en a d'im-
menses, comme on n'en voit jamais en France. Alors tu imagines ce que peuvent être les forêts, et les montagnes, et les
chutes d'eau. Il y a des fleuves si larges que d'une rive on
ne voit pas l'autre rive. Et il paraît — je ne sais plus où j'ai
lu cela — qu'ils prennent toutes les couleurs. [...] Il y a
des moments — ce doit être le matin, quand le soleil vient de
se lever — où ils sont tout roses... mais roses, tu sais, vraiment roses... Il y a d'autres moments, quand il fait très
beau, où ils sont tout bleus. On les voit aussi, avec du
brouillard à fleur d'eau, tout blancs, de vrais fleuves de lait.
Et certains jours où le ciel est couvert, orageux, ils devien-

---

[20] Act I, tableau 2, pp. 293-294.

nent tout gris, métalliques, comme des fleuves de plomb...
(*Un silence. Elle demeure immobile.*)
GÉRARD. (*Timidement.*) Et puis? [21]

Marie-Louise's feminine *pudeur* comes into play here to prevent
her from directly embellishing Philippe. But her oblique idealization
(like her muted idealization in the photograph scene) is no less evident
for being oblique. Her lyrical embroidery, which transforms Argentina
into a land of such colour and dimension, is a way of attributing
charm, beauty and perfection to Philippe, is an attempt to create a
décor worthy of him. In these haunts, infinitely more varied, infinitely
less dreary than her fir-forest, a part of her accompanies Philippe.

That her description is governed by the association she makes
between Argentina and Philippe is manifest to the audience; but not
to her interlocutor. She is making a prolonged stage whisper to the
audience, for whom her words have a resonance and significance they
do not have for Gérard; his function is solely catalytic, and the
geography lesson is an expedient which no one will fail to detect. [22]
By introducing this lesson, Bernard was choosing a simple way of
exploiting a standard device of his 'unexpressed' plays; this involves
'dialogue' on two levels, one mental and therefore hidden, the other
verbal; Marie-Louise talks of Philippe while appearing to talk of
Argentina. The effect is one of monologue in dialogue, of which we
saw a less complex example in *Martine*. [23] There, the focus was on
the person hearing the monologue; here, the reverse applies: the
monologue — missed by the listener — is the indirect sign of an unconscious operation within the speaker.

Stored in Marie-Louise's memory are various images derived from
her reading of the customary, colourful descriptions of distant lands.
These images merge with those in Baudelaire's 'L'Invitation au voyage'
and, under the control of her own imagination, effectively inspire her
evocation of Argentina. The fact is that she has rapidly and astonishingly developed a taste for Baudelaire, whom she had professed

---

[21] Act II, pp. 311-313.
[22] Marcel Azaïs relates: "Le soir où j'ai vu *L'Invitation*, [...] le public
ne se gênait pas pour montrer qu'il avait vu la ficelle, [...] et les rires cla-
potaient. Au fond, je sais bien qu'il riait pour cacher ses larmes, car, une
fois admise la fiction simplette du raccord, la scène est touchante." *Le Chemin
des Gardies*, Paris, Nouvelle Librairie Nationale, 1926, p. 386.
[23] See above, p. 84.

to dislike; it appears that she finds particularly agreeable his 'L'Invitation au voyage,' and, of late, instead of playing on the piano her favourite Chopin nocturne, she has taken to playing Duparc's *L'Invitation au voyage*.

A crucial event has taken place in Marie-Louise's mind, an event which neither she nor any character in the play mentions, but which is largely responsible for her behaviour: she has discovered in Baudelaire's poem a secret message from Philippe. We are left to provide for ourselves her mental progression towards this discovery: Philippe must have known in advance that he was about to go away; if he gave her that particular book of poetry he must have had his reasons; perhaps he secretly fell in love with her; [24] he probably was too timid to approach her directly; from far away, over the waves, in the land of order and beauty, Philippe hopes that she will divine his signals:

> Mon enfant, ma sœur,
> Songe à la douceur
> D'aller là-bas vivre ensemble! ... [25]

She becomes so imbued with the feeling of this poem that she unconsciously echoes some of its words. For instance, when she hears of Philippe's return to France, she declares frantically to her sister: "Il vient du bout du monde vers moi" — in order to gratify her slightest desires, she fails to add. [26]

For Marie-Louise then, as for Emma Bovary, literature has a stealthily pernicious effect. But Flaubert is able to inform us of the effect of Emma's reading on her imagination, and of her inner motives:

> Elle avait lu *Paul et Virginie* et elle avait rêvé la maisonnette de bambous.
>
> ... ...
>
> Avec Walter Scott, [...] elle s'éprit de choses historiques, rêva bahuts, salle des gardes et ménestrels.
>
> ... ...

---

[24] At one point she says to Jacqueline, "Rien ne permet de croire qu'il ne m'aime pas" (Act III, tableau 1, p. 332).

[25] Charles Baudelaire, 'L'Invitation au voyage,' *Les Fleurs du Mal*, Paris, José Corti, 1968, p. 112.

[26] Act III, tableau 1, p. 331.

Elle lut Balzac et George Sand, y cherchant des assouvisse-
ments imaginaires pour ses convoitises personnelles. [27]

Bernard, for his part, gives few details about the actual content of
Marie-Louise's reading, and as dramatist he is without the novelist's
freedom to comment widely. A certain amount of unverifiable supposition is therefore involved in any attempt to trace the influence of
literature on our protagonist.

The author does not specify which of Baudelaire's poems (apart
from 'L'Invitation au voyage') are included in the volume Marie-Louise
has, but our assumption is that Philippe gave her a copy of *Les
Fleurs du Mal*. It is easy to imagine how Marie-Louise, invaded by
an overpowering sense of boredom, depression and monotony, could
see herself reflected in a certain Baudelairean mood:

> Rien n'égale en longueur les boiteuses journées,
> Quand sous les lourds flocons des neigeuses années
> L'ennui, fruit de la morne incuriosité,
> Prend les proportions de l'immortalité. [28]

Again, a person of her temperament would readily have participated
in the dream of "une île paresseuse où la nature donne / Des arbres
singuliers et des fruits savoureux," [29] or of that "paradis parfumé, /
Où sous un clair azur tout n'est qu'amour et joie." [30] On the other
hand, however, the disillusioning lesson of the returned voyagers would
probably have been overlooked:

> Nous avons vu des astres
> Et des flots; nous avons vu des sables aussi;
> Et, malgré bien des chocs et d'imprévus désastres,
> Nous nous sommes souvent ennuyés, comme ici. [31]

The process is selective. Marie-Louise, like most of us, finds what
she seeks, notices what she wants to see, identifies herself with impressions to which she is already responsive, likes that with which

---

[27] *Op. cit.*, pp. 33, 35, 54.
[28] *Op. cit.*, pp. 143-144 ('Spleen').
[29] *Op. cit.*, p. 61 ('Parfum exotique').
[30] *Op. cit.*, p. 128 ('Moesta et Errabunda').
[31] *Op. cit.*, p. 259 ('Le Voyage').

she can identify herself, and ignores the rest. Hence her preference for 'L'Invitation au voyage.'

The question of Baudelaire and Marie-Louise leads to the question of Baudelaire and Bernard; the latter, as if there were shame involved in recognizing the patronage of Baudelaire, has given us a dry admonishment:

> Quelques personnes ont vu, dans ma pièce [...], une transposition dramatique du poème de Baudelaire et de la musique de Duparc. C'est une explication très séduisante à laquelle je finirai forcément par me rallier. En attendant, je puis encore dire la vérité. [...]
> Cette jeune femme lisait un poète que lui avait laissé l'absent. Ce poète devint bientôt Baudelaire. Le morceau qu'elle lisait fut d'abord un sonnet quelconque. Et j'avais écrit la dernière ligne de la dernière scène quand je pensai à 'L'Invitation au voyage,' qui m'apparut comme un couronnement, me donnant à la fois le titre et le symbole.
> J'avais donc accompli le chemin inverse de celui que l'on pourrait croire, et j'imagine que cela doit arriver quelquefois. [32]

Bernard's declaration poses once again the familiar problem of how much credence we should give to an author's statements about the genesis of his work, without being disrespectful, without imputing dishonesty. The case of Chekhov who thought *The Three Sisters* was a vaudeville is by no means the only one of its kind; [33] such warning cases should deter us from embracing too hurriedly every statement of intention.

We may concede that it would be restrictive to consider Bernard's play simply as a dramatic transposition of the poem and music. But the play, as it stands, certainly invites speculation in this direction. In order to counter this, Bernard uses an unfair argument. When he

---

[32] Bernard, 'L'Invitation au voyage,' *Le Journal*, 23 fév. 1924, p. 4.

[33] Elsa Triolet relates: "Tchékhov croyait avoir écrit un vaudeville; or, à une discussion sur la pièce, au 'Théâtre d'Art,' tout le monde parlait de 'drame.' Tchékhov, d'abord stupéfait, se mit finalement en colère et quitta la réunion. K. S. Stanislavski raconte qu'à peine la discussion terminée, il se précipita chez Tchékhov, et le trouva chez lui, chagriné et hors de lui... 'Il était persuadé d'avoir écrit une comédie gaie; or à la lecture, on avait accueilli la pièce comme un drame et pleuré en l'écoutant.' " A. Tchékhov, *Théâtre*, Paris, Club des amis du Livre progressiste, 1963, p. 263.

claims that he thought of the poem only after he had written the last line of the play, he cannot be referring to the first performed version of *L'Invitation*, where both the poem and the music are specifically mentioned; [34] he is speaking of an early draft. He is therefore accusing the critics of making wrong inferences from the play as it was performed, and producing private evidence from a draft with which no one but himself is acquainted. In any event, once we begin to ask whether the idea of the play preceded the idea of the poem or *vice versa* (whether too Marie-Louise's exotic vision preceded her reading of the poem or *vice versa*) we are embarking on the famous 'chicken-and-egg' debate. The idea of the play and the idea of the poem, Marie-Louise's vision and the poem, interlock. It is ironical, though, that while Bernard implies in the play that Baudelaire's poem forms an unconscious point of departure for his protagonist's chimerical Argentina, he should be reluctant to acknowledge the possible unconscious element of infiltrating literary reminiscences in himself.

To return to Marie-Louise, it is obvious that her interest in Baudelaire springs originally from the fact that Philippe gave her the volume; a major part of the unconscious operation we observe in her has to do with her consecration of objects connected with him. Her destruction of his photograph is not as contradictory and sacrilegious as it might at first appear, because she no longer identifies it with Philippe. As for the rest, the author relies greatly on little incidental details. She does not allow Jacqueline to use the chair that Philippe used to sit on; [35] she gets nettled when Jacqueline plays with the fan which Philippe had given to her, and which she had previously claimed to find distasteful; [36] she objects to Gérard's touching the volume of Baudelaire. [37] Her actions indicate that she has developed a guilt complex round this volume, less on account of its content than on account of its association with the donor. She hastily puts it away every time her husband enters.

We grasp the full extent of Marie-Louise's internal evolution, and see the wide area covered by her reverie, when Jacqueline informs

---

[34] Act II, p. 314.
[35] Act I, tableau 2, p. 292.
[36] *Ibid.*
[37] Act II, p. 309.

her of Philippe's return to France. Having found secret messages in Baudelaire's poem, she is convinced that Philippe has been pining away for her in Argentina. Through the lenses of her imagination, little nothings assume a special importance and provide her with proof for the conclusions she has already formed. She gives us an effective object-lesson in self-delusion:

> MARIE-LOUÏSE. Il s'agit... il s'agit... mais oui... de toute ma vie.
> JACQUELINE. Toute ta vie?
> MARIE-LOUÏSE. Peut-être le vrai bonheur manqué... et par ma faute...
> JACQUELINE. Par ta faute?... Quelle idée?
> MARIE-LOUÏSE. Pour un mot que je n'ai pas dit... Lui répondre, simplement... Et je n'ai pas osé...
> JACQUELINE. Lui répondre... Mais il ne t'avait rien demandé.
> MARIE-LOUÏSE. Rien demandé!
> JACQUELINE. Quoi?
> MARIE-LOUÏSE. En tout cas, c'est tout comme. Il y a des questions qui sont au bord des lèvres. Il ne dépendait que de moi de les faire naître...
> JACQUELINE. Est-ce que tu rêves?
> MARIE-LOUÏSE. Oh! j'ai des souvenirs qui ne me trompent pas... Des paroles, des regards, des serrements de main, des façons, à table, de me passer les plats, ou, au tennis, de m'envoyer la balle... et tant de choses encore que tu ne sais pas...
> JACQUELINE. Eh bien, dis-les...
> MARIE-LOUÏSE. Est-ce que ça s'explique... Des impondérables que je comprends aujourd'hui. [38]

Marie-Louise begins to convince herself that Philippe has returned because of her, and she quickly progresses from the interrogative — "s'il m'attendait?" [39] — to the definite — "il m'attend, Jacqueline, c'est sûr." [40] Philippe, she reasons, is deliberately tempting fortune by not informing her of his return. He speculates that she would discover eventually, and in a last desperate bid he gambles that either she will arrange to meet him or will not. The arguments that Jacqueline uses

---

[38] Act III, tableau 1, pp. 321-322.
[39] *Ibid.*, p. 327.
[40] *Ibid.*, p. 328.

to persuade her that she is beguiling herself are of course wasted. Marie-Louise works herself up to such a state of exaltation that when she says: "J'irai seule, j'irai à pied, s'il le faut. Je veux le voir, Jacqueline, je veux le voir," [41] it is clear that nothing will stop her from fulfilling what has become her mission. Henry Bidou remarks:

> Avec l'impétuosité sans merci des forces naturelles, le rêve trop longtemps flatté échappe et tend à son objet. Toutes les puissances de l'âme, orientées vers l'image lointaine de cet homme, se précipitent vers lui maintenant qu'il est proche. Tout est emporté dans cet orage. Point de projet, mais un besoin impérieux de voir le voyageur. [42]

We mentioned above that Jacqueline played the part of the traditional confidante in L'Invitation. [43] She is, according to May Daniels, "one of those perspicacious characters whom Bernard often places besides his 'case' in order to elucidate the unexpressed or subconscious emotion." [44] At the end of the scene between the two sisters, there is in effect little that has been left unexpressed. Unlike Martine, Marie-Louise is not usually choked by emotion. Naturally, she is incapable of relating her semi-conscious acts of idealization and her flights of romantic fancy, but she states directly to Jacqueline her pressing desire to see Philippe, her sense of imprisonment, and her rebellion:

> Raisonner! raisonner! Est-ce que je n'ai pas fait cela toute ma vie?... Si on peut appeler vivre, mon existence! Vois où j'en suis... Je ne suis pas plus avancée qu'à dix ans. Ma prison dorée n'a fait que changer de geôlier. Papa d'abord, Olivier ensuite.
> ... ...
> Il y a des années que j'étouffe, tu le sais bien, toi! Tu devrais comprendre, toi! Je n'en peux plus! Je n'en peux plus. [45]

---

[41] Ibid., p. 331.
[42] Henry Bidou, 'La Semaine Dramatique,' Journal des Débats, 7 avril 1924, p. 3.
[43] P. 123.
[44] May Daniels, The French Drama of The Unspoken, Edinburgh at the University Press, 1953, p. 201.
[45] Act III, tableau 1, pp. 330, 333.

But all of this, which would undoubtedly have been of interest to Olivier, will never be revealed to him. Neither will Philippe know from Marie-Louise of the influence he has exerted on her. Despite her outspoken nature, Bernard preserves intact a hard core of unexpressed feeling when he places her in the presence of the two men.

Earlier we described the unconscious process according to which Marie-Louise's attraction towards Philippe was masked by her apparent dislike for him and his gifts. [46] We notice now that even when in conversation with her confidante she shies away from certain words:

> JACQUELINE. Est-ce que je t'aurais prise à part pour t'annoncer cette nouvelle si je n'avais pensé qu'elle te ferait un certain effet?
> MARIE-LOUISE. En voilà un amusement!
> JACQUELINE. Pas plus extraordinaire que ton béguin.
> MARIE-LOUISE. Ah! qu'est-ce que c'est que ce mot stupide?
> ... ...
> JACQUELINE. Il va repartir pour l'Argentine, on me l'a dit. Et puis, si tu l'as... aimé...
> MARIE-LOUISE. Jacqueline!...
> JACQUELINE. Mais oui, si tu l'as aimé, tu ne l'aimes plus, n'est-ce pas? (*Marie-Louise ne répond pas.*) [47]

It may be that Marie-Louise feels that the word *béguin* trivializes her real sentiments; it may be that her recoiling at the word *aimer* is an unrehearsed attempt to conceal and repress a love that actually exists, in the way that her avowed displeasure with Philippe's gifts screens a liking for him. Without entering into a semantic inquiry about 'inclination,' 'attraction' and 'love,' however, we think it is inexact to say that Marie-Louise is at any time *in love* with him. Her capacity for day-dreaming and self-delusion is too great. If she is in love, she is in love only with the idealized absent person who has no existence outside her mind. In the *roman d'amour* she has created, she and Philippe love each other. Their reunion does not take place on the stage. It later becomes obvious, though, that the shock of seeing the real Philippe was sufficient to wrest her from her fantasies,

---

[46] Pp. 125-126.
[47] Act III, tableau 1, pp. 319-320, 323.

and to dissuade her from throwing herself into his arms and declaring her imaginary passion. He will remain ignorant that he had transformed her life.

If there is a 'hero' in the play it is Philippe. It is he who controls most of the action, but, without actually doing anything. In this respect, his rôle resembles that of Yelena in *Uncle Vanya*, as seen by the Russian critic V. Ermilov:

> Le mouvement interne de la pièce est dans la transformation cachée, imperceptible des personnages: Voïnitzki, Sonia, Astrov. Se transforme leur optique de la vie, d'eux-mêmes. Pour tous les trois cas, il y a perte: perte d'espoir, perte d'inspiration, de la poésie dans la vie. [...] Dans toutes ces transformations, dans toutes ces pertes, le rôle décisif est joué par Elena Andréevna. [...] Or, ce qui caractérise Elena Andréevna, c'est justement qu'elle n'agit pas. [48]

Yet Yelena is frequently seen on the stage; Philippe is completely invisible as well as being inactive. *L'Invitation* must surely be one of the first plays to make such extensive use of the invisible 'hero.' [49] In the first version of the play (the version under present discussion) we are aware that Philippe is at the beginning staying with Olivier and Marie-Louise. But the only tangible sign of his presence occurs when, from off-stage, he dazzles Marie-Louise with a mirror. In the revised version, Philippe is even more absent, and when the curtain rises he is already on his way to Argentina. Doubtless, by keeping him out of sight the author succeeds in making the idea outweigh the person; Philippe's remoteness and insubstantiality are in harmony with the immateriality of Marie-Louise's dreams. But, as Frank Chandler remarks, "in the older drama, the scene of her reunion would have been regarded as a sure *scène à faire*, [whereas] here it is merely reported." [50] It might appear to some that Bernard, in order to keep the figure of Philippe constantly blurred, was *forced* to jettison a naturally dramatic scene that was clamouring to be shown. Within the scheme of Bernard's theatre however, the suppression of such a key scene was more a calculated act than an unavoidable accident, the author being especially keen on inverting the traditional

---

[48] Quoted by Elsa Triolet in A. Tchékhov, *Théâtre*, p. 434.
[49] A more recent and famous example is of course *En attendant Godot*.
[50] Frank W. Chandler, *Modern Continental Playwrights*, p. 250.

order of dramatic effect. The importance ascribed to that which is lacking, whether spatially or acoustically, is consistently considerable.

The unexpressed element in *L'Invitation* centres on Marie-Louise's relationship with her husband Olivier after Philippe's departure. Olivier is not insensitive to the process of transformation taking place inside Marie-Louise, and he admits to her that she is becoming a stranger to him. He finds her so much more preoccupied than before; her head seems so full of secret thoughts. He begins to consider practical means of curing her apparent dissatisfaction, wondering whether his personal shortcomings account for it. He would like to spoil her, take her to Paris, buy her more books, more clothes, more jewels, a car; she responds nonchalantly with a series of monosyllables, making Olivier (and the spectator) acutely aware that her dissatisfaction does not lie on such an earthly plane. In addition, she says significantly to him a few moments later:

> L'essentiel est que Jacqueline soit heureuse... (*Songeuse.*) Et elle saura l'être. Son mari lui donnera tout ce qu'elle peut désirer: un intérieur, la paix bourgeoise, un budget bien équilibré, des enfants, Paris deux fois par an, des amis de leur milieu, des petits potins... Jacqueline n'a pas beaucoup... d'aspirations. [51]

There is a hint here of an assumed superiority over those less privileged women who have no obscure aspirations, a hint of a certain snugness in her privileged state of dissatisfaction. Be that as it may, Olivier, who has noticed her sudden appetite for Baudelaire, her bizarre attitude to the chair Philippe used to sit on, and to the fan, is understandably disquieted by the change in his wife.

After her description of Argentina to Gérard, Marie-Louise begins to play *L'Invitation au voyage*.

> (*Olivier est entré sur les derniers vers. Il reste devant la porte, regardant Marie-Louise. Il fait maintenant presque sombre. La musique s'affaiblit, semble mourir sous les doigts... Marie-Louise se tait et rêve... Alors Olivier tourne un bouton. Vive lumière. Marie-Louise se lève brusquement en fermant le couvercle du piano, où elle s'appuie du corps et des deux mains, toute déséquilibrée, comme une femme prise en faute.*)

---

[51] Act II, pp. 306-307.

OLIVIER. *L'Invitation au voyage* ... Décidément, Baudelaire ...

MARIE-LOUISE. (*Avec effort, essayant de sourire.*) Mais non ... mais je ... j'ai fait travailler Gérard.

OLIVIER. (*Surpris.*) Travailler Gérard?

GÉRARD. On a appris ma géographie, papa. L'Amérique du Sud. (*Long regard entre Olivier et Marie-Louise.*)

OLIVIER. (*D'une voix blanche.*) Laisse-nous, mon petit ... (*Gérard sort. Silence. Ils sont l'un en face de l'autre. Il la regarde fixement. Elle soutient son regard. Visiblement, il attend une parole, mais elle ne dit rien. Elle hésite, sa poitrine se gonfle, puis, soudain, elle baisse la tête, traverse la scène et sort sans un mot. Il l'a suivie des yeux avec stupéfaction. Dès qu'elle a disparu, il court vers la porte en l'appelant.*) Marie-Louise! ... Marie-Louise! ... (*Au bout d'un instant, elle reparaît sur le seuil. Il lui prend la main et l'attire en tremblant vers le milieu de la pièce.*) Écoute ... Je voudrais ... te ... Je suis si ... tourmenté ...

MARIE-LOUISE. (*D'une voix blanche.*) Tourm ... (*Elle le regarde. Elle n'achève pas.*)

OLIVIER. Tu n'as ... rien à me dire? ...

MARIE-LOUISE. (*La tête basse.*) Quoi?

OLIVIER. Vraiment rien?

MARIE-LOUISE. Mais ... Olivier ... non ...

OLIVIER. Pourtant ...

MARIE-LOUISE. Quoi?

OLIVIER. ... Je ne sais pas.

MARIE-LOUISE. Alors ... (*Elle fait un mouvement pour sortir. Mais, au dehors, on entend une cloche. Ils écoutent, immobiles. Puis ils se regardent ... Un silence. Et elle va vers lui.*) La cloche du dîner ... qui nous appelle ... qui nous appellera ainsi ... Viens, viens ... (*Elle le prend par l'épaule et le pousse doucement. Et derrière lui, furtivement, elle essuie une larme.*) [52]

In this scene we see in operation unexpressed thoughts which underlie and counterbalance the truncated words and sentences. The effect is that of a study in inarticulateness on the part of two persons who are not by nature inarticulate. Without having recourse to the traditional aside, Bernard enables us to intercept the mental processes of the two speakers. The silent part of the discussion revolves round Philippe, though his name is not even pronounced. Having been

---

[52] Act II, pp. 314-315.

caught in the act of dreaming about Argentina (and presumably about Philippe) Marie-Louise can sense the suspicion present in Olivier's mind; but she reasons with herself that to choose to mention Philippe and volunteer a reassurance would probably be to strengthen in Olivier an unfounded suspicion.

Olivier, for his part, assumes that her dissatisfaction must be motivated, and that there must be a substantial reason why she misses Philippe, as she appears to do. It is difficult to see how he could imagine anything else when so much in her attitude suggests guilt; but he knows that his suspicions are vague, and while he would dearly like to have the situation elucidated, he is fearful of making a wrong move. This apprehension is translated by his insistent, questioning look — a timid attempt to end his uncertainty without making hasty accusations. Bracing himself for the worst, he therefore waits for Marie-Louise's confession or explanation.

The stupefaction with which he watches her departing without a word is likely to be shared by a large portion of the audience. By this, it might begin to seem as if Bernard takes mischievous pleasure in carefully building up our expectations and then deliberately dashing them. He does it twice in quick succession, whetting our appetite for the explanation, which eventually never comes, with Marie-Louise's return after her brief exit. On closer examination, however, we can see that Bernard's decision to make the scene culminate in non-explanation was not whimsical.

The scene is akin to those in which we waited in vain for Martine to make a coherent declaration. We saw that on one occasion her combined sense of rejection, unworthiness and inferiority prevented her from unbosoming herself to Julien. [53] Even so, at least there would have been something concrete for Martine to declare. This does not apply to Marie-Louise. Her dissatisfaction is primarily self-begotten, and while it is true that she idealizes Philippe in his absence, it is also true that there has never been the slightest semblance of a passionate relationship with him. From our privileged viewpoint we, unlike Olivier, can see that there are no grounds for a 'show-down' and that there is really nothing material for her to confess.

Then there is the question whether, given the inclination, Marie-Louise would be capable of explaining everything that has been taking

---

[53] See above, pp. 76-77.

place within her. We behold in her an entangled interplay of conscious thought and unconscious forces. She is aware of her boredom and depression; but her virtual paraphrase of the Baudelaire poem (in her description of Argentina) is on a less conscious plane; and her idealization of the absent Philippe lies somewhere on the hazy border between the conscious and the unconscious. She certainly does recognize that her attitude towards him has been modified, but it is doubtful whether she is wholly aware of the nature, progress or extent of this modification, and whether, therefore, she is in a position to offer a precise explanation for it.

The non-verbal confrontation justifies itself on various levels. At the end of the scene, however, Olivier is still plunged in uncertainty. His apprehensions with regard to his wife are multiplied by his discovery, the morning after Marie-Louise suddenly left for Épinal, that Philippe is in Épinal:

> OLIVIER. (*Essayant de se dominer.*) Gustave savait que ce monsieur était à Épinal... Jacqueline le savait donc aussi...
> LANDREAU. Sans doute.
> OLIVIER. Elle a dû le dire à Marie-Louise...
> LANDREAU. Eh bien? (*Il le regarde.*) Quoi! vous lui en voulez de ne vous l'avoir pas dit?
> OLIVIER. (*Lointain.*) Mais non... mais non...
> LANDREAU. (*Après un silence.*) Si vous attachez de l'importance à ces choses, mon cher, vous êtes fou... (*Il reste un instant rêveur et puis, d'une voix changée, un peu inquiète.*) Vous êtes fou...
> OLIVIER. (*Reprenant ses papiers.*) Ah! parlons d'autre chose...
> LANDREAU. Pas avant de...
> OLIVIER. (*Se lève brusquement et va ouvrir la fenêtre de droite; puis se retournant au bout d'un instant.*) Vous n'avez rien entendu?
> LANDREAU. Non...
> OLIVIER. (*Refermant la fenêtre.*) Il m'avait semblé... (*Il revient s'asseoir; il ouvre distraitement une lettre.*) Une réponse du Comité des Forges au sujet de notre différend avec... Ce n'est pas très important... (*Il ouvre une autre lettre.*) Une lettre de la maison Huchart. Tiens! cela me paraît sérieux. On demande si nous pouvons augmenter nos envois de vingt pour cent. Oui, sans hésiter... Vous le pensez aussi? (*Il le regarde et s'aperçoit que Landreau, rê-*

veur n'écoute plus. Il se penche.) Vous ... le pensez aussi ...
La maison Huchart ...
LANDREAU. *(Tressaillant.)* Huchart! ... Oui, oui ... Gros-
se maison ... solide, très solide ... Ils vous demandent quoi?
D'augmenter ... Oh! sûrement! Huchart, je crois bien.
*(Maintenant, c'est Olivier qui n'écoute plus. Il regarde sa
montre et la remonte machinalement.)*
OLIVIER. *(Après un silence.)* Quelle heure avez-vous?
LANDREAU. *(Tirant sa montre.)* Onze heures moins
dix ...
OLIVIER. C'est cela ... *(Il prête l'oreille, lève un doigt.)*
Attendez ... *(Après un silence.)* Non ...
LANDREAU. *(Qui a gardé sa montre à la main et la remonte tout en parlant.)* J'ai beaucoup connu le père Huchart, celui qui a fondé la maison. Il avait une propriété près
de Saint-Dié. Un brave homme. Il venait parfois, en passant.
Ses enfants, à sa mort, se sont associés avec le gendre, San-
terre, un des fils des 'courroies agricoles.' Je n'ai plus gardé
que des relations d'affaires ... *(Il regarde Olivier, puis replace sa montre dans son gilet.)* Allons, je vous laisse. Vous
ne paraissez pas avoir la tête au travail ni à la conversation ...
OLIVIER. *(Désignant le bureau.)* Je vais finir tout de
suite ...
LANDREAU. Oui, oui, vous n'avez pas besoin de moi
pour cela. Il n'y a d'ailleurs rien de pressé ... *(La porte
s'ouvre avec bruit. Les deux hommes se retournent brusquement. Mais c'est Gérard qui entre en coup de vent.)* [54]

In *L'Invitation* Bernard does not concentrate his attention on one
character, as he had in *Martine*. He also uses the technique of the
unexpressed to insinuate the reactions of those surrounding the protagonist. Having stated that Marie-Louise probably knew beforehand
that Philippe was in Épinal, there is no real need, either from the
point of view of the spectator or from that of Landreau, for Olivier
to enunciate the direction his thoughts are taking. Through a most
elementary form of thought-transmission, infinitely more frequent in
real life than on the stage, his uneasy suspicion is passed on to
Landreau. But at this moment when Marie-Louise is at the forefront
of both their minds, they will proceed to talk of anything but Marie-
Louise. They must neither stop talking altogether nor mention her,

---

[54] Act III, tableau 2, pp. 338-340.

as they reciprocate empty talk and fits of abstraction. Olivier is perhaps about to succeed in diverting his own attention when he opens the Huchart letter, but Landreau's abstractedness, the cause of which he can guess, denies him the opportunity. Landreau himself makes a gallant attempt to keep alive a 'business-as-usual' conversation with his information about the Hucharts; but his wish to depart is his tacit avowal of failure. The fact is that their efforts to fool themselves that they are not preoccupied about Marie-Louise is evidence that they are — as surely as negation is so often in Bernard a telling sign of admission.

The author skilfully employs pause and visual image in a combination that gives a deceptive impression of effortlessness and simplicity. He informs us of Olivier's unspoken fear that Marie-Louise might never return by underlining everyday signs of restless expectation: listening intently to noises from outside, looking anxiously through the window, worrying about the time. The watches which both Olivier and Landreau wind absent-mindedly perform the same dramatic function as the nervously smoked cigarettes in other plays.

When Gérard raises a false alarm by entering in the place of the much awaited Marie-Louise, the present-day reader may be reminded of the boy's entrances in *En attendant Godot*. There the images of the tramps' expectation are given great prominence and are repeated:

> [Estragon] se lève péniblement, va en boitillant vers la coulisse gauche, s'arrête, regarde au loin, la main en écran devant les yeux, se retourne, va vers la coulisse droite, regarde au loin. [55]

At the beginning of Act II it is Vladimir's turn to scan the horizon. In both plays we see dialogue trying to inhibit silent reflection on the urgent concerns of the moment. The tramps, however, make no effort to conceal either that they are waiting or that their endless patter is only one way of passing the time while waiting. Indeed it may be argued that *Godot* rejoins the traditional drama where *L'Invitation* diverges from it, in that the characters in Beckett's play show that they grasp the significance (at least in part) of their actions and attitudes by their comments on them.

---

[55] Samuel Beckett, *En attendant Godot*, Paris, Éditions de Minuit, 1952, Act I, p. 19.

Olivier's wait is not futile, for Marie-Louise eventually arrives. Her return is evidently intended as a moment of intense interest, and the audience shares in Olivier's suspense. Operating by stealth, he does not begin with accusations. He does not reveal that he knows Philippe was in Épinal; he waits to see if Marie-Louise will try to hide this information. Intonation, physical attitudes and, in particular, the movements of the eyes have as important a function here as the words exchanged. He scrutinizes her, searching perhaps for positive signs of guilt, while she tries to be calm and natural, though unable to look him in the face. Finally she is unnerved by his gaze, and mentions as unconcernedly and parenthetically as she can: "Ah! je ne te disais pas... Sais-tu qui j'ai vu? Philippe Valbeille." [56] This is Olivier's cue to bombard her with questions:

> Tu savais... que monsieur Valbeille était à Épinal? [...]
> Pourquoi es-tu allée à Épinal? [...] Comment t'a-t-il ac-
> cueillie? [...] Quand dois-tu le revoir? [57]

Finally, then, we have a confrontation between Olivier and Marie-Louise during which Philippe is avowedly the subject of discussion. None the less, the couple move along two different channels of feeling which are not seen to meet. The reason is that Marie-Louise's internal evolution has not been wholly visible to Olivier. We recall that at the outset she had remarked to Jacqueline:

> Veux-tu que je te dise ce que c'est, Philippe? Le fils d'un
> marchand de clous. D'ailleurs, qu'est-ce qu'il est venu faire
> ici? Voir comment on fabrique des clous. Et qu'est-ce qu'il
> fera en partant? Il ira voir fabriquer d'autres clous. Et tou-
> jours comme ça. Et finalement ce sera un monsieur comme
> son père. [58]

From this mockingly realistic view of Philippe, she progresses to a semi-conscious glorification of his figure, only to return to a level-headed awareness of his lack of sparkle. Her recent meeting with him in Épinal leads her to review the signal work of transfiguration performed by her imagination during his absence, and to recognize that

---

[56] Act III, tableau 2, p. 347.
[57] *Ibid.*, pp. 348-350.
[58] Act I, tableau 1, p. 276.

she had idealized a man who in flesh and blood has never been, and will never be, more bewitching that the next nail-merchant. We realize that she has (at least for the moment) been cured of her romantic yearnings when she says to her husband, who is demanding to know the content of their conversation:

> Il m'a dit qu'il avait huit cents employés et qu'il débitait six cent mille clous par jour... Il m'a dit qu'il était associé avec un nommé Dupont et que leur seule concurrence sérieuse était une maison allemande, Beckmann ou Stockmann, enfin quelque chose en 'mann'... Il m'a dit qu'il était vice-président de la chambre de commerce de Buenos-Ayres et qu'il avait fondé je ne sais pas quoi pour les accidents du travail... Il m'a dit que les rues de Buenos-Ayres étaient toutes tirées au cordeau et qu'il n'allait jamais au théâtre... Il m'a dit... il m'a dit que le commerce extérieur de l'Argentine... de la République Argentine... Enfin, tu vois... des choses comme ça. [59]

The fact, however, is that her words have a significance for us that they do not have for Olivier, partly because of our privileged standpoint, partly because he is at the moment solely concerned to discover details of a relationship which he assumes has been improper. His question — "Quand dois-tu le revoir?" — comes after the passage just quoted, and indicates the extent of his present conviction that there has been a long-standing illicit relationship between his wife and Philippe, of which he has only recently been made aware. His attitude towards the end of the scene resembles that of a husband willing himself into tolerance, partially satisfied that at least he now knows.

The confrontation therefore only goes half-way, essential details being left unstated and unclarified on both sides. They do not linger on the subject of Philippe; they seem to conspire not to have any compelling explanations before our eyes. Olivier for instance, after his broadside of questions, allows his relief at her return to show, and will not let her speak freely:

> Non, non, pas aujourd'hui. (*Avec une joie contenue.*) Il ne faut rien me dire, Marie-Louise. [60]

---

[59] Act III, tableau 2, p. 349.
[60] *Ibid.*, p. 350.

"Ce grand drame," Marcel Azaïs observes, "se sera déroulé sans qu'ils soient allés entre eux au-delà de quelques allusions." [61]

The result is that the *rapprochement* which is real to them is illusory to us. Marie-Louise has conveyed to Jacqueline her sense of being enveloped in monotonous triviality; but nowhere does she make this plain to Olivier. Furthermore, she does nothing to assure him that she has not in effect gone astray. Indeed Marie-Louise presumes so much on his intuition and tacit comprehension that the curtain falls on a misunderstanding: her symbolic discarding of the consecrated objects is taken by Olivier as a pledge to terminate an 'affair,' whereas it signals the end of a mental phase:

> ([*Le regard d'Olivier*] *va se fixer sur la petite table. Le regard de Marie-Louise a suivi le sien et s'accroche au même point* ... *Et, soudain, elle saisit le Baudelaire et le porte à la bibliothèque. Puis, ayant pris l'éventail sur le piano, elle va le mettre dans le tiroir de la table. Enfin elle va au petit fauteuil et le tire loin du poêle* ... *En reculant, elle arrive à la hauteur d'Olivier qui n'a cessé de la suivre des yeux avec une émotion contenue* ... *Longue étreinte* ... *C'est Marie-Louise qui se dégage la première. D'un pas léger, elle va au piano et commence le morceau qu'elle jouait au début de la pièce.*)
> OLIVIER. (*D'une voix étranglée.*)   Oui, oui, ce *Nocturne* de Chopin ... que tu aimais tant ... (*Il se penche sur elle.*) Merci ...
>   RIDEAU [62]

With *L'Invitation*, we have moved away from those concrete, definable sentiments that are relatively easy to treat in a play, and are in the domain of the imponderables. "Dans le plan profond," Henry Bidou says, "apparaît à demi tout un monde de larves, de sentiments à demi formés, d'aspirations confuses." [63] Bernard attempts to convey this indistinct, embryonic world to his audience through the building of impressions, and visual images are indispensable to this process.

The visual element is here more prominent than in *Martine* and *Printemps*; Olivier's anxiety when awaiting his wife's return, Marie-

---

[61] Marcel Azaïs, *Le Chemin des Gardies*, p. 391.
[62] Act III, tableau 2, p. 351.
[63] Henry Bidou, 'La Semaine Dramatique,' *Journal des Débats*, 7 avril 1924, p. 3.

Louise's guilt complex, her dissatisfaction, her pensive sadness are translated mainly through repeated images. The stage directions frequently indicate that she is furtively wiping away tears, or is lost in dream. The Stendhalian woman in love, who

> à son métier à broder, ouvrage insipide et qui n'occupe que les mains, songe à son amant, tandis que celui-ci, galopant dans la plaine avec son escadron, est mis aux arrêts s'il fait faire un faux mouvement. [64]

comes to mind when we see Marie-Louise communing with herself over her needlework, in a memorable picture of calm domesticity:

> (Olivier [...] range des papiers, prend des notes. Marie-Louise [...] travaille à un ouvrage, assez distraitement.)
> OLIVIER. (Sans s'arrêter.) Qu'est-ce que tu fais? (Marie-Louise ne tourne même pas la tête. Elle n'a pas paru entendre. Un long silence. Les mêmes jeux de scène continuent de part et d'autre.)
> MARIE-LOUISE. (Sans lever la tête, comme un écho lointain.) Qu'est-ce que tu fais? [65]

The most important visual image combines motion with immobility:

> JACQUELINE. Tu as tout ce qu'il faut pour être heureuse: un bon mari, un bel enfant. Je ne vois pas de quoi tu te plaindrais.
> MARIE-LOUISE. Mais je ne me suis pas plainte, Jacqueline... (Elle remonte vers le fond et reste un moment rêveuse, les yeux fixés sur la forêt.) [66]

It need hardly be said that by itself this action is not particularly conspicuous or dramatic. It becomes significant through repetition, and through the remarks of Marie-Louise which succeed it. For it is at this point, we recollect, that she insinuates to us her response to the fir-forest: the fact that the trees never lose their leaves, and encompass the house in innumerable columns makes them the representation of her sense of tedium and captivity. The second time we

---

[64] De l'Amour, p. 53.
[65] Act II, p. 297.
[66] Act I, tableau I, p. 274.

see the image, therefore, (shortly after the sudden announcement of Philippe's impending departure) we know what state of soul it is supposed to evoke:

> MARIE-LOUISE.   ... L'Argentine... Oui, c'est drôle de se dire cela quand on est enfermé quelque part.
> JACQUELINE.   Enfermé? *(Marie-Louise ne répond pas. Elle est remontée au fond et regarde la forêt.)* [67]

The image also directs our attention to Marie-Louise's aspiration to be beyond the fir-forest, and her hasty flight to Épinal can be interpreted as her eventual fulfilment of this sustained ambition. Naturally, such an aspiration is dependent on her feeling of imprisonment; we discern these two symbiotic impressions when, on the third occasion that we see the image, she opens the window, on the pretext that the room is stuffy. [68] In all, the image is used five times, and on each occasion it accompanies and highlights the same mood in Marie-Louise. [69] Its function is obviously to mark important emotional and dramatic junctures, in the manner of the now commonplace cinematographic techniques of cut-back and flashback. In effect, this particular recurring image forms in *L'Invitation* a pictorial leitmotif, corresponding to the verbal leitmotifs of a poem or novel, and to the musical leitmotifs of a Wagnerian opera.

Music is another auxiliary to the transmission of mood in *L'Invitation*. Chopin and Duparc compete for the protagonist's favour and give her the opportunity to confide her humour to the piano. Because of her habitual tendency towards reverie and melancholy, the Chopin nocturne which she performs at the beginning appears ideally suited to her nature. But when she becomes addicted to Baudelaire, she also becomes addicted to Duparc's *L'Invitation au voyage*. One of the most delightful moments of the play occurs immediately after Marie-Louise's fanciful description of Argentina to Gérard:

> L'enfant la regarde, interdit. Elle va vers le piano. Elle se laisse tomber sur le tabouret, devant le clavier, et rêve un moment. Elle commence à jouer très doucement, puis à chanter *L'Invitation au voyage*, dans la mélodie de Duparc.

---

[67] *Ibid.*, pp. 283-284.
[68] Act I, tableau 2, p. 290.
[69] *Ibid.*, p. 295; Act II, p. 307.

[. . .] La musique s'affaiblit, semble mourir sous les doigts . . .
Marie-Louise se tait et rêve. [70]

Music is used here as a prolongation of dream, as a substitute for
absolutely silent reverie, and, because of the accompanying words, it
leaves us in no doubt as to the escapist direction of her dream.

It is not until after the disillusion of her reunion with Philippe
that she reverts to what Maurice Coindreau has felicitously termed
"le bon Chopin des familles, sensuel mais anodin, musique pour jeune
fille bien élevée, symbole des joies permises de l'amour conjugal et
bourgeois." [71] When, at the end of the play, she again performs her
favourite nocturne, the melody serves to inform us that she has returned to her normal state of melancholy and reverie without escapism.

L'Invitation, then, presents a case of cristallisation, although in
this instance the woman does not really love the man in question,
and he himself is indifferent to her; [72] this woman is the familiar
figure of the idle provincial wife, injected with bovarysme, playing
the piano, reading widely, basking in her dissatisfaction; she is the
imaginative romantic figure, disorientated and isolated in an uncap-
tivating environment, hankering after different climes. She is in fact
an amalgam of literary resonances, and the play is to a large extent
a parable about the rôle of literature in some people's lives. Again,
this is where the venturesome nature of Bernard's project becomes
apparent: he has undertaken to subdue to the dramatic form a subject which, at the outset, looks anything but suited to this form. The
insubstantial is so paramount that many a dramatist would have been
daunted by the very idea of the play. But this insubstantiality was
neither daunting to Bernard nor injurious to his over-all design.
Indeed it provided him with solid justification for the use of his techniques of the unexpressed. It is unnecessary to emphasize that even
in a play belonging to the essentially verbal tradition, the heroine
would have been incapable of expatiating on her slow internal evolution, on the formation of her dreams, on her vague yearnings, and
on the crystallization process of which she is not even wholly aware.

★ ★ ★

---

[70] Act II, pp. 313-314.
[71] Maurice Coindreau, La Farce est jouée, New York, Éditions de la
Maison Française, 1942, p. 218.
[72] See above, pp. 126-127.

The three plays we have just discussed were not conceived as a trilogy; but they reveal a fundamental continuity in the way they embody the author's struggle with the limitations of his medium, and illustrate his belief in the limitless reverberations of unexpressed sentiment. None of the main recurrent features of these plays (among them: pregnant silence, wordless communication, indirect dialogue, dialogue on different levels, cross-illumination of detail, suggestion and allusion) was first exploited by Bernard. His task consisted in making a combined and concentrated use of them, in order to transmute into dramatic form certain aspects of human conduct and linguistic behaviour. The three plays we have examined are those where, in conveying the unexpressed (and sometimes inexpressible) thoughts and experiences, he has best been able to extend the experience of the spectator and reader beyond what is directly presented in the drama, and deepen the imaginative significance of the play.

CHAPTER FIVE

FURTHER CONSIDERATIONS ON BERNARD'S THEATRE OF THE UNEXPRESSED

> The debate will always rage — a vain but healthy debate — between those who insist that the theatre must be literature above all and live through the poetry which it animates, and those who balk at eloquent tirades, at the exuberance of imagery, at heroism dangerously verging on inhumanity and fostering boredom in unmoved audiences. [1]

Theatre and Literature

IT IS NOT INCONCEIVABLE that in some future era it will rest with cassette libraries, record libraries and film libraries to preserve theatrical performances for subsequent ages. For the present, however, it is still true that most of the plays that have come down to us have done so through the written word. This manner of survival is one important cause of the dichotomy between the play-in-the-book and the play-in-performance that has tended to develop with regard to some authors in the literate public at large. One finds, for instance, that the admiration which many have for a Shakespeare play is not in essence different from that which they might have for his Sonnets. Only a step from the actors, directors and spectators who are constantly drawn to the Shakespeare play-in-performance, there is an audience which pays stricter allegiance to the play-in-the-book, and which would claim to obtain from it a completeness of experience that

---

[1] Henri Peyre, 'Paul Claudel (1868-1955),' *Yale French Studies*, Winter 1954-55, p. 94.

the dramatic performance is incapable of providing. Gide was a member of the second group:

> Été entendre *Coriolan* à l'Odéon. Je ne m'accorde plus que des places de poulailler, connaissant mon trop peu de patience au théâtre; et en effet, hier encore, malgré ma grande satisfaction — ou peut-être à cause d'elle — je n'ai pu me retenir à ce spectacle, passé le troisième acte. Copeau et Ghéon m'ont vivement reproché de n'avoir point attendu la scène avec Aufidius. Le vrai c'est que je suis rentré pour la lire. [2]

Gide was representative of a group for whom the purely literary qualities of a play count most, and for whom mental performance suffices. Presumably, it is to this class of audience that Hardy destined *The Dynasts*, Hardy being among the authors who incline to the view that actual performance presents impediments to the dramatist's freedom, and can be dispensed with:

> Readers will readily discern [...] that *The Dynasts* is intended simply for mental performance, and not for the stage. [...] By dispensing with the theatre altogether, a freedom of treatment was attainable in this form that was denied where the material possibilities of stagery had to be rigorously remembered. [...] Whether mental performance alone may not eventually be the fate of all drama other than that of contemporary or frivolous life, is a kindred question not without interest. [3]

---

[2] André Gide, *Journal: 1889-1939*, Paris, Gallimard, 1955, p. 297. Cf. also Charles Lamb's remarks on *Macbeth*: "When we no longer read it in a book, when we have given up that vantage-ground of abstraction which reading possesses over seeing, and come to see a man in his bodily shape before our eyes actually preparing to commit a murder, if the acting be true and impressive, [...] the painful anxiety about the act, the natural longing to prevent it while it yet seems unperpetrated, the too close pressing semblance of reality, give a pain and an uneasiness which totally destroy all the delight which the words in the book convey." 'On the Tragedies of Shakespeare, Considered with Reference to their Fitness for Stage Representation' in *English Critical Essays: Nineteenth Century* (ed. Edmund D. Jones), London, Oxford University Press, 1971, p. 94.

[3] Thomas Hardy, 'Preface,' *The Dynasts* (An epic-drama of the war with Napoleon, in three parts, nineteen acts, & one hundred & thirty scenes), London, Macmillan, 1910, p. x.

The opposite view that drama should not aim solely or primarily at the reader has of course never been unsupported. Here again a theatre/literature divorce is apparent, as in Bernard's "le théâtre n'a pas de pire ennemie que la littérature." [4] What this statement also reflects is the fact that besides 'well-made play' and 'theatrical,' *littérature* had in the twenties already begun to acquire a pejorative nuance — a fact further reflected in Copeau's tribute to *Le Paquebot Tenacity*: "Ah! quelle reconnaissance de tenir entre ses doigts, enfin, quelque chose qui ne pue pas le théâtre et la littérature." [5] Yet the great demerit of Bernard's comment is that it is apt to foster misunderstandings of the type that can be found in Jean Kiehl's *Les Ennemis du Théâtre*:

> Cet excellent avocat d'une mauvaise cause écarterait de la scène Claudel et Giraudoux. Le relâchement du style serait ainsi promu au rang des vertus. Ce sont les mots eux-mêmes, leur éclat, leur musique qu'attaque l'auteur de *L'Ame en peine*. [6]

To be sure, Claudel's and Giraudoux's plays incorporated many of the elements that Bernard's theatre of the unexpressed eagerly avoided; none the less, an examination of the latter's attitude to these dramatists would lead beyond Kiehl's error, and show that Bernard, with an open-mindedness not always found among the avant-garde, was singularly unshackled by dogma.

Claudel embodied a paradox: he was intensely fascinated by the technical problems of scenic representation, and took an active interest in the staging of his plays; [7] and yet it is doubtful whether he ever completely got rid of what might be called the closet-play syndrome. Though *L'Échange*, *Partage de Midi*, *L'Otage* and *L'Annonce faite à Marie* show a greater consideration for the necessities of *le plateau*

---

[4] Bernard, 'Le silence au théâtre,' *La Chimère. Bulletin d'Art Dramatique*, mai (2) 1922, p. 67.

[5] Jacques Copeau, 'Le Paquebot Tenacity,' *L'Art Libre*, mars 1921, p. 40. It is noticeable that even with relation to the novel and to poetry, *littérature* has during this century steadily acquired a pejorative nuance.

[6] Jean Kiehl, *Les Ennemis du Théâtre*, Neuchâtel, Éditions de la Baconnière, 1951, p. 151.

[7] This is adequately demonstrated by the collection of articles, lectures and letters compiled by Jacques Petit and Jean-Pierre Kempf in Paul Claudel, *Mes idées sur le théâtre*, Paris, Gallimard, 1966.

than his earliest plays, [8] one is inclined to hold that their significance as theatre is far outstripped by their incontestable significance as poetry. Claudel, though, had the good fortune to encounter a producer dedicated to dispelling the belief that his plays were undesigned for, and unsuited to, the stage; there has been unanimity of applause for Barrault's production in 1943 of *Le Soulier de Satin*. What is often disregarded is the distance at which the play that Barrault staged lay from the one that Claudel wrote, the original play having been abridged and reorganized into a manageable stage-version. [9] Whereas the idea of writing a play solely for mental performance was foreign to Bernard's conception of drama, Claudel's attitude appears at times to have approached that of the Hardy of *The Dynasts*.

Claudel's verbal exuberance was contrary to the verbal nudity towards which Bernard tended. But the latter was not a man to make sweeping condemnations. In his opinion, it mattered little whether a dramatist was verbose or not, provided that his dialogue contained substance and was rich in *prolongements*. To illustrate what he meant he cited Paul Raynal's *Le Tombeau sous l'Arc de Triomphe*, maintaining that in spite of its extreme diffuseness the play derived greatness from its abundant resonances. [10] It is in keeping with this attitude that when speaking of Claudel, Bernard has consistently adopted a tone of respect:

> Paul Claudel, que j'ai peu connu comme homme, demeure l'ami secret qui transporta ma jeunesse, et Violaine reste une enfant de mon univers. [11]

Equally manifest has been his esteem for Giraudoux:

> Son style n'est ni recherché, ni alambiqué, c'est la pensée qui est chatoyante, et parfois déconcertante, et ce qui est miraculeux, c'est précisément qu'un style aussi pur soit au service d'une pensée aussi rare. [...] Son génie éblouissant réussit, en quatre ou cinq ouvrages qui sont des chefs-d'œuvre, le mariage paradoxal des contraires. [...] [Dans

---

[8] Notably *Tête d'Or* and *La Ville*.

[9] The final section of *Le Soulier de Satin,* adapted by Jean-Pierre Granval, was first staged in the summer of 1972, again through the efforts of Barrault.

[10] See Bernard, *Témoignages,* Paris, Coutan-Lambert, 1933, pp. 30-31.

[11] Bernard, *Mon Ami le Théâtre,* Paris, Albin Michel, 1958, p. 156.

Siegfried] la littérature [...] montre l'oreille, mais reste encore assez contenue. C'est en cela justement que *Siegfried* est une grande pièce. [12]

The fifth scene of the third act of *Siegfried* may well have held a special appeal for Bernard. It is a scene which exploits the silence of the third person, which, as we have said, is part of what Bernard understood by the unexpressed. Giraudoux allows us to divine behind Siegfried's lengthy silence a mental conflict that parallels the debate taking place between Geneviève and Eva. Siegfried occupies the position of judge and jury in a dispute in which he is himself the cause of litigation; the arguments advanced by Geneviève to convince Eva that she should permit him to become Jacques Forestier again, and those advanced by Eva to convince Geneviève that she should let him remain Siegfried are the arguments which, once learnt, he balances silently in an effort to resolve his dilemma. [13] Be that as it may, the manipulation of words, rather than the dramatic manipulation of silence, was Giraudoux's forte, and his characters, with their ability to reason eloquently and analyse themselves perceptively, are of a species alien to Bernard's *théâtre de l'inexprimé*.

Bernard's attitude to Claudel and Giraudoux demonstrates a respect for talent that went beyond simple considerations of doctrine. His admiration for those who displayed qualities that he was loath to pursue is less a contradiction than a sign of his lack of arrogance. For Bernard never even implied that all French drama should obey his personal conceptions, and his 'unexpressed' plays were an attempt at an alternative theatre that did not seek to supersede other forms:

> Je ne prétends nullement que les instruments nouveaux que je cherche à apporter doivent supplanter des instruments usés. Je ne veux pas m'opposer à qui que ce soit. L'effort de chacun de nous est comme le complément, plus ou moins fructueux, de tout ce qui a été fait avant lui, de tout ce qui est fait à côté de lui. [14]

---

[12] *Ibid.*, pp. 129-131.

[13] Jean Giraudoux, *Siegfried*, Paris, Bernard Grasset, 1949, Act III, sc. 5, pp. 143-151. Cf. above, pp. 92, 111, 122.

[14] Bernard, 'Quelques précisions, après deux récentes expériences,' *Comœdia*, 7 avril 1924, p. 2.

A few months after identifying *littérature* as the theatre's worst enemy, Bernard enlarged upon the topic and clarified what he meant by *littérature*. He contended that there was a literature which was particular to the theatre, and which was distinct from the literature of the novel, defining the novel as an art of analysis and development, and the theatre as an art of synthesis and suggestion. [15] This distinction is visible in Bernard's work. We examined earlier the scene in *Martine* where Julien has just returned home to his wife Jeanne, and Martine, instead of making a discreet withdrawal, remains in pained silence. [16] In *Le Roman de Martine* the corresponding scene takes place outdoors:

> Tous trois repartent bras dessus bras dessous, Jeanne au milieu. Mais la conversation est un peu guindée. Jeanne et Julien parlent de choses indifférentes. Martine ne dit rien ou ne répond que par monosyllabes, s'isole elle-même. [...]
> Elle souffre plus encore de leur indifférence et de sentir qu'en réalité elle ne les gêne pas.
> [The couple take leave of her.]
> Longuement, elle regarde ces deux formes qui diminuent, vont atteindre l'horizon. Jusqu'à la dernière seconde, elle garde l'espoir qu'ils vont penser à elle, se retourner, l'appeler. Mais les amoureux égoïstes ont disparu sans un regret. Alors, devant l'horizon vide, Martine, toujours couchée, sent les larmes lui monter aux yeux. Et seule, seule au monde, désespérément seule, pour ne pas voir toute sa tristesse, elle colle son visage au sol et mêle à l'herbe arrachée ses cheveux blonds secoués par les sanglots. [17]

The author is here in the traditional mould of the authoritative novelist, telling us what to think of his characters, providing discursively an inside view of Martine. When the omniscient, descriptive, explanatory novelist changes to the 'dramatist of the unexpressed,' such an insight is suggested — no more than suggested — by self-sufficient non-verbal images. All the same, it should be noted that when Bernard adapted his novel *Madeleine Landier* into *Le Jardinier d'Ispahan*, the

---

[15] See Henri Rambaud et Pierre Varillon, 'Enquête sur les maîtres de la jeune littérature: Les Auteurs dramatiques' (Bernard's reply), *La Revue Hebdomadaire*, 16 déc. 1922, p. 333.

[16] See above, pp. 89 ff.

[17] Bernard, *Le Roman de Martine*, Paris, Flammarion, 1929, pp. 229-233. The novel, though published later, was composed before the play.

play's protagonist — a figure far more complex than Martine — became too much of a mystery; the inherent weakness of this method became manifest. With justification, Edmond Sée complained of the difficulty of interpreting Madeleine's silences, seizing her complicated motives, and following her multifarious reactions:

> Ici l'on aurait besoin que le romancier de *Madeleine Landier* vînt expliquer, compléter [...] bien des choses à peine indiquées, suggérées tacitement par l'auteur dramatique. [18]

Bernard's *littérature du théâtre* is not to be confused with another kind of literature of the theatre, the kind to which George F. Reynolds refers in his article 'Plays as Literature for an Audience':

> Oratory, narrative, lyric should all find easy admission into drama, for all have been in the past and still can be effective literature for an audience. [...] Even purely decorative passages may be effective if they are not too long and if they avoid the methods of poetry for the individual reading alone. [19]

There are no "purely decorative passages" in Bernard's theatre of the unexpressed. The culmination of Martine's despair towards the end of the passage quoted is accompanied by language of an exalted quality; but we encounter no equivalent of this, no vehement and lyrical soliloquy, in the play. It would, nevertheless, be inaccurate to state that Bernard never found it useful to introduce a lyrical strain; [20] it would be equally inaccurate to claim that he took lightly the business of composition and declined to exploit the resources of language. He chose not to make his presence as author unduly obvious, not to intervene to defend causes or provide character-portraits. Yet he was constantly present and active — searching for the mode of expression that would involve simultaneously an act of eloquence and a refusal of eloquence, for the phrase that would be both rich in implications and ordinary in appearance; consciously developing certain motifs, choosing what to tone down and what to heighten; employing, in

---

[18] Edmond Sée, 'L'œuvre dramatique,' *Le Jardinier d'Ispahan* (Press cuttings in the *Collection Rondel*), p. 15.

[19] Pp. 14-15 in *University of Colorado Studies*, July 1953.

[20] Cf. below, p. 168.

fact, many of the stylistic devices that are usual in the more word-centred drama. Bernard's dialogue is often striking for its use of suggestive omission; it cannot be denied, though, that the words appearing on the page have their own intrinsic value and appeal as conscious (and at many times conventional) penmanship. But Bernard firmly repudiated the notion of theatre as a mere branch of written literature, and this repudiation entailed a conscientious shunning of ornateness for its own sake.

The Bias towards Sober and Naturalistic Expression

There is in *Miss Julie* an ironical comment on the theatre's efficiency in inculcating good speech in the theatre-goer:

> JEAN. My natural modesty forbids me to suppose that you would pay a truthful compliment to one so humble as myself, so I assumed you were exaggerating, for which I believe the polite word is flattering.
> MISS JULIE. Where did you learn to talk like that? You must have spent a lot of your time at the theatre.
> ... ...
> MISS JULIE. Do you know you're quite a *raconteur*? Did you ever go to school?
> JEAN. A bit. But I've read a lot of novels, and gone to theatres. And I've heard gentlefolk talk. [21]

The fact is that a major portion of post-Renaissance European drama has been greatly concerned with elegance of expression; so much so that by the time we get to the nineteenth century, verbal beauty has come to be considered a prerequisite. In this connection, Strindberg's remarks do not apply only to Sweden:

> When anyone in the 1860's and 1870's submitted a full-length play to the Royal Theater, he had to observe the following requirements if he were to get it performed. [...] The end of an act should be the place for applause, which was aroused by an oratorical figure [...]. Within the plays were 'numbers' for the actor which were called 'scenes'; the soliloquy or monologue was permitted and frequently was the high spot or climax; a longer emotional outburst or a

---

[21] Strindberg, *Miss Julie*, pp. 123, 131 in *The Plays. Volume One* (Translated by Michael Meyer), London, Mercury Books, 1964.

speech of condemnation or an exposure was almost necessary; one could even relate something — a dream, an anec-
dote, an event.

But roles were required, too — rewarding roles for the
stars of the theater. [22]

It is certainly true that the history of drama offers numerous examples of the non-verbal method being applied to intense feeling.
Sophocles' characters alternate between restraint and discourse in
times of distress. On finding Ajax impaled upon his sword, Tecmessa
is full of vocal woe; towards the end of *Antigone* Creon allows his
grief a no less eloquent outlet. But in *Antigone* Eurydice, on hearing
of her son's suicide, prefaces her own suicide with a forcible silence
which arouses notice:

> CHORUS. What makest thou of this? The Queen has gone
> Without a word importing good or ill.
> MESSENGER. I marvel too, but entertain good hope.
> 'Tis that she shrinks in public to lament
> Her son's sad ending, and in privacy
> Would with her maidens mourn a private loss.
> Trust me, she is discreet and will not err.
> CHORUS. I know not, but strained silence, so I deem,
> Is no less ominous than excessive grief. [23]

In the main, however, the informing ethos of Western drama from
the time of the Greeks has been that in moments of crisis words
increase in quantity and rise above the level of everyday language;
the strong passion provokes an explosion of volubility that corresponds
to, and is justified by, the emotional state of paroxysm.

There is no denying the dramatic potential of the passage of declamation; the *morceau de bravoure,* which in the wrong hands can
become an undistinguished piece of ranting, does, when handled with
skill and conviction by the actor, create a telling impact. It is primarily in the interests of verisimilitude that Bernard abstained from
it. "The speaker of a *tirade,*" Ronald Peacock aptly observes, "mar-

---

[22] Strindberg, *Letters to the Intimate Theatre* (Translated by Walter
Johnson), London, Peter Owen, 1967, pp. 16-17.

[23] *Antigone*, pp. 409-411 in *Sophocles I* (Translated by F. Storr), London,
Heinemann, 1962.

shals the arguments and ideas that justify his feelings or actions or desires in a given situation and he utters them with all the weight of which his feelings make him capable. This happens in real life, but of course the concentration, eloquence, and rhetorical purposefulness of a *tirade* transcend in their formal skill anything that real situations normally produce." [24] Such a realization was basic to Bernard, who was concerned to reproduce, with all its hesitant disjointedness, the pattern of ordinary human speech, and whose 'unexpressed' plays are best served by a naturalistic mode of diction and bodily expression.

Bernard's was an attempt to exploit the dramatic possibilities of unmethodical conversation, sustain dialogue simultaneously on different planes, and provide insights into the significant content behind apparently insignificant words:

> Il y a sous le dialogue entendu comme un dialogue sous-jacent qu'il s'agit de rendre sensible. [...] Un 'couplet' en dit toujours moins qu'une réplique en apparence indifférente. [25]

The subtextual complexity of this type of drama necessitates from the actor a combination of balance, control and subtlety that could be daunting even to the extremely skilled performer. As well as finding the proper intonation for the truncated words and sentences, the actor is required to focus the audience's attention on, and convey the meaning behind, a certain quality of silence, the movements of the eyes, a gaze upon a certain object, a fleeting facial expression, an instinctive gesture, a particular movement from one part of the stage to the other. The actor's task would be considerably easier if he were not performing before an immense auditorium; there the problem of focus would be most acute, and naturalistically feeble utterances would be in danger of being lost. [26]

The bias towards naturalistic delivery leads, then, to the impasse represented by the limitations of the medium. For, as everyone knows, it is not the sheer love of vociferation that has made so much of the

---

[24] Ronald Peacock, *The Art of Drama*, London, Routledge & Kegan Paul, 1957, p. 175.

[25] Bernard, 'Le silence au théâtre,' *La Chimère. Bulletin d'Art Dramatique*, mai (2) 1922, p. 67.

[26] This mode of drama would, of course, be ideally suited to cinema and television. Cf. above, pp. 24 ff.

acting in Western drama tend towards the declamatory; rather it is the acoustic conditions under which the drama has developed. In the open-air amphitheatres, in the theatres that were partly open to the sky, at those periods when the actors had habitually to contend with the excessive rowdiness of wags in the audience, the voice of thunder was an indispensable possession. Today even, in spite of improved acoustics, the large theatre often demands that that which in real life would be conveyed in a quiet tone be voiced more in the manner of Antony's address to the Romans. Stanislavski was probably right in saying that there is scarcely any use at all for loudness on the stage, and that "in the great majority of cases it serves no purpose except to deafen those who have no understanding of art," [27] but the fact still remains that loudness is sometimes the only way to grapple with the problem of acoustics. It is because he was aware of the impasse facing naturalistic delivery in the vast theatre that Strindberg sought a small home for his *Intima Teatern*:

> We looked for a *small* house, because we wanted the voices to be heard in every corner without forcing the actors to shout. There are, you know, theaters so large that the actors must strain their voices so that every utterance becomes false, and where a declaration of love has to be shouted, a confidence revealed as if it were a military order, the secret in one's heart whispered with full voice, and where it sounds as if everyone on the stage were angry or were in a hurry to get offstage. [28]

Whether dramatists, actors and producers have a great deal to gain by aiming at strict verisimilitude will always be a subject of discussion. One is constantly reminded that even if the actors eat real food they will be obliged to drink a harmless liquid from the cup of poison. An attempt at naturalism is obviously no guarantee of artistic worth, and it would be absurd to condemn the myriad playwrights who do not seek to follow the supposedly 'natural' model. There can be no shame attached to Robert Bolt's admission that he made the

---

[27] Constantin Stanislavski, *Building a Character* (Translated by Elizabeth Hapgood), London, Reinhardt & Evans, 1950, p. 147.

[28] Strindberg, *Letters to the Intimate Theatre*, pp. 20-21.

characters of *The Tiger and the Horse* "unnaturally articulate and unnaturally aware of what they 'stood for'." [29]

Bernard's bias towards naturalistic dialogue is best understood within the historical context. His feeling was that dramatists of the rhetorical tradition tended to falsify experience through their attachment to "unnaturally articulate and unnaturally aware" characters; he endeavoured to counter this tendency. In particular, his predisposition towards the patterns of everyday speech was a sign of his eagerness to see the theatre eliminate the declamatory excesses which had been part of the former century's appurtenances. "Musset mis à part," he contended, "le romantisme n'a guère servi le théâtre. Il l'a encombré de toute une verroterie, de toute une ferraille dont il n'est pas entièrement débarrassé." [30] In fact, the Romantic drama crossed the bridge from the sort of elevated expression that found justification in the character's emotional state to a more gratuitous and parasitical lyricism; part of Hugo's legacy to French drama was the oratorical passage that existed primarily, if not solely, for its decorative effect. Bernard's call for a literature of the theatre was an appeal for a halt to that trend, and for a movement towards greater sobriety:

> Pas de phrases à effet, pas de tirades, pas de cavatines pseudo-lyriques; pas de morceaux destinés à se loger dans les mémoires. [...] Pas, non plus, de ces analyses où le personnage, toujours clairvoyant sur lui-même, n'ignorant rien de ses plus subtils sentiments ou pensées, étale son 'moi' comme aucun de nous ne serait capable de le faire aux heures moralement décisives, c'est-à-dire aux heures les plus troubles pour l'esprit et le cœur ou les deux. [31]

Contained in these lines are a dissociation from what we have termed the informing ethos of Western drama, and a rejection of the soliloquy in its traditional form.

---

[29] Robert Bolt, 'Preface' (to *A Man for all Seasons*), *Three Plays*, London, Mercury Books, 1963, p. 98.

[30] Bernard, 'Le Théâtre de Demain,' *La Revue Mondiale*, 1er mars 1923, p. 8.

[31] Bernard, 'Sur le Présent et l'Avenir prochain du Théâtre en France,' *Comœdia*, 30 juillet 1923, p. 1.

Monological Statement

Una Ellis-Fermor saw Bernard's theatre of the unexpressed as one of a number of solutions that have been offered throughout the ages to "the problem of conveying to the audience thought which cannot naturally form part of the dialogue." [32] Among these solutions she considered that provided by the Greek chorus. Discussing its capacity for communicating "a body of common thought and feeling without which the dialogue would be bleak and limited, yet which the main actors in those circumstances could never utter themselves," she mentioned instances where "we meet choric speeches which, though they might be interpreted as commentary, deduction or reflection arising from the passions or events, seem rather an amplification or extension of the thought of the main agents and to belong more properly to them than to the speakers." [33] One may add to this another function of the chorus (a function sometimes fulfilled by the confidant in seventeenth-century France), of which *Trachiniae* affords a good example. The audience has to be apprised of the significance of Deianira's action in sending the robe to Heracles; we have to be told of her resentment at the presence of Iolè in her house, and of her desire, with the help of the 'charmed' robe, to wean Heracles from Iolè. This information is conveyed to us when she purportedly consults with the chorus:

> Friends, while our herald guest is in the house
> Conversing with the captives, ere he leaves,
> I have stolen forth to speak with you alone;
> Partly to tell you what my hands have wrought,
> And to command your sympathy ... ...
> ... ...
> But how by love-charms I may win again
> My Heracles and wean him from this maid,
> This I have planned — unless indeed I seem
> O'erwanton; if ye think so, I desist. [34]

---

[32] Una Ellis-Fermor, *The Frontiers of Drama*, London, Methuen, 1964, p. 97.

[33] *Ibid.*, pp. 102-103.

[34] *Trachiniae*, pp. 301-305 in *Sophocles II* (Translated by F. Storr), London, Heinemann, 1961.

The chorus, as a materialized conscience that listens and speaks, allows the heroine to reason aloud, and thereby to impart to the audience her most intimate considerations.

Such an address to a chorus is not substantially different in function from a certain type of soliloquy. This device is one which Una Ellis-Fermor also examined as a solution to the problem of communicating unspoken thought. She observed, for instance, how the soliloquy could reveal "what we could not otherwise divine of the depths of the speaker's mind, compressing into some twenty lines of vivid illumination what might else have taken the better part of an act to convey." [35] Gloucester's self-profile at the beginning of *Richard III* performs just this function. Implicit behind that self-expository monologue is the feeling, common to much of the traditional drama, that the central figure should be clear-sighted enough to know when he is engaged in wrongdoing, and to know the motives behind such wrongdoing. This assumption is obviously not implicit in Bernard's *Printemps,* where any analysis by the protagonist (whether in soliloquy or in dialogue) of the causes of her mischievous acts is precluded, inasmuch as these acts are unconscious and unintentional. Bernard mirrors thereby the twentieth century's acute insight into the fact that people are often incapable of disinterring their own motives, that 'villainy' often involves a subtle mixture of instinct and gratuitousness. With this insight, one might be tempted to suggest that Gloucester's exposition of his motives implies on the part of Shakespeare a misapprehension of the psychology of the villain. When Gloucester announces:

> And therefore, since I cannot prove a lover,
> To entertain these fair well-spoken days,
> I am determined to prove a villain,
> And hate the idle pleasures of these days. [36]

one may well wonder whether this is the ordinary procedure of villainy, whether it is with such deliberation that the villain seeks, finds, sets forth the reasons for his villainy, and plans its future course.

---

[35] *Op. cit.,* pp. 105-106.
[36] *Richard III,* Act I, sc. I, ll. 28-31. The line numbering is that of Shakespeare, *Complete Works* (ed. W. J. Craig), London, Oxford University Press, 1971.

Yet this would be to judge the conventions of one era by the expectations of a later one. It is doubtless true that, as Trilling remarks,

> The hypocrite-villain, the conscious dissembler, has become marginal, even alien, to the modern imagination of the moral life. The situation in which a person systematically misrepresents himself in order to practise upon the good faith of another does not readily command our interest, scarcely our credence. [37]

But it is worth remembering that this has not always been the case.

In Elizabethan England and seventeenth-century France, author and audience concurred in the recognition and acceptance of soliloquy as a non-realistic but convenient way of advancing the action, giving circumstantial information, and transmitting the speaker's inmost thoughts. Today, on the other hand, monological statement has clearly ceased to command respect; in Beckett we even see this type of statement ridiculing itself by declaring its own identity:

> HAMM. Et moi? Est-ce qu'on m'a jamais pardonné, à moi?
> CLOV. (Baissant la lunette, se tournant vers Hamm.) Quoi? (Un temps.) C'est pour moi que tu dis ça?
> HAMM. (Avec colère.) Un aparté! Con! C'est la première fois que tu entends un aparté? (Un temps.) J'amorce mon dernier soliloque. [38]

The decline and discredit of monological statement has of course corresponded to the rise of naturalism in the drama. Bernard was predisposed towards naturalistic dialogue; but, at the same time, he recognized the usefulness and effectiveness of asides and monologues; his theatre of the unexpressed shows signs of an attempt to reconcile this recognition with that predisposition, of an attempt to circumvent the limitation created by the commitment to naturalism. While, at a hurried glance, his theatre might appear devoid of asides and monologues, an attentive look allows one to realize that he has ingeniously merged a number of 'asides' into his dialogues, and to determine the

---

[37] Lionel Trilling, Sincerity and Authenticity, London, Oxford University Press, 1972, p. 16.
[38] Samuel Beckett, Fin de partie, Paris, Éditions de Minuit, 1957, p. 102.

points at which he approaches, and departs from, conventional forms and uses of monologue.

Absent from Bernard's theatre is the type of aside during which one character, or more, says something that is heard by the audience but not by other characters. The type of aside he frequently employs occurs when a character communes with himself during a lull in the *exchange* of dialogue:

> MARIE-LOUISE.   L'essentiel est que Jacqueline soit heureuse... (*Songeuse.*) Et elle saura l'être. Son mari lui donnera tout ce qu'elle peut désirer: un intérieur, la paix bourgeoise, un budget bien équilibré, des enfants, Paris deux fois par an, des amis de leur milieu, des petits potins... Jacqueline n'a pas beaucoup... d'aspirations... (*Un malaise. Elle est remontée vers le fond et regarde la forêt.*) [39]

> CLARISSE.   Et puis, moi, je ne suis pas de ces femmes qu'on amuse d'un rien. (*Rêveuse.*) C'est que ma vie, monsieur... J'ai perdu mon mari toute jeune. Vous imaginez les hommages qui ont pu se presser autour d'une veuve de vingt-cinq ans... Et celui auquel j'ai répondu avait pris une place si entière... (*Brusquement.*) Pourquoi est-ce que je vous parle de cela, à vous?
> ... ...
> CLARISSE.   Vous devez me trouver bien abattue, bien éteinte...
> MAURICE.   Éteinte? Oh! ne dites pas cela...
> CLARISSE.   (*Avec un sourire.*) Merci... (*Rêveuse.*) Vous voyez pourtant une femme pour qui quelque chose s'est brisé... Certains... attachements peuvent être plus étroits que des liens légitimes... (*Changement de ton.*) Mais cela n'est pas intéressant, allez! [40]

By making these 'asides' audible to the interlocutor, by placing them half-way between self-address and outward communication, Bernard was aiming at realistic credibility. His refusal of situations in which the audience hears what is unheard by other characters was inspired by the same aim. These attempts at realistic credibility, however, may have been caused by a misinterpretation of the traditional aside — a misinterpretation apparently made by many adherents of

---

[39] *L'Invitation*, Act II, pp. 306-307 in *Théâtre I*, Paris, Albin Michel, 1925.
[40] *Printemps*, Act I, pp. 196, 197 in *Théâtre I*.

naturalism. Considered on one level, Macbeth's asides are unrealistic because Banquo and others should be able to hear what we as audience hear:

MACBETH. (Aside.)   Two truths are told,
As happy prologues to the swelling act
Of the imperial theme. I thank you, gentlemen.
... ...
BANQUO.   Look, how our partner's rapt.
MACBETH. (Aside.) If chance will have me king, why, chance
                                              [may crown me,
Without my stir ... ...
BANQUO. Worthy Macbeth, we stay upon your leisure.
MACBETH. Give me your favour: my dull brain was wrought
With things forgotten. [41]

The truth is, though, that these asides (they may also be regarded as an interrupted monologue) represent the thought rather than the actual speech of Macbeth. The Thane of Cawdor ruminates in silence, while the actor playing Macbeth becomes the voice of his silence. Because the dramatist transmits the amplified thoughts on a wavelength reserved for character-audience communication, they cannot be heard by the other characters — though Banquo notices the meditative stance. The Thane apologizes for pondering; Clarisse is apologetic about her audible confidences. [42]

The Thane of Cawdor is cut off from his companions as a result of his meditative silence. On many instances, Bernard has been able, with his type of aside, to achieve a similar isolation of the self-communing character:

MARIE-LOUISE. (Tout à fait lointaine.) Il y a des moments — ce doit être le matin, quand le soleil vient de se lever — où [les fleuves] sont tout roses... mais roses, tu sais, vraiment roses... Il y a d'autres moments, quand il fait très beau, où ils sont tout bleus. On les voit aussi, avec du brouillard à fleur d'eau, tout blancs, de vrais fleuves de lait. Et

---

41 *Macbeth,* Act I, sc. 3, ll. 127-150.
42 It is interesting to note that certain film versions of Shakespeare's plays have exploited the capacity of that medium to present people who are not visibly talking, but whose thoughts are audible. Meanwhile, the tape recorder has enabled the stage-manager to make audible the thoughts of a non-speaking character.

certains jours où le ciel est couvert, orageux, ils deviennent
tout gris, métalliques, comme des fleuves de plomb... (*Un
silence. Elle demeure immobile.*)
GÉRARD. (*Timidement.*) Et puis?
MARIE-LOUISE. (*Sursaute, comme arrachée à son rêve.*)
Et puis?... (*Elle regarde le petit et, soudain, lui prend la
tête à deux mains.*) Oh! toi, peut-être que tu peux encore
comprendre... Ah! qu'est-ce que je dis? [43]

The difference between the significance of Marie-Louise's words for
Gérard and their significance for the audience is patent; he hears a
description of rivers and sees his mother in a sort of trance, but he
is too innocent to detect her oblique idealization of Philippe. Marie-
Louise has begun to speak on a different wavelength, somewhat in
the manner of Julien in the following passage:

MARTINE.   Par exemple, quand je vous ai vu arriver sur
la route, il y a quinze jours, sous le pommier... Je n'ou-
blierai jamais ça...
JULIEN.   Nous ne l'oublierons jamais... Il n'y a pas de
meilleur lien que le souvenir... Oui, comme il était grand,
ce tout petit pommier... Un autre beau souvenir, c'est la
moisson. Je vous verrai toujours arrêtée sur un tertre, de-
bout, la faux sur l'épaule, dans le ciel bleu... (*Elle le regarde un peu interloquée. Il se tourne vers la fenêtre. Elle
ne le quitte pas des yeux. Il reste ainsi un long moment et
puis il finit par murmurer:*)
Je tiendrai la faucille ou la faux recourbée
Et devant mes pas l'herbe ou la moisson tombée
Viendra remplir ta grange en la belle saison...
MARTINE. (*Après un silence.*) Qu'est-ce que vous dites?
JULIEN.   Des vers...
MARTINE.   Des vers? [44]

To all intents and purposes Julien is speaking a language foreign to
Martine; to all intents and purposes Martine has *heard* nothing; she
notices how her partner is rapt. The abrupt introduction of a lyrical
language provokes a change in our understanding of relationships on
the stage; Bernard's use of the different wavelength serves to emphasize the lack of affinity between Martine and Julien, and, conse-

---

[43] *L'Invitation*, Act II, p. 313.
[44] *Martine*, tableau 2, p. 123 in *Théâtre I*.

quently, to give greater relief to the affinity between Jeanne and
Julien. For when Julien later speaks in the same vein to Jeanne, she
hears and understands, and what was little more than an aside when
Martine was present becomes part of a dialogue:

> JULIEN. Je parlais une langue étrangère et je retrouve
> un parler familier. [...]
> JEANNE. C'est imprévu! Julien est devenu bucolique...
> D'ailleurs, je vous comprends si bien...
> JULIEN. (S'animant.) Vous me comprenez, n'est-ce pas?
> Voyez ce champ de blé intact. Regardez la forme que dessine
> cette masse d'épis lourds: une corne d'abondance.
> JEANNE. Tiens, c'est vrai. C'est bien émouvant...
> JULIEN. N'est-ce pas que c'est émouvant? Tout à l'heure,
> je regardais cela et, comme malgré moi, je me suis mis à
> murmurer des vers:
> Je tiendrai la faucille ou la faux recourbée...
> JEANNE. (L'arrête d'un geste et, à sa joie, continue len-
> tement:)
> ...Et devant mes pas l'herbe ou la moisson tombée
> Viendra remplir ta grange en la belle saison
> Afin que nul mortel ne dise en ta maison...[45]

In that it is audible to other characters the Bernardian aside is
analogous to the overheard soliloquy. This device has, not unexpectedly, been important for its comic possibilities — as witness Malvolio's
well-known discourse.[46] A recent variation is to be found in Ionesco's
Macbett:

> MACBETT. Tiens, voici Banco. Que vient-il faire ici,
> tout seul? Cachons-nous. Écoutons ce qu'il va dire.

Macbett listens attentively to Banco's monologue, which expresses
distrust of Macbett, and the ambitious hope that the witches might
reconsider their prediction so as to enable Banco himself, and not
only his descendants, to reign. When Banco goes off, Macbett begins
his own monologue with

> J'ai tout entendu, traître.[47]

---

[45] Tableau 2, pp. 129-131.
[46] *Twelfth-Night*, Act II, sc. 5.
[47] Eugène Ionesco, *Macbett*, Paris, Gallimard, 1972, pp. 81-83. The overheard soliloquy also occurs in more staid circumstances, as is the case with

In France, however, outside farce and comedy, the overheard soliloquy has never gained great favour. Corneille for one thought it inadmissible:

> Surtout le poëte se doit souvenir que quand un acteur est seul sur le théâtre, il est présumé ne faire que s'entretenir en lui-même, et ne parle qu'afin que le spectateur sache de quoi il s'entretient, et à quoi il pense. Ainsi ce serait une faute insupportable si un autre acteur apprenait par là ses secrets. [48]

In view of this argument that the soliloquist is engaged in silent rumination, it appears that Corneille and Racine were making an unnecessary concession to a false sense of verisimilitude in requiring absolute solitude for the speaker of a monologue, and in ensuring that he always noticed the approach of others. Thus, the type of aside we observed in *Macbeth* is as rare in French classical tragedy as it is in Bernard's drama, and the possibility of another character's catching the soliloquist reflecting is made considerably remote:

> CINNA.   Et laisse-moi, de grâce, attendant Émilie,
> Donner un libre cours à ma mélancolie.
> Mon chagrin t'importune, et le trouble où je suis
> Veut de la solitude à calmer tant d'ennuis.
> ... ...
> Mais voici de retour cette aimable inhumaine. [49]

> ROXANE.   Laissez-moi: j'ai besoin d'un peu de solitude.
> Ce jour me jette aussi dans quelque inquiétude;
> J'ai, comme Bajazet, mon chagrin et mes soins;
> Et je veux un moment y *penser* sans témoins.
> ... ...
> Que de justes raisons... Mais qui vient me parler?
> Que veut-on? [50]

Henry VI (*Henry VI, Pt. 3*, Act III, sc. I), and with Annabella ('*Tis Pity She's a Whore*, Act V, sc. I).

[48] Pierre Corneille, *Trois discours sur le Poème dramatique* (ed. Louis Forestier), Paris, Société d'Édition d'Enseignement Supérieur, 1963, p. 68.

[49] Corneille, *Cinna* (ed. Marcel Barral), Paris, Bordas, 1967, Act III, sc. 2, ll. 857-860; Act III, sc. 3, l. 905.

[50] Racine, *Bajazet* (ed. Eugène Berest), Paris, Bordas, 1965, Act III, sc. 6, ll. 1061-64; Act III, sc. 7, ll. 1095-96. My emphasis.

The soliloquist who is overheard is, like the Bernardian character during the passage of dreamy distraction, engaged in actual speech. The difference is that the Bernardian character is only partly oblivious of the other character (to whom he nominally addresses his remarks) whereas the overheard soliloquist genuinely believes he is alone (except, of course, in a sham monologue). Again, it is Bernard's preoccupation with realistic credibility which prevented him from introducing scenes where characters are indisputably *holding loud discourse* with themselves.

We emphasize "holding discourse" because there are two conspicuous occasions in *Martine* on which the performer is required to speak when alone:

> (*[Martine] regarde vers la gauche avec attention, tout à coup s'assied et, à moitié soulevée sur ses deux poings, murmure:*) Qui est-ce? (*Après quelques secondes.*) C'est un homme. (*Vivement elle baisse sa jupe, relève ses cheveux, en tapote les extrémités sur les tempes, défripe son corsage, remet ses paniers droits.*) Un jeune homme... (*Elle regarde silencieusement.*) Qui est-ce qui peut bien venir de Bateux à cette heure-ci? (*Elle regarde plus fixement.*) Comme il a chaud!... (*Elle paraît de plus en plus intriguée.*) Mais où est-ce que j'ai vu une tête comme ça?... (*Nouveau silence et, brusquement, elle détourne la tête.*) Le voilà! (*Elle regarde le bout de ses pieds, arrache un brin d'herbe et le mordille d'un air indifférent.*) [51]
>
> ... ...
>
> JULIEN. (*Après avoir rêvé un instant à la fenêtre, se retourne et regarde le milieu de la pièce.*) ... Jeanne... (*Il regarde de nouveau dehors.*) Est-ce qu'elle sentira cela?... (*Il rêve un long moment et, soudain, regarde plus fixement.*) ... Mais c'est... mais oui, c'est Martine. (*Il se penche par la fenêtre.*) Eh! Martine... Eh! vous ne montez pas... Elle rougit... elle monte... (*Très agité, il court vers la porte du fond.*) Elle monte... (*Il ouvre la porte. Martine paraît.*) [52]

The words spoken by the actress and actor can be interpreted as the respective character's unvoiced thoughts (except, of course, when Julien hails Martine), as the character's actual speech, or as a mix-

---

[51] Tableau 1, pp. 97-98.
[52] Tableau 2, pp. 120-121.

ture of the two. What is clear is that Bernard has reserved a large area for the non-verbal. The automatic reflex with which Martine 'makes herself presentable' belongs to the category of pre-linguistic instinct, and, appropriately, is given no spoken equivalent. The monologues fulfil one of their conventional functions (the announcement of entrances), but, deprived of the full complement of words that accompany thought in the traditional theatre, they proceed by telegraphic notation rather than by well-couched statement and argument. The discontinuous speech testifies to Bernard's hostility to the concept of the play as verbal show-piece, his hostility to the idea of writing the sort of monologue that could provide a pretext for declamation.

We have already touched upon Bernard's rejection of the monologue of self-analysis. His view was that "the more acute the experience the less articulate its expression"; [53] his argument was that the moments of great moral decision, the moments when mind and heart are in turmoil are precisely the moments when one often lacks the capacity for the coherent formulation of searching self-enquiry. [54] When, therefore, such moments occur in Bernard's theatre they are overlaid with silence. Hence a number of what can be described as non-verbal or unspoken monologues:

> [Jacqueline] sort. Marie-Louise reste agitée, anxieuse, et puis, en tremblant, elle va vers la petite table et, d'une main, sans s'asseoir, ouvre le Baudelaire et le feuillette machinalement... Silence. Et soudain, ayant entendu du bruit, elle referme le livre et s'écarte d'un air détaché. Jacqueline entre avec Olivier. [55]

The passage has, naturally, to be considered with the preceding action: Marie-Louise has convinced herself that Philippe has returned to France on her behalf, and she has just instructed Jacqueline to tell Olivier, without mentioning that Philippe is in Épinal, that she (Marie-Louise) is going to Jacqueline's home in Épinal. As she communes, then, through the Baudelaire medium, with Philippe, she is already representing to herself her future reunion with him, wondering for example how they will greet each other after their long separation.

---

[53] As Pinter was to put it almost half a century later in 'Writing for the Theatre,' *Evergreen*, August-September 1964, p. 81.

[54] Cf. above, p. 162.

[55] *L'Invitation*, Act III, tableau 1, p. 325.

And, at the same time, she is apprehensive lest Olivier's suspicions should be aroused. Scenes like this may now be commonplace; but when in the traditional drama the heroine, in a state of palpitation, was left alone in this fashion she was expected to say something. Here, so contrary to the manner of the traditional theatre is the moment of intense mental and emotional activity presented, that the unsuspecting spectator of the twenties might well have believed the actress had forgotten her lines.

This is also true of the scene in which Clarisse awaits Maurice (she has promised Gilberte to discourage him from going riding with Madame Desgrées), and in which her lipstick becomes the object of a fine muted apostrophe:

> Restée seule, Clarisse demeure un moment immobile. Et puis elle s'assied près de la table, les yeux fixes, lointains. Sa main s'égare sur son petit sac. Elle le prend, l'ouvre et d'un geste habituel, tout à fait machinal, en sort un bâton de rouge. Mais, au moment de le poser sur ses lèvres, elle le regarde, comme si elle le découvrait pour la première fois, avec un mélange de surprise et d'anxiété. Et elle le remet dans son sac, d'un air las, morne, découragé. Peu après, on entend du bruit dans l'antichambre. Elle se retourne brusquement. Maurice entre. [56]

Clarisse, who feels herself declining in attractiveness, has to remind herself that Maurice is her son-in-law, that he left the room just a few minutes earlier, and that she need not beautify herself for his reappearance. The *acte manqué* subtly suggests that subconsciously Maurice is equated with the gallants who showered her with attentions after her husband's early death. But the precise nature of her internal discourse can only be guessed at; whatever questions she might be asking herself about the significance of her gesture remain locked inside her head. Dispensing with the conveniently instructive address to the spectator, Bernard in effect obliges the latter to collaborate in the composition of the monologue.

These 'monologues' invite also a few reflections on the stage direction. Together with the two succinct monologues of *Martine* (and, to a lesser degree, the asides) Bernard's non-verbal monologues bear witness to his assiduity in prescribing the details of scenic presenta-

---

[56] *Printemps*, Act II, pp. 230-231.

tion. Here May Daniels's remarks about *Martine* are specially apposite:

> The beginnings of love show in little instinctive movements and hesitations; dismay at its hopelessness, agitation at the sight of her cultured rival, anguish at the torments thoughtlessly inflicted on her by the one she loves — all appear in attitude, gesture and expression. Stage directions are part of the structure of the play and are as important as the text. [57]

Indeed the reader of Bernard's plays quickly notices that the author delegated to the stage direction a responsibility far greater than that of simply indicating entrances and exits, and that he relieved the actor's text of many of the subsidiary functions that it was made to perform in the traditional drama.

To move from Aeschylus or Sophocles in the Greek to the work of many modern playwrights is to move from a form of dramatic writing marked by a scarcity of stage directions to one where stage directions sometimes cover a large area of the page. [58] We do not intend to draw a chronological survey of the independent stage direction, a task that would be complicated by the fact that editorial additions of stage directions are not always recognizable as such. Still, it is to be noticed that of the French classical authors only Molière had stage directions of any substantial length in the published text. Without manuscripts available for examination we cannot say whether these stage directions were in the author's script before rehearsals, or whether they are a record of the *jeux de scène* that had been decided on during rehearsals. It would seem, though, that Molière was an exception to the general rule that the concept of the ancillary guiding text was prevalent neither in seventeenth-century France nor in Elizabethan England. [59] When a silence occurs, then, it is indicated by the spoken text. In the passage we quoted from *Antigone* Eurydice's silence is highlighted by speculative comment on its significance. [60] In like manner, the

---

[57] May Daniels, *The French Drama of The Unspoken*, Edinburgh at the University Press, 1953, p. 184.

[58] This trend, already apparent in Ibsen and Shaw, has since become much more strongly marked.

[59] As is well known, Shakespeare did not write all the stage directions that modern editions offer.

[60] See above, p. 159.

silence of Shakespearean and Racinian characters is underlined when they are called upon to account for it:

LEONATO. Sweet prince, why speak not you?
DON PEDRO.   What should I speak?
I stand dishonour'd, that have gone about
To link my dear friend to a common stale. [61]

TITUS. Madame...
BÉRÉNICE.   Hé bien, Seigneur? Mais quoi! sans me répondre
Vous détournez les yeux, et semblez vous confondre! [62]

The practice of embedding the stage direction in the dialogue has the advantage of drawing attention to reactions which might not otherwise be perceptible to the audience. Such is the case when characters suddenly grow pale or blush or shiver or shed a furtive tear, and Bernard himself incorporates stage directions into the dialogue in this way:

JEANNE. Qu'est-ce qu'il y a?... Vous avez froid? [...]
Mais vous frissonnez... Décidément vous mourez de froid. [63]

CLARISSE. Ce n'est pas que parfois des larmes ne veuillent monter du cœur. Mais la gorge est trop serrée. Elles ne passent plus...
MAURICE. (Qui la regarde.) ...Oh! madame... Elles ont passé. [64]

GÉRARD. A quoi qu'il réfléchit, papa?
LANDREAU. Oh! à bien des choses... A toi, peut-être..
GÉRARD. (Qui regarde fixement son père.) Mais pourquoi qu'il a l'air de pleurer? [65]

Instances like these abound in the traditional drama. Just as frequently, however, the text spoken by the actor is meant to do what stage directions would regularly do today. The observations which the

[61] Much Ado About Nothing, Act IV, sc. I, ll. 63-65.
[62] Racine, Bérénice (ed. Gabriel Spillebout), Paris, Bordas, 1967, Act II, sc. 4, ll. 595-596.
[63] Martine, tableau 3, pp. 144-145. See above, pp. 83 ff.
[64] Printemps, Act I, p. 200.
[65] L'Invitation, Act III, tableau 2, p. 342.

Doctor and the Waiting-Gentlewoman make on Lady Macbeth's actions during the sleep-walking scene are in this category. So too is Britannicus's

> D'où vient qu'en m'écoutant, vos yeux, vos tristes yeux
> Avec de longs regards se tournent vers les cieux? [66]

Entrances are often indicated by Shakespeare, Corneille and Racine in the following manner:

PROTEUS.　Adieu, my lord: Sir Valentine is coming. [67]

ELVIRE.　Elle va revenir; elle vient, je la voi. [68]

PHŒDIME.　On vient, Madame, on vient; et j'espère qu'Arcas Pour bannir vos frayeurs porte vers vous ses pas. [69]

We may consider the manner in which the disposition of the stage is sometimes specified:

> ANTIOCHUS.　Souvent ce cabinet superbe et solitaire
> Des secrets de Titus est le dépositaire.
> C'est ici quelquefois qu'il se cache à sa cour,
> Lorsqu'il vient à la Reine expliquer son amour.
> De son appartement cette porte est prochaine,
> Et cette autre conduit dans celui de la Reine. [70]

We may also consider the way the effects of the storm are created in *King Lear*:

> LEAR.　Blow, winds, and crack your cheeks! rage! blow!
> ... ...
> You sulphurous and thought-executing fires,
> Vaunt-couriers to oak-cleaving thunderbolts,
> Singe my white head! And thou, all-shaking thunder,
> Strike flat the thick rotundity o' the world! [71]

---

[66] Racine, *Britannicus* (ed. Maurice Martin), Paris, Bordas, 1970, Act V, sc. I, ll. 1501-02.

[67] *The Two Gentlemen of Verona*, Act III, sc. I, l. 50.

[68] Corneille, *Le Cid* (ed. N. Scarlyn Wilson), London, Harrap, 1959, Act III, sc. I, l. 771.

[69] Racine, *Mithridate* (eds. Jean Boullé & Claude Labrosse), Paris, Bordas, 1965, Act V, sc. I, ll. 1509-10.

[70] Racine, *Bérénice*, Act I, sc. I, ll. 3-8.

[71] *King Lear*, Act III, sc. 2, ll. 1-7.

Yet another of the multiple subordinate functions of the actor's text
is to proclaim the speaker's death. [72] The slow-working poison which
causes Hamlet's death allows him thrice to announce his decease before
"The rest is silence." [73] And, it has been suggested that the main
reason why Racine had Phèdre poison herself (instead of hanging
herself, as in Euripides) was that she could thereby die an eloquent
death. Bernard resolutely followed the opposite course, restricting the
spoken text to that which, in his opinion, people would normally say
in real life, and consigning other information to his stage directions.
The *ne plus ultra* was reached in the unspoken monologues, where
the voice yields as the medium of self-expression to detailed movement,
gesture and attitude.

Attitudes to the Denouement and to the Hero

So far in this chapter we have concentrated upon divergences in
the character and function of dialogue existing between Bernard's
théâtre de l'inexprimé and the traditional mainstream. There are at
least two other points of divergence, unrelated to language, which may
also be usefully considered. The first concerns the denouement, the
second the dramatic hero. Here, as in the preceding discussion, it will
be found that attitudes in evidence in Bernard's work are not entirely
peculiar to him, but rather range with the more global tendencies of
modern drama.

The haste with which Molière regularly finished off his plays has
frequently attracted comment, and there seems little need for us to
join the chorus of reproach for the general lack of verisimilitude of
his endings. All the same, his denouements do represent attempts to
resolve situations, and in this they still respect the concept of completeness within the play. This is a concept which Ibsen did not
always heed (as is obvious from the inconclusive endings of *A Doll's
House* and *Ghosts*), and one which has been increasingly mocked and
disregarded during this century. Two types of play immediately come
to mind: those whose action proceeds indefinitely, and those which
discard all pretence of a 'natural' ending with a bold and direct announcement. Among the second category are Pirandello's *Each in*

---

[72] This is apt to be mirth-provoking, as with Polonius's "O! I am slain."
Hamlet, Act III, sc. 4, l. 24.

[73] Act V, sc. 2, l. 372.

His Own Way (where the audience is informed that owing to unfortunate incidents the performance cannot continue), and Genet's *Le Balcon,* where Irma tells us:

> Il faut rentrer chez vous, où tout, n'en doutez pas, sera encore plus faux qu'ici . . . Il faut vous en aller. [74]

Among the other category are the circular plays of Ionesco and Beckett, Sartre's *Huis clos,* and the 'unexpressed' plays of Bernard.

The 'unending' play is the diametrical opposite of a *Hamlet* or a *Bajazet,* which both testify to the preponderant rôle of Death in bringing the movement of plays to a definitive close. The refusal to terminate the action (at times an attempt to transmit through the work a heightened sense of infinitude) represents a rebellion against the arbitrariness of Aristotle's leading principle of beginning, middle and end. "S'il faut une fin," Ionesco says, "c'est parce que les spectateurs doivent aller se coucher. [. . .] On lève le rideau sur quelque chose qui a commencé depuis longtemps, on le ferme parce qu'on doit s'en aller, mais derrière le rideau, cela continue indéfiniment." [75] It is precisely this impression of the drama transcending the fall of the curtain that emerges from Bernard's plays. To quote Paul Blanchart,

> Ce sont des pièces qui 'finissent mal,' ou, plutôt, qui ne finissent pas en ce sens que, le rideau tombé, le drame pourrait continuer dans l'être intime et secret des personnages. [. . .] La crise terminée et la pièce finie, on sait qu'un autre drame inexprimé, prolongement du premier, se jouera en ces personnages qui, par le miracle de l'art, sont devenus réels et survivent en l'esprit du spectateur. [76]

Indeed Clarisse's misfortune commences as the final curtain falls. Ridden by the guilt that follows her awakening, she begins as an outcast her lonely wanderings. [77] Marie-Louise no longer idealizes Philippe, but one imagines it will not be too long before she starts

---

[74] Jean Genet, *Le Balcon,* tableau 9, p. 135 in *Œuvres Complètes IV,* Paris, Gallimard, 1968.

[75] Quoted by Claude Bonnefoy, *Entretiens avec Eugène Ionesco,* Paris, Pierre Belfond, 1966, p. 95.

[76] Paul Blanchart, *Jean-Jacques Bernard,* Paris, Coutan-Lambert, 1928, p. 14.

[77] The echoes of *Œdipus Rex* are not difficult to discern.

another chapter of escapist reverie; furthermore, as we saw earlier, the husband-wife reconciliation at the end is based on a dangerous misunderstanding. [78] Martine, tied to her well-meaning and insensitive Alfred, will rear children, mind the farm, put flowers on Madame Mervan's grave, and slip unobtrusively into an inconspicuous old age. Her chances of earthly happiness have been irrevocably destroyed, and the author is careful not to suggest that we have come to the conclusion of an unhappy episode. In these plays, then, pathos emerges not from a contemplation of corpses, not from a spectacle of great men brought low, but from a presentation of commonplace existence and its abiding ingredients, from an evocation of the everlasting loneliness, dissatisfaction and frustration of little people. For the tragedy which appealed to Bernard was the tragedy of little people, one that passes unnoticed by many, but is none the less real and poignant. Without following Maeterlinck all along his mystical path, Bernard too was in favour of "un tragique quotidien qui est bien plus réel, bien plus profond et bien plus conforme à notre être véritable que le tragique des grandes aventures." [79]

Mademoiselle Mars, we are told, was irritated at having to remain silent for 'lengthy' periods in *Hernani*. [80] One can imagine how she might have reacted at being asked to convey the dramatic effectiveness of self-effacement in *Martine,* at being asked to be shadowy and reticent, at not being allowed to deliver a single *morceau de bravoure* — the hallowed hallmark of the dramatist's inspired skill with words that has always been relished by *Comédie-Française* audiences and French tragediennes. The fact is that Bernard's theatre of the unexpressed is singularly wanting in sparkling 'star-rôles,' singularly unsuited for the self-advertisement of the *monstre sacré,* singularly lacking in heroes and heroines, as we normally understand these words. Whereas we commonly find among the attributes of the conventional hero a readiness to fight against even the most overwhelming odds in pursuance of his aims, an urge to defy the gods and reverse the dictates of Fate, we find in Bernard's characters little vigour and resolution.

---

[78] See above, p. 146.
[79] Maurice Maeterlinck, *Le Trésor des humbles,* Paris, Société du Mercure de France, 1896, p. 179.
[80] See p. 41 of Alexandre Beaujour's introduction, *Hernani,* Paris, Bordas, 1964.

Ronald Peacock observes that "in drama proper the basic formula is that persons make decisions and act on them, which has consequences involving other persons, and complications and crisis follow." [81] Obviously, though, this is not the formula with which Bernard complied in his 'unexpressed' plays; it is only in later plays like *A la recherche des cœurs, Jeanne de Pantin* and *De Tarse, en Cilicie...* that we encounter characters who are endowed with strong convictions and a fixity of purpose. Marie-Louise's energy is spent on daydreams; for a moment, as she resolves to see Philippe at all costs, she seems to rise above herself; but her crestfallen return to her dull existence the following morning robs her action of its hardihood. Martine's love has nothing of a driving force; she resignedly withdraws into her shell the instant Jeanne appears. Clarisse too does not engage in assertive action, but her position is, of course, far from identical to Martine's.

Bernard proposed the following as a definition of 'Fate':

> L'ensemble des poussées intérieures et secrètes qui sont en chacun de nous et déterminent le destin de chaque individu, souvent contre son propre cœur et sa propre raison. [82]

This represents a significant deviation from the scheme where the hero is acutely conscious of an external agent, with which he feels himself at variance, and against which he makes aggressive gestures. Bernard's insight into the unconscious led him in *Printemps* towards a different type of conflict. For Clarisse is imperfectly aware of the contending pressures within her; she cannot observe her inner conflict with the lucidity with which Corneille's characters, for instance, examine the contradictions between their imperious duties. While, then, she does not actively struggle against her unwholesome incitements, this passivity, this failure to fight are a logical necessity rather than a sign of moral weakness.

Whether it is avoidable or unavoidable, however, the inertness characterizing the protagonists of the 'unexpressed' plays gives no scope for the dramatic display of heroic attitudes. But the little people

---

[81] Ronald Peacock, *The Art of Drama*, London, Routledge & Kegan Paul, 1957, p. 160.

[82] Bernard, '*Le Jardinier d'Ispahan* n'est pas une pièce persane,' *Le Jardinier d'Ispahan* (Press cuttings in the *Collection Rondel*), p. 1.

who lack energy, whose aspirations are never fulfilled but on whose lives these unfulfilled aspirations exert an overbearing influence, are clearly no less representative of humanity than the superior beings. Underlying Bernard's challenge to the dominance of the hero who is uniformly perspicacious, articulate and energetic was the reluctance to modify character from the commonplace norm of real life. The peculiar merit of this form of theatre derives from a combination of incisiveness and delicacy which allowed Bernard to give to the ordinary sentiments of unexceptional figures, involved in no momentous events, an unusually poignant and persuasive quality, which allowed him to use to advantage the selfsame elements that in life are undynamic.

The Challenges of the Theatre of the Unexpressed

The more disinclined the spectator to lay aside rigid views about what theatre should be, the greater the likelihood that he will reproach Bernard for not writing precisely the type of play he did not want to write. If one feels that the theatre should expose personages to the full glare of the spotlight, one is apt to object to the way Bernard stealthily lifts a shaded lamp to the faces of his self-effacing figures. If one feels that a play should not be dramatically languid but overtly dynamic, that subjects should be tackled head-on and strong situations not allowed to lose their vigour, that experience should be removed from the realm of humdrum actuality, that emotions should spur the hero towards articulation and urge him to valiant action, the theatre of the unexpressed will provide a number of disappointments. "Si vous demandez au théâtre," Régis Gignoux wrote, "des oppositions plus vives où des caractères s'affrontent, où des passions éclatent comme des fruits mûrs, ne vous adressez pas à [M. Bernard]; mais si vous voulez voir la vie couler, comme elle coule chaque jour, demeurez à son côté." [83] What appear to be the obvious 'defects' of the *théâtre de l'inexprimé* are methods that Bernard deliberately employed as alternatives to conventional methods, following his initial decision to deal with themes and situations that were not usually given sustained emphasis in the theatre. The non-observance of the rules concerning 'good drama,' the unwillingness to adopt a limiting definition of the

---

[83] Quoted by Robert de Beauplan, '*L'Invitation au voyage* au théâtre de l'Odéon,' *La Petite Illustration*, 29 mars 1924, page not numbered.

term 'drama' affirm a concern not with what theatre should be, but with what it could be, and testify to a conception of theatre far in advance of that which was current in the twenties. This conception was in turn served by the mettlesome spirit of enterprise and experimentation that perpetually animates the avant-garde.

In the *théâtre de l'inexprimé*, then, Bernard was questioning many accepted notions about what a play should be, and was seeking to exploit the value of the unexpressed in a genre where the verbal expression of feelings, passions, conflicts and ideas had previously reigned unchallenged. Some might regard this as a regrettable and dangerous endeavour to drain away the life-blood of the drama, to dispense with the indispensable. Others might contend that Bernard's characters would be happier in the novel, where their slow-motion existence could be better portrayed, and where authorial comment could adequately make up for their failure to analyse themselves and lay bare their hearts. It need not be stressed, though, that to censure Bernard simply for his fearless approach to the problem of conveying unspoken thought, or simply for his attempt to extend the frontiers of the theatre to include personages and subjects that were held to be reserved for poetry, music and the novel, would be to begrudge the artist his freedom to demur at received conventions and to experiment. [84] It is from other sources that the most legitimate objections spring.

The techniques of the unexpressed were ideally suited to the material which Bernard undertook to dramatize; even so, although their intermittent use can be effective within almost any given play, their consistent and intensive application from play to play would inevitably limit the playwright to one particular type of material. We are not saying that Bernard was unaware of this; the plays succeeding *Martine, Printemps* and *L'Invitation* certainly do not form a steady progression of further explorations into the unexpressed. Yet this inherent limitation of the method we are discussing is one that has to be noted. There are other points, more specifically concerned with Bernard's dramatic practice, which might also be raised. When one

---

[84] In connection with the musical potentiality of Bernard's themes, it is useful to consider that as early as 1922 Henri Rabaud felt the urge to compose a score for *Martine*; arranged as an opera, libretto by Bernard, music by Rabaud, *Martine* was first performed at Strasbourg in 1947.

has taken into account the deliberate nature of Bernard's enterprise, one still has to admit that the achievement is not uniformly deserving of praise; *Martine, Printemps* and *L'Invitation* may be his three most arresting plays; but they are obviously not flawless. It is not merely that the characters surrounding Martine are not convincingly delineated, not merely, either, that Bernard over-estimated the evocative power of the unexpressed at the beginning of *L'Invitation*; [85] the more significant fact is that having started with the well-grounded observation that too often in drama characters indulge in unjustified wordiness, Bernard has at times touched the other extreme. One feels, on occasion, that the silence and inarticulateness of his characters do not spring directly enough from their emotions or from their circumstances; one is sometimes aware of an almost obsessive evasion on the part of the author of the medium of direct speech — as in the final scene of *L'Invitation,* when Olivier so stubbornly refuses to pursue his enquiry. [86] At such moments, one suspects that the method of the unexpressed, though for the most part successfully and subtly used, was becoming an end in itself.

In composing his 'unexpressed' plays, Bernard encountered a series of challenges which he readily accepted. With regard to *Printemps,* he declared:

> J'ai essayé d'atteindre des couches de plus en plus profondes, de montrer l'envers des âmes, leur vérité cachée, de puiser la vie à sa source et d'en rendre sensibles les mouvements les plus mystérieux. On a dit que cela était plutôt l'affaire du roman ou de la musique. Pourquoi? Parce que ce serait plus facile? La mauvaise raison! Et pourquoi d'ailleurs hésiter devant ce qui n'a pas été fait? [87]

A few weeks earlier he was saying with reference to *L'Invitation*:

> Aussi a-t-on pu dire que j'avais mis à la scène un sujet de roman, de poème ou de symphonie. C'est possible, mais qu'est-ce que cela fait? Je ne pense pas qu'il y ait des formules au nom desquelles on puisse *a priori* écarter un sujet.

---

[85] See above, pp. 87 ff., 122.
[86] See above, p. 145.
[87] Bernard, 'Quelques précisions, après deux récentes expériences,' *Comœdia*, 7 avril 1924, p. 2.

[...] Et il me semble que la difficulté apparente d'une tâche
est la plus forte raison de la tenter. [88]

It is clear from these and other statements that Bernard's anxiety to
avoid the most trodden paths was an anxiety to avoid the easiest
paths. Setting out from a position of disdain for the more facile
inventions of some of his contemporaries — the "vaudeville de basse
qualité" and the "mélodrame de confection" [89] — he was only too
willing to decline the formulas that were guaranteeing commercial
success to others.

This attitude merged into a posture of self-imposed austerity:

> Quelle joie, précisément, de tenter la pièce difficile!
> ... ...
> La règle générale de la création artistique est de ne pas fuir
> la difficulté, *et même de la rechercher, de foncer dessus fran-
> chement.* Toute esquive est une défaite. [...] Le créateur
> doit sans cesse avoir à l'esprit cette phrase d'Emerson:
> 'Fais toujours ce dont tu as le plus peur.' [90]

The posture was also apparent in his account of the genesis of *L'Invitation*:

> J'imaginai un jour ce très mauvais sujet de pièce: la femme
> d'un patriote français a été la maîtresse d'un espion alle-
> mand... Sujet aussitôt écarté, mais sous lequel j'eus l'in-
> tuition, quelques semaines plus tard, qu'il y avait mieux à
> chercher. Alors se produisirent des épurements successifs.
> D'abord tomba l'idée d'espionnage, puis l'idée d'adultère, un
> peu après l'idée de guerre, enfin l'idée même de passion
> vraie. Et, par l'élimination progressive des circonstances acci-
> dentelles, un sujet finit par se dégager: la cristallisation des
> aspirations secrètes d'une jeune femme heureuse autour de
> l'image d'un indifférent parti pour un pays lointain. [91]

The tenor of this account suggests an analogy with a chemical process:
the original matter undergoes distillation; the author-distiller leaves
behind as unwanted substances the melodramatic, the impure, the

[88] Bernard, 'L'Invitation au voyage,' *Le Journal*, 23 fév. 1924, p. 4.
[89] Bernard, *Témoignages*, Paris, Coutan-Lambert, 1933, p. 19.
[90] *Ibid.*, pp. 19, 34. My emphasis.
[91] Bernard, 'L'Invitation au voyage,' *Le Journal*, 23 fév. 1924, p. 4.

concrete; only when he is sure that he has extracted from the crude oil a refined *essence*, that he has something more vaporous than corporeal, is he content. But his satisfaction at this achievement is slightly disturbing. His attitude too closely resembles that of the artist who seeks primarily to give an exhibition of technical athleticism. To refuse to shirk difficulties that present themselves during the creative process is entirely commendable and worth-while; the pursuit of difficulty for its own sake fails to move us profoundly.

Bernard treated an even more restrictive and intractable theme in *L'Ame en peine*, a play about which Lucien Dubech remarked:

> Il a [...] battu son propre record, si l'on ose s'exprimer ainsi, quand il nous a fait voir [...] une pièce dont les deux personnages principaux étaient attirés l'un vers l'autre pendant trois actes par un penchant si irrésistible qu'ils vivaient et mouraient l'un par l'autre, et cependant, ils réussissaient ce tour de force de ne pas s'adresser la parole. [92]

The play is based on the Platonic theory of twin souls; the feeling of unfulfilment that nags Marceline and Antoine (they are complete strangers) is relieved only at random moments when Fate places them in close proximity. Marceline waits for an indefinable something, Antoine seeks he knows not what. The play, underpinned by a fragile hypothesis, is best described in negative terms: a drama of what has failed to happen, a history of non-recognition, a non-consummation of Destiny. The final scene, in which Marceline goes insane on discovering Antoine's dead body on her doorstep, presents the definitive termination of their non-union.

Today's critic, used to the even more tenuous and negative subjects of Ionesco, Beckett and Pinter, should be less astonished than Dubech:

> Qu'un auteur aille chercher un pareil sujet, on n'arrive pas à épuiser son étonnement. On a comparé sa besogne à celle d'un jardinier qui voudrait faire pousser un arbre qui n'aurait que des branches, et, par principe, pas de tronc. Extraordinaire gageure. [93]

---

[92] Lucien Dubech, 'Les écoles dans l'art dramatique en 1926,' *La Revue Universelle*, 15 août 1926, p. 509.

[93] Lucien Dubech, 'Le Théâtre: Les Ames en peine,' *La Revue Universelle*, 1er mai 1926, p. 383.

The word *gageure* is well chosen, for it connotes the defiance which is implicit both in Bernard's extension of the limits of the theatre, and, more generally, in the multifarious attempts of twentieth-century artists to reach new dimensions. Yet, initially at any rate, these accomplishments will seem forbidding to many, while others will tend perhaps to overprize a particular feat of skill. In the nature of things, this play, in which Bernard took so extreme a course, was itself extremely divisive:

> Sortie de mon cœur, plus personnelle ainsi que d'autres ouvrages, *L'Ame en peine* devait inévitablement m'attirer des approbations plus ardentes, mais aussi des résistances plus marquées. [94]

L'Ame en peine may have been written with heart; it undoubtedly has emotional vigour. But one is required to surrender unconditionally to this vigour in order to appreciate the play sympathetically. One is required to ignore the nebulous quality of this modernized allegory, to ignore the fragility of its hypothesis, and to view the whole through spiritual lenses. Pitoëff's swift decision to mount the play suggests that he responded in this way, [95] but, not surprisingly, *L'Ame en peine* proved to be of limited appeal.

The relationship between Bernard and the audience deserves examination here. At the Eighth Congress of the International Theatre Institute (held in Helsinki in June 1959), France was represented by Bernard and Ionesco. In an address that followed Ionesco's Bernard stated:

> Quand Ionesco nous parle de la nécessité des laboratoires, je suis tout à fait d'accord avec lui. Quand il nous dit que l'adhésion du public est inutile, alors là, je ne peux pas être tout à fait d'accord car, en vérité, pourquoi écririons-nous si nous négligions complètement cet élément essentiel de l'œuvre dramatique qu'est le public? [96]

---

[94] Bernard, 'Avant-Propos,' *Théâtre II*, Paris, Albin Michel, 1927, p. 6.
[95] See above, p. 60.
[96] Quoted by Paul-Louis Mignon (ed.), *Les Entretiens d'Helsinki ou les tendances du théâtre d'avant-garde dans le monde*, Paris, Michel Brient, 1961, p. 35.

At a subsequent stage in the discussions Ionesco reassured the assembly that he was not arguing for the closet play:

> Lorsque je disais 'théâtre sans public,' c'était surtout une façon de parler; je voulais dire, en tout cas, que l'artiste doit risquer de n'être pas d'accord avec son public et avec la mentalité officielle. [97]

As often happens, then, initial ambiguities of expression made a disagreement appear where none really existed, for Bernard was always prepared to run the risk of which Ionesco spoke, and, at an early stage, he evinced the pride which members of the vanguard invariably take in reaching 'the enlightened few':

> Le public des théâtres ordinaires est devenu très mauvais. De nouveaux éléments s'y sont introduits, qui l'ont abaissé. Tandis que la hausse des prix en exilait des catégories de lettrés qui auraient pu faire contrepoids. Heureusement, nous avons nos publics de ces théâtres d'avant-garde où ont eu lieu, depuis la guerre, les expériences les plus intéressantes et d'où sortira peu à peu un art très différent de celui qui triomphe encore sur certaines scènes du boulevard. [98]

Bernard's disdain for the rites held dear by *Tout-Paris*, his refusal to write plays that could serve as titillating interludes to social gatherings at the playhouse made him a bad commercial prospect. Like many other innovatory playwrights, he could not easily gain access to the main theatres, and was obliged to address himself elsewhere. But his "nos publics de ces théâtres d'avant-garde" savours of such cliquishness that one suspects Bernard vacillated on the watershed between a willingness to risk not winning universal acclaim and a desire, it may be unconscious, to exclude the ranks. It is not without significance that James Agate, in praising *Printemps* as "a small masterpiece" and as "one of the best plays performed in London for a very long time," should have remarked:

> This is not a piece for the vulgar, who will see nothing in it, but for the connoisseur in craftsmanship. [99]

---

[97] *Ibid.*, p. 50.

[98] Bernard, 'Sur le Présent et l'Avenir prochain du Théâtre en France,' *Comœdia*, 30 juillet 1923, p. 1.

[99] James Agate, *The Contemporary Theatre: 1926*, London, Chapman & Hall, 1927, pp. 94, 96.

The same critic, speaking later of *Le Jardinier d'Ispahan*, was to confess:

> Frankly, I don't know what this play is about. Let me put down some of my guesses. [100]

Similar reactions had greeted the play in France, where Lucien Dubech and Edmond Sée complained that they could not always follow. [101] To a greater extent than Clarisse, Madeleine of *Le Jardinier d'Ispahan* is a mysteriously inconsistent figure, and the play presupposes on the part of the spectator perhaps too great a readiness to piece together inconspicuous bits of evidence. The problem does not exist of course for the reader, and, as with some of Ibsen's plays (*Hedda Gabler*, for example), one is inclined to think that the author over-estimated the audience's ability to grasp the psychological subtleties that would present little difficulty to the average reader. On the other hand, however, *Le Secret d'Arvers* requires no particular brilliance from the spectator; but if we are to believe Lucien Dubech, it also met with the audience's incomprehension.

The celebrated soirées held by Charles Nodier at the *Bibliothèque de l'Arsenal* in the 1820s made the *Arsenal* a favourite meeting place for the young Romantic school. Hugo and Vigny are among those who, in the course of their numerous visits to Nodier, left samples of their verse in his daughter's album. Also in the album is a sonnet by the less illustrious Félix Arvers, which has assured him a position — albeit a modest position — in the history of French Romantic poetry. The figure emerging from the sonnet was specially suited to the theatre of the unexpressed:

> Mon âme a son secret, ma vie a son mystère:
> Un amour éternel en un moment conçu.
> Le mal est sans espoir, aussi j'ai dû le taire,
> Et celle qui l'a fait n'en a jamais rien su.
>
> Hélas! j'aurai passé près d'elle inaperçu,
> Toujours à ses côtés, et pourtant solitaire,

---

[100] James Agate, *The Contemporary Theatre: 1944 and 1945*, London, Harrap, 1946, p. 90.

[101] See *Le Jardinier d'Ispahan* (Press cuttings in the *Collection Rondel*), pp. 12-15.

Et j'aurai jusqu'au bout fait mon temps sur la terre,
N'osant rien demander et n'ayant rien reçu.

Pour elle, quoique Dieu l'ait faite douce et tendre,
Elle ira son chemin, distraite, et sans entendre
Ce murmure d'amour élevé sur ses pas;

A l'austère devoir pieusement fidèle,
Elle dira, lisant ces vers tout remplis d'elle:
'Quelle est donc cette femme?' et ne comprendra pas. [102]

As is usual in such cases, there have been attempts to divine the
source of inspiration; Michel Salomon relates:

> Théodore de Banville souhaitait que l'on ne découvrît jamais
> le nom de l'ingrate ou de l'aveugle: 'Comme elle n'a pas
> deviné l'amour chaste du poète, comme elle ne lui a donné
> ni une consolation ni un sourire, il faut aussi qu'elle ne
> marche jamais sur le tapis triomphal qu'il avait étendu de-
> vant ses pieds dédaigneux.' Ce 'tapis triomphal,' elles furent
> deux à se renvoyer l'honneur d'y marcher. Marie Nodier elle-
> même et Mme Victor Hugo, savaient que l'on soupçonnait
> en l'une d'elles l'auteur du 'mal sans espoir,' et chacune se
> défendait en riant. [103]

That Bernard opted for Marie Nodier is illustrated by his one-act
play *Le Secret d'Arvers,* in which he projected an imaginary view of
the circumstances surrounding the sonnet.

The play is set in 1831, about a year after Marie, the muse of
the *Arsenal,* the nymph of Romanticism, had married a *fonctionnaire*
(Jules Mennessier), thereby disappointing the best hopes of her father
and other members of the coterie. One of these was Antoine Fontaney,
who at the beginning of the act is speaking of his unremitting love for
Marie. Arvers listens and says little; we note, though, that he is upset
when Fontaney touches the piano — Marie's piano. Arvers' inspiration
comes when Marie mentions in passing that he is the only one of
her friends who has not written in her album. There and then he
contributes his sonnet, only to see Marie skim over it with a painful

---

[102] See *The Oxford Book of French Verse* (ed. P. Mansell Jones), Oxford
at the Clarendon Press, 1968, p. 387.
[103] Michel Salomon, *Charles Nodier et le Groupe Romantique,* Paris,
Perrin et Cie, 1908, pp. 122-123.

lack of intuitive appreciation. But she is worried about Fontaney's ill health; she is twice interrupted by her mother; she is thinking of the reception to be held at the *Arsenal* that evening; the concierge brings in the copy of *Les Feuilles d'automne* which Hugo has just sent to her father. In ensuring that the sonnet receives only a small part of her attention, Bernard ensures the fulfilment of the prophecy in the second tercet.

One may legitimately remain unconvinced by Marie's inability to understand. Nevertheless, in seeking to make it plausible, Bernard has unintentionally given *Le Secret d'Arvers* the status of an allegoric beacon with regard to the 'unexpressed' plays as a whole. Marie does not understand because she reads distractedly; but Bernard suggests also that it is because she has been conditioned by the tributes she habitually receives to warm to a different order and quality of poetic utterance. In her album there is, she says, "une déclaration de Guttinguer à rendre Fontaney jaloux"; [104] as she reads the sonnet she remembers a poem in her album, dedicated to her by Émile Deschamps, which she quotes with fervour:

> Les belles sont aussi des reines;
> Il faut bien que ces souveraines
> Entendent quelques vérités. [105]

After the hymns loudly and ardently addressed to Marie's regal beauty, after the wind, the earthquake and the fire, comes Arvers' discreet "murmure d'amour" — the still small voice that Marie does not hear. Her bankruptcy of intuition indicates a failure to attune herself to an unfamiliar accent. It is easy to see, then, what moral the fable holds for both Bernard and his spectator. In coming to the theatre of the unexpressed from that in which characters provide a running commentary on their various states of mind, the spectator needs to make a crucial adjustment in perspective. If he does not, there is the danger that Bernard's 'murmurs' might suffer the same misadventure as that of his protagonist Arvers.

According to Lucien Dubech,

---

[104] *Le Secret d'Arvers*, p. 30 in *Théâtre II*, Paris, Albin Michel, 1927.
[105] *Ibid.*, p. 39.

Le public a été comme l'héroïne du sonnet, il a dit: 'Quelle était cette femme?' et il n'a pas compris. Comme il est trop naturel, les spectateurs ont refusé de se casser la tête à déchiffrer des rébus. Ils ne viennent pas au théâtre pour travailler, et quand ils veulent exercer leur intelligence divinatrice, ils préfèrent les mots en croix de M. Bernard le père. [106]

If in fact the spectators did not understand, this is attributable more to a defect of imagination on their part, more to their failure to attune themselves to an unfamiliar accent, than to any troublesome problems posed by the play. It is immaterial whether or not the members of the audience are acquainted with the sonnet and with the speculation concerning Marie Nodier's inspirational rôle. By the time Marie has completed her oft-interrupted and repetitive reading of the poem, even the least observant spectator should have been able to form a picture of the discreet, hopeless passion of a diffident and reserved Arvers. It is true, none the less, that Bernard did not handle the pivotal ironical situation with his usual precision. The form of irony whereby the words and attitudes of one character assume an importance for the spectators that constantly escapes another character necessitates a nice tightrope exercise; we are supposed to discern without undue difficulty the significance of those words and attitudes, and, at the same time, we are to believe in the interlocutor's unawareness. The balance is achieved in *L'Invitation,* where we, unlike Olivier, become familiar with Marie-Louise's internal drama, and where Olivier's ignorance strikes us as convincing. But with *Le Secret d'Arvers,* we cannot readily give credence to Marie's incomprehension, though, in our view, the play should be within the grasp of the entire audience.

So despite Bernard's reliance on the active collaboration of his audience, it would be wrong to suggest that he made conscious and sustained efforts to baffle the spectator and overtax his intelligence. Only the spectator who expects everything to be explained to him, and who seeks complete mental relaxation in the theatre could take exception to the elementary mental exercises that Bernard normally asks of him. If there is a genuine complaint about the mental strain on the audience, it has to be made with reference not to *Le Secret*

---

[106] Lucien Dubech, *La crise du théâtre,* Paris, Librairie de France, 1928, p. 76.

d'*Arvers*, but to *Le Jardinier d'Ispahan*. Even in the latter play, however, a capital rôle is apportioned to the audience's imagination and sensibility. For the anti-prescriptive nature of the theatre of the unexpressed often makes it just as important for one to respond to a certain mood and surrender to individual reverie, as to treat fact and statement with intellectual power. In this matter, we can do no better than turn to Paul Blanchart, who has excellently expressed the essence of Bernard's technique:

> En définitive, il s'agit de faire surgir sur le théâtre, ou, plutôt, de suggérer dans l'esprit du spectateur toute la vie secrète, toutes les complexités mystérieuses que les êtres dissimulent sous leurs apparences quotidiennes.
> Le théâtre ainsi conçu n'est pas seulement une 'analyse.' Il devient presque une intuition, une 'divination.' Il rejoint la poésie et la musique en ce qu'elles contiennent d'inexplicable, de mystérieux — de divin.
> ... ...
> Un art essentiellement de sensibilité [...] le contraire d'un art intellectualiste ou cérébral. [...] La part du cœur et celle de l'esprit s'y équilibrent et s'y mêlent harmonieusement. *Comprendre* y devient synonyme de *sentir*. [...] D'où cette formule, qui résume tout, et qui, désormais, peut suffire: 'Le Théâtre de Jean-Jacques Bernard ou *l'intelligence de la sensibilité*.' [107]

---

[107] Paul Blanchart, *Jean-Jacques Bernard*, Paris, Coutan-Lambert, 1928, pp. 10-11, 27-28.

CHAPTER SIX

THE LATER DESTINIES OF *L'INEXPRIMÉ*

THE INEFFECTUAL AND SELF-EFFACING protagonist of the intimist
drama constituted a new species of 'hero,' a hero deficient in vital
energy, unprovided with the will to power — in short, the antithesis
to the Superman. [1] Marie-Louise's gesture in rushing off to Épinal to
see Philippe is but a shadow of the uncompromising action to which
a heroine like Ibsen's Nora commits herself. Other Bernardian characters do not even make such gestures. Theirs is a reluctance to act
resolutely in order to secure their aims, an infirmity of purpose
conjoined with a devotion to compromise, a prompt acceptance of
the futility of efforts to escape from unexciting, non-ideal lives.
Whatever impression of inescapability there is, is achieved not through
the presence of an actively hostile Fate, but through the failure of the
characters to exercise their will. Benjamin Crémieux, in his discussion
of Vildrac's *Madame Béliard*, has remarked upon this bankruptcy of
energy:

> Nous touchons là à la caractéristique essentielle du théâtre
> intimiste : caractéristique qui est peut-être en même temps
> la marque de l'époque où il triomphe. Ce théâtre ne nous
> peint que des héros inconsistants, résignés, qui abhorrent la
> bataille, autrement dit le contraire des véritables héros dra-
> matiques qui ne vivent que dans et par le conflit. Martine,
> Michel Auclair [2] s'effacent, l'héroïne d'*Aimer* [3] ne quitte pas

---

[1] The ascendancy of this species of 'hero' is of course one of the dominant
characteristics of twentieth-century literature.

[2] Protagonist of Vildrac's *Michel Auclair*.

[3] By Géraldy.

son mari. M. Un Tel [4] laisse partir sa femme et le geste de Madame Beudet [5] ne s'accomplit pas. [6]

Crémieux was right to suggest a relation between this characteristic of intimism and the period at which it made its appearance; the Intimists' movement towards quietude may indeed be seen as one of the repercussions of the upheavals of their recent past. [7] Crémieux's reference to characters who "hate battle" is particularly apt, for such characters are the fictional embodiment of the real faltering will to wage war during the later stages of the 1914-18 hostilities. [8] After fulfilling the rôle of a spur to action, the War began to act as a check to enthusiasm, the zealous energy of the French mobilization being overtaken by creeping war-weariness. The apparent endlessness of the slaughter, the growing awareness that the central issues were being decided away from one's own battlefield — away even from all the battlefields — were severely undermining faith in the effect of individual action, and feathering the shaft of defeatist propaganda. It is the intimist drama which, of all the post-war dramatic trends, best recaptured this propensity towards aboulia.

Bernard's plays cannot correctly be described as period pieces. He did not attempt particularized portraits of life in the twenties or at any specific time. [9] The contemporary setting remains inconspicuous during the presentation of everyday people, whose ordinary sentiments and behaviour do not belong exclusively to any time or place. Being based on a number of elementary truths about the ways in which language is used, the theatre of the unexpressed offers situations and characters that are as valid and convincing in the seventies as they were in the twenties. It is nevertheless true that Bernard is one of those authors whose good fortune it was to appear at the opportune moment. Many admired his virtuosity in treating with deliberately

---

[4] Protagonist of Amiel's *Monsieur et Madame Un Tel....*

[5] Protagonist of Amiel and Obey's *La Souriante Madame Beudet.*

[6] Benjamin Crémieux, 'Le Théâtre,' *La Nouvelle Revue Française,* 1er déc. 1925, p. 748.

[7] Amiel, Bernard, Géraldy and Vildrac all saw active combat during the First War.

[8] As manifested by the refusal of several French regiments to return to the line in May 1917.

[9] We are obviously not referring here to his historical dramas such as *Louise de la Vallière* and *Marie Stuart, Reine d'Écosse.*

reduced means what looked like unpromising material, and his endeavour to extend the frontiers of the theatre from the inside rather
than through the use of external artifice; but to this admiration was
added the same sense of relief that greeted the efforts of Copeau and
the *Cartel des quatre*. His success, then, was largely that of one who
held a promise of deliverance for the theatre, who showed signs of
redeeming if from the cheapness which seemed inherent in it at the
time, and of wresting it from its technically unadventurous routine.
For though the distaste for the rhetorical drama and the run-of-the-
mill Boulevard output was certainly not universal, there was a growing
desire for the emergence of a new breed of dramatist, who would
have less recourse to the stock-in-trade of purple patches, tumultuous
effusions, and spicy *hors-d'œuvres*. Responding to a need for novelty,
and for a drama that put art before commerce, Bernard's 'unexpressed'
plays corresponded to a certain post-war mood — a mood of restraint
in speech, a mistrust of speechification and of words at their face
value, which were part of the legacy of the First War. [10] Bernard's
theatre, without being contemporary or modish in a superficial sense,
was in a number of ways profoundly and intimately in accord with
the sensibility of the time.

It is useful to recall here that it is precisely the shifts in taste,
sensibility and expectation which help to account for the variations
in responses to art from one era to another. To be sure, these shifts
constantly accompany the passage of time, and what Benjamin Crémieux said in 1939, on reviewing *Le Jardinier d'Ispahan*, is worth
recording:

> Il y a quinze ans, aux temps heureux du proustisme et du
> théâtre du silence, on n'aurait pas songé à opposer la moindre
> résistance au *Jardinier d'Ispahan*. On eût admiré sans ré-
> serve cette tragédie fourrée, ce drame secret, ce mélange de
> raffinement extrême, de cruauté impitoyable et d'animalité
> déchaînée. On accorde aujourd'hui moins de prix à ces dé-
> licatesses, à ces réticences; on rêve plutôt d'un théâtre poé-
> tique et brutal, où s'affrontent avec violence des passions
> avouées et qui n'ont pas honte d'elles-mêmes. L'intimisme

---

[10] Luc Hommel, for instance, has written of "cette éloquence des mots
dont nous avons failli périr et dont la guerre a guéri, en partie, les nouvelles
générations tout au moins." 'Le Théâtre de Jean-Jacques Bernard,' *La Revue
Générale*, 15 mai 1925, p. 596.

traverse une mauvaise passe. Il n'en est pas condamné pour cela et il est permis de souhaiter que *Le Jardinier d'Ispahan* contribue, en dépit des circonstances contraires, à le remettre à la mode. [11]

Yet, as is well known, the changes in mood are often precipitated by historical event, and in this century they have doubtless been precipitated by the two Wars. One finds that the Second War's influence on the spiritual disposition of the French nation at large has adversely affected the destinies of Bernard's theatre where the post-1918 temper had been more auspicious. [12]

Four facets of the alteration in humour due to the Second War are particularly relevant to Bernard. It is clear, first of all, that the activities of the Resistance provided an outlet for the instinctive desire to continue the struggle against the enemy, and that this persistence in action, against all the odds, constituted a riposte to that defeatism of which the armistice was a symbol — for many Frenchmen a humiliating and discreditable symbol. It is unfortunately impossible to talk of the actual impact of Bernard's plays during the Occupation, since they were banned; one is inclined to submit, however, that the moment was less propitious for the resignation of a Martine than for Sartre's Oreste to hold out in defiance of Jupiter, and for the lesson in intransigence from Anouilh's Antigone. Secondly, with the added urgency which the War brought to the problem of the human condition, the existential mystery of man and his metaphysical plight were threatening to replace psychology as a leading preoccupation of the man of letters. At the same time, the tenets of commitment, though not new in any essential way, were receiving a new lease of vitality — another consequence of the pressure of circumstances. It is worth observing, in this connection, that Bernard himself, who in former days had proclaimed his opposition to artists who

---

[11] Benjamin Crémieux, 'La lumière sur la scène,' *Le Jardinier d'Ispahan* (Press cuttings in the *Collection Rondel*), p. 17.

[12] The following entry which Vildrac made in his diary in 1944, concerning his own play, is an important point of reference in assessing the impact of the War: "Je suis tombé sur des comptes rendus de presse de *Madame Béliard*, la plupart élogieux. Mais tout cela m'a paru vain, lointain, mort. La pièce elle-même. Cette guerre donne à tout ce qui l'a précédée, le caractère du révolu, du démonétisé." *Pages de Journal: 1922-1966*, Paris, Gallimard, 1968, p. 138.

sought in their work to serve causes other than that of their art, [13] has produced with *De Tarse, en Cilicie* ... (one of the major plays he has written after the Second War) a piece with a definite politico-economical content. It has been remarked before that the doctrine of Art for Art's sake tends to lose adherents in the midst of widespread injustice and repression, and there is little reason to doubt that Bernard's experiences during the Second War [14] contributed to the modification of his vision of his responsibilities as a writer.

The fourth point about the shift in sensibility occasioned by the Second War concerns silence. As Marc Beigbeder has judiciously observed, events added a new facet to silence, without depriving it of its fundamental character:

> [Le silence] est devenu le fait, le drame, la tragédie (et éventuellement la terrible comédie) de ne pouvoir parler: on a été contraint au silence, dans l'émotion, la souffrance, la mort, la faim, l'honneur. La meilleure œuvre en prose de la littérature résistante — et peut-être la seule — ne s'appelle-t-elle pas, de reste, *Le Silence de la Mer*, et le drame n'y est-il pas, non de savourer le silence, mais de n'y pouvoir, de n'y pouvoir devoir parler? [15]

Little of that mood of restraint in speech, which was part of the sequel to the First War, followed the silence into which France had plunged during the Occupation.

In a genre characterized by unpredictability and instability of tastes, plays which were closely tied to the sensibility of a particular era, plays which provided responses to particular contemporary needs, plays whose success was in large measure founded on a sense of relief, will no doubt appear in the retrospect to have been doomed to evanescence. Two kindred questions occur here: whether Bernard's theatre has in fact been short-lived, and whether impermanence is in itself a flaw.

---

[13] Cf. Bernard, *Témoignages*, Paris, Coutan-Lambert, 1933, pp. 38-39.

[14] The placing of his plays on the proscribed list, his arrest and internment at Royallieu, the arrest of his father, the deportation of one of his sons.

[15] Marc Beigbeder, *Le Théâtre en France depuis la libération*, Paris, Bordas, 1959, pp. 179-180.

In attempting to answer the vexed question whether durability is a viable criterion for assessing a dramatist's worth, it may be useful to repeat a few first principles. A play lives its real life during first performances and during revivals; it goes into a state of dormancy, consigned perhaps to a library, whenever it is not being performed. The longer the uninterrupted state of dormancy, it seems, the slighter the chances that the piece will ever again see the light of day. The majority of plays enter this state of limbo, obliged by the unrelenting governing laws of the theatre, the laws of taste, commerce and reason, to make way for newer or more interesting or more adventurous or even worse plays. Most people will admire the dramatist who manages the feat of having his plays translated into many languages and continually performed centuries after his death. But such an author is evidently exceptional. It would be a supreme injustice for us to turn an exceptional quality into an indispensable virtue, and follow the example of those who, demanding a constant flow of immortal masterpieces, wield as the most damning strictures "Will not last," and "Has dated."

An account of the dissemination of Bernard's work will serve to show that his plays have not suffered from the almost immediate evanescence that has befallen myriad plays whose names fill dramatic histories. The year 1926 saw the first London productions of *Printemps* (at the Everyman Theatre) and *Le Feu qui reprend mal* (at the Academy Theatre); the latter play was revived in 1934 at the Gate Theatre. In 1928 (the year that *Martine* and *L'Invitation* opened in New York) the Apollo Theatre presented *L'Ame en peine*; it was revived at the Westminster Theatre in 1931 in a Tyrone Guthrie production. *Martine* was staged at the Gate Theatre in 1929, was revived at the Ambassadors' Theatre in 1933, and *L'Invitation* was produced at the Everyman Theatre in 1930 and revived at the Gate Theatre in 1937. Four of Bernard's plays have been shown on B.B.C. Television: *Martine* in May 1947, and, in a new production (directed by Kenneth Tynan, with Claire Bloom as Martine and Denholm Elliott as Julien) in May 1952; *Printemps* in October 1948; *Nationale 6* in June 1953; *Le Feu qui reprend mal* in June 1958. [16]

---

[16] Many of Bernard's plays have at various times been broadcast on B.B.C. Radio; the latest occasion was in August 1965, when the Home Service presented *Martine*.

Two of Bernard's plays have been shown on I.T.V.: *Martine* in July 1956, and *Printemps* in November 1957. Apart from being performed in London and New York, *Martine* has been performed in Belgium, Holland, Scandinavia and Switzerland, *L'Invitation* in Algeria, Belgium, Czechoslovakia, Holland, Italy, Luxembourg and Switzerland, and *Nationale 6* in Czechoslovakia, Sweden and Tunisia. Monaco saw the first productions of *L'Ame en peine*, and Switzerland the first productions of *A la Recherche des Cœurs*, *La Louise*, *Marie Stuart, Reine d'Écosse* and *Louise de la Vallière*. [17] This dissemination of Bernard's plays outside France was matched with consecration at home. In 1929 *Le Feu qui reprend mal* entered the repertoire of the *Comédie-Française*, where it was joined by *Martine* in 1934. [18]

In the chronicle of modern drama the *théâtre de l'inexprimé* is a symbol of a battle against the excesses of the rhetorical tradition. Naturally, such a battle loses at least a particle of its immediate relevance once the excesses disappear, and, in fact, they have largely disappeared from French drama; even the characters of Montherlant and Giraudoux — perhaps the major representatives in twentieth-century France of the rhetorical tradition — have not as a rule reverted to the orgies of introspective verbalization in which their nineteenth-century counterparts engaged. It is clear, then, that the specific function which the theatre of the unexpressed needed to fulfil is unlikely to recur. It is equally clear that after an active life of some twenty to thirty years Bernard's plays have become dormant. We have seen that this does not in itself constitute a flaw, and that inevitably most plays retire to a resting-place away from the boards. The bigger mischief is that with the advances in the theatre over the last twenty-five years, the revolutionary force of Bernard's assault upon convention has diminished to such an extent that the theatre of the unexpressed is apt to be bracketed, in the contemporary mind, with what is pejoratively called *Théâtre bourgeois*.

Le Cid and *Andromaque* have become classics; *La Cantatrice chauve* and *La Leçon* have become a tourist attraction at the *Théâtre*

---

[17] The last-mentioned play was to have a two-year run at the *Odéon* after the Liberation.

[18] *Le Feu qui reprend mal* has so far been performed twenty-six times at the *Comédie-Française*: 1929(16), 1930(6), 1932(2), 1936(2). *Martine* has been performed sixty-seven times: 1934(16), 1935(3), 1936(4), 1937(6), 1939(1), 1940(2), 1945(12), 1947(22), 1948(1).

de la Huchette. The history of drama provides countless instances of the process according to which, the initial thrust having been made, the vanguard is reincorporated into the main body, and replaced by a fresher vanguard. When one looks back on the activities of the vanguard, they are seen to derive from the rites of self-sacrifice, for in hastening advancement the vanguard hastens, in a sense, its own effacement. Martin Esslin has made some useful comments on the destinies of progressive theatre:

> In the West End of London early Shaw and Ibsen have become safe after-dinner entertainment for the suburban business community, the equivalents of Scribe, Sardou, and Dumas fils in their own day — the very authors whom they wanted to replace because they were safe and establishment-minded.
>
> Such, however, is the dialectical law of historical development: each hour has its own necessity, its own imperative; and what is essential is precisely the insight and the courage needed to obey it. Once the hour is passed, the new moulds have been created, lesser spirits will inevitably continue to use them; and that is how the revolutionary contents and forms of yesteryear turn into the safe, conservative clichés of today. [19]

The theme has also been treated by Roland Barthes:

> Au-delà du drame personnel de l'écrivain d'avant-garde, et quelle qu'en soit la force exemplaire, il vient toujours un moment où l'Ordre récupère ses francs-tireurs. [...] L'avant-garde poursuit rarement jusqu'au bout sa carrière d'enfant prodigue: elle finit tôt ou tard par réintégrer le sein qui lui avait donné, avec la vie, une liberté de pur sursis. [20]

The conquests of the battle against the excesses of the oratorical heritage abide, and of these conquests others have availed themselves — perhaps unknowingly. It is widely felt in France that Bernard's *théâtre de l'inexprimé* is a latent power behind a sizeable portion of

---

[19] Martin Esslin, *Brief Chronicles*, London, Temple Smith, 1970, pp. 21-22.

[20] Roland Barthes, 'A l'avant-garde de quel théâtre?,' *Théâtre populaire*, Ier mai 1956, p. 2.

contemporary drama. Henri Crémieux, who has been actively associated with the French stage for over half a century, has stated:

> Le théâtre de l'inexprimé a aidé à faire comprendre que tout
> n'est pas dans le verbe, dans le discours. [...] C'est une for-
> mule qui a apporté beaucoup de choses. Elle a éloigné du
> théâtre tout ce qui a été introspection verbale. [...] C'est
> un élément de transformation sans lequel le théâtre d'au-
> jourd'hui ne serait pas le même. [21]

To this statement and to Alfred Simon's assertion that

> Bien des auteurs débutants retrouvent aujourd'hui encore la
> technique de *Martine* qui ne le disent pas et ne le savent
> peut-être même pas. [22]

one may add the following comments by Jean-Jacques Gautier:

> Nous sentons un certain nombre de traces, de cheminements
> ou de phénomènes de résurgence de ce théâtre du silence;
> ces résurrections ne sont pas conscientes. Aucun des auteurs
> du théâtre moderne, contemporain (anglo-saxon par exemple),
> qui ne dit pas ce qu'il dit; qui dit autre chose, ou rien;
> qui procède par allusion, mystère, ou dérivation, sinon par
> impuissance à formuler, ne pense, ne dit, ni ne sait, qu'il
> s'inscrit plus ou moins dans la lignée de J.-J. Bernard. [23]

The techniques of the unexpressed have become public; [24] the avoidance of over-statement, the use of indirect dialogue, of dialogue on
different levels, of impercipient, unrhetorical and inarticulate leading
characters have long since passed into the common domain.

Referring to the progressive trends in the Parisian theatre of the
twenties and thirties, Dorothy Knowles states:

> It is doubtful whether some of the most successful of pre-
> sent-day Parisian playwrights, be it Jean-Paul Sartre, or
> Samuel Beckett, or Eugène Ionesco, would ever have cap-
> tured the attention of the general public, or would ever even

[21] Henri Crémieux, interview with the author, 22 January 1972.
[22] Alfred Simon, *Dictionnaire du théâtre français contemporain*, Paris,
Larousse, 1970, p. 95.
[23] Jean-Jacques Gautier, letter to the author, June 1972.
[24] They are part of the daily routine in cinema and television.

have thought of writing for the theatre, had it not been for the *avant-garde* [...] that prepared the way for them. [...] As for the 'anti-theatre' of the fifties, had it not been for the liberalizing of traditional dramatic conceptions by the playwrights of the inter-war years, it is questionable whether such completely free forms could have come into being at all — in France at any rate. [25]

This welcome acknowledgement of the significance of the inter-war renewal puts us in mind of the sentiments which Bernard expressed in 1924:

> L'effort de chacun de nous est comme le complément, plus ou moins fructueux, de tout ce qui a été fait avant lui, de tout ce qui est fait à côté de lui. De l'ensemble des efforts peut naître, un jour, une petite flamme nouvelle. Ce n'est qu'en tremblant d'émotion qu'on ose s'abandonner à l'espoir d'y avoir un peu contribué. [26]

The hope has been fulfilled beyond Bernard's modest expectations; the second half of this century has been witness to a conflagration (rather than "une petite flamme"), in the course of which time-honoured dramatic formularies have been reduced to ashes. The 'conflagration' would probably have taken place without Bernard. Even so, the fact remains that in addition to merging into the dramatic mainstream, many of the techniques he employed, and many of the general ideas underpinning their use, have been at the roots of some of the major developments in the contemporary avant-garde. Bernard's rôle as a precursor allows us to set the theatre of the unexpressed against a wide background of theory, experiment and achievement in twentieth-century drama.

There is no denying that Artaud's *Le Théâtre et son Double* contains a number of challenging and provocative concepts. It is on the question of the practicality of the author's proposals that the book is least satisfactory. Despite the obvious ubiquity in avant-garde drama of elements which *seem* to be in response to his suggestions, it is doubt-

---

[25] Dorothy Knowles, *French Drama of the Inter-War Years 1918-39*, London, Harrap, 1967, p. 5.

[26] Bernard, 'Quelques précisions, après deux récentes expériences,' *Comœdia*, 7 avril 1924, p. 2.

ful whether any one play can be accurately described as a faithful representation of the Artaudian vision. One suspects that his impact on the theatre is overstated, and that there enters into the fascination for Artaud a sense of reverence for the poet-madman who dreamt of an idealized theatre that no one could ever hope to achieve. One suspects also that there is too much emphasis placed on Artaud's rôle as originator, and not enough said about his status as successor.

One insufficiently explored question relating to Artaud's thought is the extent to which *Le Théâtre et son Double* is a restatement of some of the leading principles of Baty, Bernard, and other *Compagnons de la Chimère*. The common terrain is not immediately discernible. In the first place, Artaud's passionate professions of antagonism towards the traditional theatre of the Western world are couched in extreme and incandescent terms; Bernard's and Baty's declarations were nothing near so virulent. Secondly, though Bernard avoided the usual discursive treatment of personality, sentiment and thought, his plays still had an unmistakable psychological bias; Artaud, for his part, advocated no less than an eradication of psychology from the drama. For the rest, there is a notable absence in Artaud's writings of references to Baty, or to the latter's refusal to pay allegiance to *Sire le Mot*; [27] Baty is the sole member of the *Cartel des quatre* with whom Artaud never worked; Henri Crémieux, one of the *Compagnons*, cannot remember seeing Artaud at any of the group's activities. [28] It is improbable, however, that Artaud, a practising and alert man of the theatre, remained unaware of the debate being generated in the twenties by the *Compagnons'* declarations of intent, by their avowed ambition to orientate "le théâtre de demain dans la voie du drame intégral, où le mot ne règne plus seul, mais où les autres éléments reprennent tout leur pouvoir d'expression." [29] It could well be that the germ of Artaud's doctrine issued from their call for total theatre, and that his encounter with the Balinese theatre in 1931, far from suddenly flooding him with insights into the language of gesture and movement, gave impetus to the formulation of concepts that had been, until then, in the seminal state. Certainly the juxtaposition of

---

[27] See above, pp. 66-67.
[28] Henri Crémieux, interview with the present author, 22 January 1972.
[29] *La Chimère. Bulletin d'Art Dramatique*, avril 1922, p. 33.

one of the essential statements of Artaud's doctrine and the manifesto of Baty's *Compagnons* reveals a similarity. The latter affirmed:

> Pour nous, l'art dramatique reste l'art suprême en qui tous les autres s'exaltent, plus beaux d'être réunis. La sculpture donne l'attitude, le geste, la danse; la peinture, le costume et le décor; la littérature, le texte; la musique, la voix de l'acteur, les bruits, le chant parfois et souvent la symphonie. [...] Au-delà des mots, la pensée achève de s'exprimer par le geste, la couleur et le son. [30]

Artaud argued for

> La substitution à la poésie du langage, d'une poésie dans l'espace qui se résoudra justement dans le domaine de ce qui n'appartient pas strictement aux mots. [...] Cette poésie très difficile et complexe revêt de multiples aspects: elle revêt d'abord ceux de tous les moyens d'expression utilisables sur une scène, comme musique, danse, plastique, pantomime, mimique, gesticulation, intonations, architecture, éclairage et décor. [31]

Artaud, Baty and Bernard, fully aware that the verbal medium was incapable of treating analytically wide areas of experience, sternly discountenanced the notion of drama as a mere branch of written literature. Their prescription of a greater autonomy for an art form that could live its proper life only on the boards was a sign of their anxiety to see the theatre develop its own idiom. Yet the differences between Artaud's insight into the ways by which this could be achieved and that of Bernard and Baty are not to be minimized. With Baty, as with Bernard and other *Compagnons,* the absolute necessity and central importance of the dramatist, and of a text composed of clearly recognizable and understandable words, were not in question. The word had constant meaning, whether direct significance or subtextual importance. The voice was the medium for speech or for naturalistic sound. Artaud, on the other hand, was unequivocally in favour of the subordination of the dramatist to the director, and his approval of this aspect of the Balinese theatre at the Colonial Exhibition

---

[30] *Ibid.,* fév. 1922, p. 3.
[31] Antonin Artaud, *Le Théâtre et son Double,* Paris, Gallimard, 1964, pp. 55-56.

of 1931 is here instructive.[32] Also, without recommending the complete elimination of comprehensible speech, he was seeking scope for the non-naturalistic use of sound, for words that are not utilitarian in the usual sense, and for "la matérialisation visuelle et plastique de la parole":

> La parole articulée, les expressions verbales explicites interviendront dans toutes les parties claires et nettement élucidées de l'action, dans les parties où la vie se repose et où la conscience intervient.
> Mais, à côté de ce sens logique, les mots seront pris dans un sens incantatoire, vraiment magique, — pour leur forme, leurs émanations sensibles, et non plus seulement pour leur sens.[33]

Artaud made, then, some allowance for normal speech; but he evidently went many steps further than Bernard and Baty in challenging the Word's status and function. The demotion sanctioned by Bernard and Baty was intended to place the Word on a footing of greater equality with the play's other constituent parts. Artaud backed a more uncompromising and a more savagely executed dethronement. But all three shared a fundamental preoccupation, namely, to terminate the over-dominance in the theatre of verbal rhetoric. One can therefore trace back, beyond Artaud, to Bernard the refusal to hallow the Word and to let dialogue perform tasks according to the established customs of Western drama, a refusal which forms the basis of virtually the entire avant-garde movement. We propose, next, to consider the signs of this refusal in Beckett, Ionesco and Pinter, and to show that these authors have, in some respects, been animated by intuitions and premises not unlike those which had earlier animated Bernard, that they (Pinter in particular) have extended in details, though not in essentials, various methods which he had anticipated. For the plays of Beckett, Ionesco and Pinter may bear on the surface little resemblance to the 'unexpressed' plays; in the latter, plots are still basically logical and coherent, and though personality is not explicitly indicated by words, it remains a more or less fixed reality; Beckett, Ionesco and Pinter reflect to a far greater extent than Bernard

---

[32] See *Le Théâtre et son Double*, p. 90.
[33] *Ibid.*, pp. 104, 189.

(in *Printemps*, for example) the fluidity and unknowability of human personality, and are less committed to logical, coherent plots. Nevertheless, these salient differences do not obscure the fact that many of the plays of Beckett, Ionesco and Pinter are further movements away from literary theatre, further deny the dialogue its 'prerogative' to communicate thought and feeling, continue the search for substitutes for purely verbal language in the theatre, and betray a fascination for silence.

We mentioned earlier Maeterlinck's preference at one stage of his career for static drama (a preference which Bernard shared), and saw how Maeterlinck's *Les Aveugles* foreshadowed *En attendant Godot*. [34] In effect, the clowning and other stage business in Beckett's play do not conceal its lack of truly dramatic action. Interest centres not on positive acts but on the inactivity of waiting, and the major event that Godot's arrival would have constituted does not materialize. The omission of the decisive *scène à faire* and the enforced absence from the stage of an important character are also features of Bernard's plays. [35] With Beckett, as with Bernard, we are in the province of dramatic brinkmanship and non-event, and it is a significant coincidence that embedded in the dialogue of *Printemps* is the same sort of remark about the play's action ("Il ne s'est rien passé.") [36] that can be found in *Godot*:

> ESTRAGON.   Rien ne se passe, personne ne vient, personne ne s'en va, c'est terrible. [37]

Godot belongs to the category of drama without dynamism, or, to use Edith Kern's phrase, of "drama stripped for inaction." [38]

It is inaction of a physical kind that begins to figure in Beckett's subsequent plays: Nagg and Nell imprisoned in their dustbins in *Fin de partie*, Winnie protruding from the mound in *Oh les beaux jours*, the disembodied Mouth suspended eight feet above the level of the

---

[34] See above, pp. 44-45.

[35] See above, pp. 46-47, 113, 137-138.

[36] *Printemps*, Act III, p. 261 in *Théâtre I*, Paris, Albin Michel, 1925; see also above, p. 114.

[37] Samuel Beckett, *En attendant Godot*, Paris, Éditions de Minuit, 1952, Act I, p. 70.

[38] Edith Kern, 'Drama Stripped for Inaction: Beckett's *Godot*,' *Yale French Studies*, Winter 1954-55, pp. 41-47.

stage in *Not I* match with their immobility the anti-dynamic nature
of the situations of which they are part. With dramatic action, changes
in situation, and physical movement of minimal importance, it is the
play's language which rises to prominence. But, at the same time, it
receives new values and functions which differentiate it from the language of the traditional drama. One notices characters conversing on
different planes, barely listening to the supposed interlocutor; [39] one
notices dialogue becoming an ineffectual channel of communication
on account of the inability of some characters to follow the threads
of simple conversation:

> NAGG. Tu me vois?
> NELL. Mal. Et toi?
> NAGG. Quoi?
> NELL. Tu me vois?
>
> ... ...
>
> NAGG. *(Montrant le biscuit.)* Tu veux un bout?
> NELL. Non. *(Un temps.)* De quoi?
> NAGG. De biscuit. [40]

> VLADIMIR. On attend Godot.
> ESTRAGON. C'est vrai. *(Un temps.)* Tu es sûr que c'est
> ici?
> VLADIMIR. Quoi?
> ESTRAGON. Qu'il faut attendre.
>
> ... ...
>
> ESTRAGON. Tu es sûr que c'était ce soir?
> VLADIMIR. Quoi?
> ESTRAGON. Qu'il fallait attendre? [41]

Eventually, what occurs is no less than a total breakdown of inter-
communication within the play — as in *Comédie,* where each character
is surrounded by silence, unable to hear the reflections of the other
two. [42] To be sure, the timed pauses at the beginning of the play, and
the intermediate 'noise' of the three characters engaged in simulta-
neous thinking create that contrapuntal effect which Beckett often

---

[39] Cf. Bernard's use of this device in *Le Feu qui reprend mal.* See above,
pp. 48-49.

[40] Samuel Beckett, *Fin de partie* suivi de *Acte sans paroles I,* Paris, Éditions de Minuit, 1957, pp. 30, 32.

[41] *En attendant Godot,* Act I, pp. 20, 22.

[42] As is often remarked, *Comédie* bears a conspicuous resemblance to
Pinter's *Landscape.* Cf. below, p. 215.

achieves through his orchestration of sound and silence. [43] But while Bernard's frequent use of silence was obviously determined by considerations of a psychological order, these pauses are among the miscellaneous silences in Beckett's plays whose specific psychological function (or dramatic value) is not easily ascertained.

The monodrama *Acte sans paroles I* stands as a monument to Beckett's preoccupation with silence, and can be described as an example of the *théâtre de l'inexprimé* taken to its furthest possible point. One watches a man who becomes acquainted with the notion of futility, and who finally withdraws to a position of lethargic indifference. When he wants to take advantage of the shade of the tree, the palms deny him their meagre shade; all his efforts to reach the water-bottle and quench his thirst are systematically rendered fruitless. So he determines to ignore the tree and the water-bottle, and the sound of the whistle which calls his attention to them. But as he enacts the rôle of Tantalus (a rôle which merges with that of the anti-Sisyphus) not a word, not an exclamation of anger, despair or frustration is uttered. He is permitted to feel intensely and to think of ways of reaching the water, but not to enclose his feelings or thoughts within verbal language. In other words, his extended monologue is not projected outwards, but its line of development is suggested by his successive actions and attitudes. [44]

This emphasis on visual image — possibly a harking back to the idiom of the silent film — is also found in Beckett's less wordless plays; witness the scrupulous prescription in *Oh les beaux jours* of Winnie's every movement, action and reaction. But in *Oh les beaux jours* we encounter a silence that differs patently from that of *Acte sans paroles I*. Whereas the silence of the protagonist of the latter play is consistently dominant, Winnie's continual verbal interruptions of the background silence exemplify that struggle for prominence, common in Beckett's plays, between language and silence. This struggle betrays a fear of silence, an inability to endure the vacuum, and leads to a brand of wordiness where tirades and other outpourings are not argumentative, informative or emotional in the traditional sense. It is not primarily in order to reach Willie that Winnie has

---

[43] See *Comédie*, pp. 10-11 in *Comédie et actes divers*, Paris, Éditions de Minuit, 1966.

[44] For Bernard's use of the unspoken monologue see above, pp. 172 ff.

recourse to language; her endeavour is to avoid being enveloped by
the omnipresent silence, and to keep her anguish at bay. Her exercise
is not only similar to that performed by the tramps in *Godot*:

> ESTRAGON. En attendant, essayons de converser sans
> nous exalter, puisque nous sommes incapables de nous taire.
> VLADIMIR. C'est vrai, nous sommes intarissables.
> ESTRAGON. C'est pour ne pas penser. [...] (*Long si-*
> *lence.*)
> VLADIMIR. Dis quelque chose!
> ESTRAGON. Je cherche. (*Long silence.*)
> VLADIMIR. (*Angoissé.*) Dis n'importe quoi! [45]

It is also an elaboration of the exercise often performed by characters
in Bernard's 'unexpressed' plays. [46]

We are not contending, of course, that the plays of Beckett, Ionesco
and Pinter can be viewed only in relation to the *théâtre de l'inex-*
primé. We are not engaged here in an exhaustive appraisal of the
three playwrights; our concern is with their refusal to hallow the Word,
and to let dialogue fulfil tasks according to the established customs
of Western drama. We shall shortly see that in Bernard and Pinter
the actual signs of this refusal are similar. The case of Ionesco, however, is different; his early plays reveal altogether different symptoms
of this common refusal.

Having found the recipe for garrulous silence, many of Ionesco's
characters abide by the principle of talking and saying nothing. The
early plays proceed from a disillusioned view of language; the author
precludes the development of 'real' dialogue — one of the bases of
the traditional drama; communication of thought and examination
of sentiments give way to constant exchanges of hackneyed formulas,
and the accumulation of these allows the audience an intimate experience of the void of language. It is at this point that Bernard and
Ionesco, after starting from a common base, a common negation of
the conventional functions of dialogue, so widely diverge. Where
Bernard casts doubt on the adequacy and appropriateness of language
in certain circumstances, Ionesco more drastically undermines confidence in the power and usefulness of words in general. Le Vieux

---

[45] *En attendant Godot*, Act II, pp. 105-106.
[46] Cf. above, pp. 93, 142-143.

in *Les Chaises* feels sure that words will give an *a posteriori* justification to his purposeless existence. Thanks to words he will not have lived in vain, and will join the ranks of the immortal:

> Ma vie a été bien remplie. Ma mission est accomplie. Je n'aurai pas vécu en vain, puisque mon message sera révélé au monde. [47]

But his message to humanity remains in the depths of silence; the deaf-mute who is supposed to transmit it manages only to make unintelligible scribblings on a black-board and to emit various guttural sounds. The absence of meaning that emerges from his 'address' would, if we are to accept the opinion of Le Professeur in *La Leçon*, also have emerged from a more coherent speech:

> Si vous émettez plusieurs sons à une vitesse accélérée, ceux-ci s'agripperont les uns aux autres automatiquement, constituant ainsi des syllabes, des mots, à la rigueur des phrases, c'est-à-dire des groupements plus ou moins importants, des assemblages purement irrationnels de sons, dénués de tout sens. [48]

Relegating words to their rude status of vocal sounds, "des assemblages purement irrationnels de sons," is Ionesco's extreme reaction to his awareness that words have already been debased and distorted by rhetorical usage. A violent quarrel in *La Cantatrice chauve* consists of phonemes strung together to form words of insulting resonance:

> M. Smith. Kakatoes, kakatoes, kakatoes [. . .].
> Mme Smith. Quelle cacade, quelle cacade, quelle cacade [. . .].
> M. Martin. Quelle cascade de cacades [. . .].
> Mme Martin. Cactus, Coccyx! coccus! cocardard! [. . .]
> Mme Smith. Encaqueur, tu nous encaques. [49]

The author proceeds to a ceremonial disintegration of language, to the dislocation of an object which has become empty, deceptive, useless,

---

[47] Eugène Ionesco, *Les Chaises*, p. 176 in *Théâtre I*, Paris, Gallimard, 1954.
[48] *Théâtre I*, p. 77.
[49] *Théâtre I*, sc. II, pp. 53-54.

and even dangerous, [50] all with the aim of making theatrical words which have lost all theatrical vitality:

> Si [la parole] n'est que discussion chez certains auteurs, c'est une grande faute de leur part. Il existe d'autres moyens de théâtraliser la parole: en la portant à son paroxysme, pour donner au théâtre sa vraie mesure, qui est dans la démesure; le verbe lui-même doit être tendu jusqu'à ses limites ultimes, le langage doit presque exploser, ou se détruire, dans son impossibilité de contenir les significations. [51]

Bernard evidently did not reach forward to this spectacular extreme; there is little sign of kinship between *Martine* and a play like *La Cantatrice chauve*. All the same, underlying Ionesco's early plays and Bernard's 'unexpressed' plays is the feeling that the word is an inadequate agent of dramatic expression, and that the idiom of the theatre should be revitalized and structurally readjusted. The dissatisfaction with the language of the theatre which led Ionesco to distort words in his early plays (in order, he says, to "rompre le cou à la mauvaise éloquence de la scène") [52] is related to the distaste for the conventional rhetoric of the French stage which led Bernard away from literary drama, and which prompted his declaration: "Le théâtre n'a pas de pire ennemie que la littérature." [53] The traditional theatre presupposes the possibility of verbal communication, takes for granted its desirability, and holds sacred the right of words, in copious quantity, to make it possible. Bernard and Ionesco began by questioning such hallowed premises, though they interpreted their tasks differently and achieved different results. One used words sparingly and sought other purveyors of meaning, while the other was to make communication a ludicrous pattern of illogical statements; but they were both looking askance at the conventional privileges and functions of dialogue. This does not mean, however, that we are attempting to set Bernard up as the direct literary ancestor of Ionesco. The

---

[50] In *La Leçon* the word *couteau* becomes a murder weapon (*Théâtre I*, p. 89).

[51] Eugène Ionesco, 'Expérience du théâtre,' *La Nouvelle Nouvelle Revue Française*, 1er fév. 1958, p. 262.

[52] Quoted by Claude Bonnefoy, *Entretiens avec Eugène Ionesco*, Paris, Pierre Belfond, 1966, p. 189.

[53] Bernard, 'Le silence au théâtre,' *La Chimère. Bulletin d'Art Dramatique*, mai (2) 1922, p. 67.

hazards attending the popular practice of establishing literary influ-
ences are self-evident; as everyone knows, the assumption that Y's
work will bear the influence of X because the latter was a well-known
writer during Y's adolescence is often fallacious. Ionesco's own warning
in this matter should not be disregarded:

> On m'avait dit que j'étais influencé par Strindberg. Alors j'ai
> lu le théâtre de Strindberg et j'ai dit: 'en effet, je suis in-
> fluencé par Strindberg.' On m'avait dit que j'étais influencé
> par Vitrac. Alors j'ai lu Vitrac et j'ai dit: 'en effet, je suis
> influencé par Vitrac.' On m'avait dit que j'étais influencé
> par Feydeau et Labiche. Alors j'ai lu Feydeau et Labiche et
> j'ai dit: 'en effet, je suis influencé par Feydeau et Labiche.'
> C'est ainsi que j'ai fait ma culture théâtrale. [54]

Turning to Pinter, we find first a conspicuous similarity between
his doctrine and Bernard's. Pinter's statements at the Seventh National
Student Drama Festival in 1962 read like a manifesto for the *théâtre
de l'inexprimé* with which Bernard and Amiel would probably have
been proud to be associated:

> There are two silences. One when no word is spoken. The
> other when perhaps a torrent of language is being employed.
> This speech is speaking of a language locked beneath it. That
> is its continual reference. The speech we hear is an indication
> of that which we don't hear. It is a necessary avoidance, a
> violent, sly, anguished or mocking smoke screen which keeps
> the other in its place. [...] I think that we communicate
> only too well, in our silence, in what is unsaid, and that what
> takes place is a continual evasion, desperate rear guard at-
> tempts to keep ourselves to ourselves. [55]

Pinter's drama is a focal point for a fascinating interplay of different
types of silence, from the relentless, menacing silence of the Match-
seller in *A Slight Ache* to the silence of those who, to use Amiel's
phrase, "se taisent en parlant." [56] The visual *coups de théâtre* in *The
Dumb Waiter* serve to instil into Ben and Gus a growing sense of
uneasiness; but it is the fervour characterizing their discussion of mat-

---

[54] Quoted by Claude Bonnefoy, *Op. cit.*, p. 57.
[55] Reproduced in Harold Pinter, 'Writing for the Theatre,' *Evergreen*,
August-September 1964, p. 82.
[56] See above, p. 18.

ters that are in the context unimportant which reveals that they are trying to use language as an instrument to exorcize their anguish, which evinces their unavowed, unformulated anxiety. Thus their conduct mirrors the author's feeling that between people "there is continual cross-talk, a continual talking about other things, rather than what is at the root of their relationship," [57] that "often, below the word spoken, is the thing known and unspoken." [58]

Indeed the subjacent, unheard dialogue of the subjacent drama is frequently discernible in Pinter's plays. Much of the chatter we hear — trite, repetitive, infantile, amusing chatter — is a subterfuge used by people who do not say directly what they are thinking. It represents an attempt to prevent self-discovery, and to avoid revealing one's self to others. In considering the utterances of Pinter's characters then, one is well advised to heed Mick's observations on Davies, and take nothing that they say at face value. [59] But language is not always part of an act of deception, and does not always serve as a smoke-screen beyond which one may point to major unrevealed preoccupations. The questions which Meg asks Petey at the beginning of *The Birthday Party* accentuate her belief in the cardinal importance of *making* conversation at all costs, are directed, in other words, to the sacred aim of avoiding the void of silence:

> MEG. You got your paper?
> PETEY. Yes.
> MEG. Is it good?
> PETEY. Not bad.
> MEG. What does it say?
> PETEY. Nothing much.
> MEG. You read me out some nice bits yesterday.
> PETEY. Yes, well, I haven't finished this one yet.
> MEG. Will you tell me when you come to something good?
> PETEY. Yes.
> (*Pause.*)
> MEG. Have you been working hard this morning?

---

[57] Harold Pinter, interview with Kenneth Tynan, B.B.C. Home Service, 28 October 1960. Quoted by Martin Esslin, *The Theatre of the Absurd*, Harmondsworth, Penguin Books, 1968, p. 274.

[58] Harold Pinter, 'Writing for the Theatre,' *Op. cit.*, p. 81.

[59] See Harold Pinter, *The Caretaker*, London, Methuen, 1965, Act III, p. 73.

PETEY.   No. Just stacked a few of the old chairs. Cleaned up a bit.
MEG.   Is it nice out?
PETEY.   Very nice.
(*Pause.*)
MEG.   Is Stanley up yet?
PETEY.   I don't know. Is he?
MEG.   I don't know. I haven't seen him down yet.
PETEY.   Well then, he can't be up.
MEG.   Haven't you seen him down?
PETEY.   I've only just come in.
MEG.   He must be still asleep.
(*She looks round the room, stands, goes to the sideboard and takes a pair of socks from a drawer, collects wool and a needle and goes back to the table.*)
What time did you go out this morning, Petey?
PETEY.   Same time as usual.
MEG.   Was it dark?
PETEY.   No, it was light.
MEG.   (*Beginning to darn.*) But sometimes you go out in the morning and it's dark.
PETEY.   That's in the winter.
MEG.   Oh, in winter.
PETEY.   Yes, it gets light later in winter.
MEG.   Oh.
(*Pause.*)
What are you reading?
PETEY.   Someone's just had a baby.
MEG.   Oh, they haven't! Who?
PETEY.   Some girl. [60]

One's impression is of unprimed personages, of characters who have not been prepared to disclose the play's business; their seemingly improvised dialogue, of tardy rhythm and indefinite direction, is of a type we also encounter in Bernard. [61] What is particularly noticeable through all the patter — when such an opening is placed beside that of a more conventional play — is the radical modification in the function of the play's language; the dialogue no longer translates emotions, its informative value is reduced, and, only on a superficial level does it present an exchange of speech.

---

[60] Harold Pinter, *The Birthday Party and Other Plays*, London, Methuen, 1960, Act I, pp. 9-11.
[61] Cf. *Printemps*, Act II, pp. 210 ff., and *L'Invitation*, Act II, pp. 297-298 in *Théâtre I*, Paris, Albin Michel, 1925.

The lack of a substantial exchange results from the juxtaposition of a non-stop talker and an otherwise-occupied, less talkative partner. This situation occurs time and again in Pinter's plays, and when it does we are made acutely aware of the different degrees of sensitivity and response to ever-present silence. Whereas the anxiety which Ben and Gus share unites them in a silence-destroying duologue, Petey obviously does not feel with Meg the need to avert silence. But Petey does not go as far in declining invitations to avoid silence as Lenny at the beginning of *The Homecoming*, or as Mick at the beginning of the third act of *The Caretaker*. "He don't answer me when I talk to him," [62] Davies complains aloud to himself, clamouring to establish a rapport with the other person, and appearing to voice a grievance and an appeal on behalf of other characters in Pinter's plays. It is the refusal of one member of the duet to play the conversational game that transforms potential dialogues into monologues; as in Bernard's plays (where, however, it is arrived at differently) [63] the monologue in dialogue becomes a powerful affirmation of the spiritual seclusion of one individual in the presence of another. Such seclusion is the central theme of *Landscape*, a play in which Pinter has developed much further than Bernard the type of intertwined monological statements which we find in *Le Feu qui reprend mal*, and which are a common feature in Chekhov. [64] In *Landscape* we have two monologues in the guise of two interlacing sets of reminiscences; each set is on a different level and of a different tone, and each set is apparently unheard by the other character.

The list of points of correspondence between Bernard and Pinter is lengthy: the two, by bringing inarticulate people to the forefront of their plays, move resolutely away from the rhetorical tradition; the two convert into an effective dramatic idiom ordinary undecorated speech, with all its inflections, its platitudes, its ramblings and its indecisiveness; the two are able to lend immense dramatic and emotional power to unspoken sections of dialogue, to allow situations to tell their own tale, and to suggest the conflicts often existing between the words uttered and the genuine emotional and psychological processes within the speaker. Theirs is a drama which gives special

---

[62] *The Caretaker*, Act III, p. 58.
[63] See above, pp. 84, 129.
[64] See above, pp. 48-49.

prominence to the unexpressed, to allusion, and to pregnant pauses. We may consider for a moment the pauses occurring in the following passage from *The Collection*:

> JAMES. I'm going to go and see him.
> STELLA. See him? Who? *(Pause.)* What for?
> JAMES. Oh ... have a chat with him.
> ... ...
> JAMES. I want to see if he's changed from when I last saw him. [...]
> STELLA. You've never seen him.
> *(Pause.)*
> You don't know him.
> *(Pause.)*
> You don't know where he lives.
> *(Pause.)*
> When did you see him?
> JAMES. We had dinner together last night. [65]

It may be that Stella does not follow quickly enough James's train of thought, or it may be that she initially pretends not to know whom he is going to see. He therefore waits for her to stop pretending, or, alternatively, he allows her time to make the mental deduction. Only when this is done (and her question "What for?" shows clearly that it has been done) does James proceed, still without bothering to name Bill. He then suspends all verbal argument against the implied accusation of falsehood. He simply observes Stella's progress as she withdraws from her categorical assertion and concedes that he has met Bill. James's is a deliberate abstention from stating what he knows does not need to be stated to Stella. As in *Mourning Becomes Electra* when Lavinia extracts a confession of murder from Christine, as in *Printemps* when Clarisse and Gilberte silently take stock of Clarisse's sentiments, we have here a fine example of redundancy avoided through silence, through a displacement of parts of the dialogue to a purely non-verbal sphere. [66] The mechanism is not unlike that found in *The Stronger*, where the silence of Mademoiselle Y serves to wind thoughts out of Madame X "like silk from a cocoon." [67] Pinter's char-

---

[65] Pp. 29-30 in Harold Pinter, *The Collection and The Lover*, London, Methuen, 1964.

[66] Cf. above, pp. 118-119.

[67] P. 232 in Strindberg, *The Plays. Volume One* (Translated by Michael Meyer), London, Mercury Books, 1964.

acters, however, (like Bernard's before him) do not belong to the category of those whose every thought is clothed in words, and Stella's
thoughts are reduced to far fewer words than those of Madame X.

Pinter has coincided with Bernard in the belief that the dramatist
should not force a character to speak where silence would be a more
spontaneous reaction, to mention something which in an equivalent
real-life situation would not be mentioned, or to speak in a manner
that would not come naturally to that particular character. [68] Where
Bernard says:

> Pas [...] de ces analyses où le personnage, toujours clair-
> voyant sur lui-même, n'ignorant rien de ses plus subtils sen-
> timents ou pensées, étale son 'moi' comme aucun de nous ne
> serait capable de le faire aux heures moralement décisives,
> c'est-à-dire aux heures les plus troubles pour l'esprit et le
> cœur ou les deux. [69]

Pinter remarks:

> A character on the stage who can present no convincing
> argument or information as to his past experience, his present
> behaviour or his aspirations, nor give a comprehensive anal-
> ysis of his motives is as legitimate and as worthy of attention
> as one who, alarmingly, can do all these things. The more
> acute the experience the less articulate its expression. [70]

It is far from astonishing that on encountering Pinter's plays French
critics were reminded of Bernard. When in 1965 *The Collection* and
The Lover had their Paris première, Thierry Maulnier wrote:

> Sa technique n'a rien de révolutionnaire. Elle pourra même
> rappeler à certains spectateurs, par la concision allusive du
> dialogue, l'art de rendre parlants les silences, le parti pris de
> faire apparaître la vérité de la situation dans l'inexprimé, les
> débuts à la scène de Jean-Jacques Bernard. [71]

---

[68] See Harold Pinter, 'Writing for the Theatre,' *Evergreen*, August-September 1964, p. 82.

[69] Bernard, 'Sur le Présent et l'Avenir prochain du Théâtre en France,'
Comœdia, 30 juillet 1923, p. 1.

[70] Harold Pinter, 'Writing for the Theatre,' *Op. cit.*, pp. 80-81.

[71] Thierry Maulnier, 'Le Théâtre,' *La Revue de Paris*, nov. 1965, p. 137.

Meanwhile, Jean-Jacques Gautier observed in *Le Figaro*:

> Dialogue suspensif, éludé, allusif, ambigu, où les phrases
> rares veulent toutes dire autre chose que ce qu'on dit.
> Il est divertissant de voir revenir comme une trouvaille
> du dernier bateau 'le théâtre du silence' cher à Jean-Jacques
> Bernard. [72]

More recently Pierre-Aimé Touchard wrote:

> Il n'est pas impossible qu'un théâtre de l'inexprimé, avec de
> nouveaux mots, de nouveaux symboles renaisse à un moment
> donné. Dans une certaine mesure, on peut dire qu'un théâtre
> comme celui de Pinter relève de cette esthétique. [73]

Here again, though, it would probably be wiser to speak of the
zeitgeist than to announce a case of direct influence or indebtedness. [74]
Bernard's and Pinter's attitudes to dialogue fall under the canopy of
twentieth-century preoccupations with the language of drama — preoccupations which are also present in Beckett and Ionesco, but which
are not the exclusive preserve of these four dramatists. It may also
be useful to repeat that in Beckett, Ionesco and Pinter there are preoccupations, currents of feeling, mechanisms which are totally unlike
anything we find in Bernard, which reflect utterly different moods
and perceptions. What our selective survey of the three dramatists
has drawn attention to is the persistence, in the present day, of trends
that were already pronounced in the theatre of the unexpressed: the
estrangement from the linguistic conventions of the traditional theatre,
the general reluctance to use the literary language in the drama.

The methods encouraged by the *théâtre de l'inexprimé* are part
of the daily routine in cinema and television; the ingredients of this
theatre have proved their validity and their ability to endure; the
unorthodox traits of the 'unexpressed' plays have merged into the dramatic mainstream; many of the notions that actuated these plays have
been developed by the post-Second-World-War avant-garde. Outside

---

[72] Article reproduced in Jean-Jacques Gautier, *Théâtre d'aujourd'hui*, Paris, Julliard, 1972, p. 189.

[73] Pierre-Aimé Touchard, letter to the author, August 1972.

[74] In a letter to the present author, dated August 1972, Pinter stated that
he was not acquainted with the work of Bernard.

the drama, analogous developments have been taking place. Certain features of the modern novel are strongly suggestive of techniques used in the 'unexpressed' plays; [75] Maurice Blanchot speaks of the strains of expressive insignificance in novelistic dialogue in terms that would, to a large extent, be relevant to the language of Bernard's and Amiel's characters:

> Quand quelqu'un parle, c'est son refus de parler qui devient alors sensible; son discours est son silence: renfermé, violent, ne disant rien que lui-même, sa massivité abrupte, sa volonté d'émettre des mots plutôt que de parler. [76]

It is, in fact, not extravagant to say that the spirit of *l'inexprimé* has emphasized its presence in the twentieth-century novel. Two novels appear to us to illustrate this tendency in specially significant and interesting ways: *L'Étranger* and *La Jalousie*.

In considering *L'Étranger* from this angle, one notices first of all Meursault's taciturnity (for which he accounts with fitting economy: "C'est que je n'ai jamais grand-chose à dire. Alors je me tais."), [77] and the way he sometimes stops short of giving audible form to what passes through his mind:

> J'aurais voulu le retenir, lui expliquer que je désirais sa sympathie, non pour être mieux défendu, mais, si je puis dire, naturellement. [...] J'avais le désir de lui affirmer que j'étais comme tout le monde, absolument comme tout le monde. Mais tout cela, au fond, n'avait pas grande utilité et j'y ai renoncé par paresse. [78]

This, however, is not unusual in the novel; it is not uncommon for narrators to allow their readers such a privileged insight. What is more important is the silence that exists at the very core of the novel, the silence resulting from the absence in Meursault of self-interro-

---

[75] The common concern of Bernard and Nathalie Sarraute to indicate what lies concealed beneath banal words and actions might perhaps be noted here; the parallel between his attention to unexpressed sentiment and her practice of conversation and *sous-conversation* is, however, only apparent; she tries to render verbally the movement of the *sous-conversation,* where he was trying to convey the characters' inner movement by non-verbal methods.

[76] Maurice Blanchot, *Le Livre à venir,* Paris, Gallimard, 1959, p. 187.

[77] Albert Camus, *L'Étranger,* Paris, Gallimard, 1957, p. 98.

[78] *Ibid.,* p. 97.

gation and internal discourse — not merely on abstract considerations, but on the concrete and essential matter of the killing of the Arab. The reader may be tempted to explain Meursault's act as one of self-defence. But it is an explanation which the narrator does not advance (and, more astonishingly, one which is not offered to the court by the defence lawyer); as far as one can tell, Meursault has not begun to seek an explanation. His precise motivations, if at all they can be determined, are not elucidated through probing self-examination.

Not unexpectedly, this preliminary failure to enquire leaves him even more unprepared than he might otherwise have been for interrogations coming from without:

> 'Pourquoi avez-vous attendu entre le premier et le second coup?' dit-il alors. Une fois de plus, j'ai revu la plage rouge et j'ai senti sur mon front la brûlure du soleil. Mais cette fois, je n'ai rien répondu. [. . .] 'Pourquoi, pourquoi avez-vous tiré sur un corps à terre?' Là encore, je n'ai pas su répondre. Le juge a passé ses mains sur son front et a répété sa question d'une voix un peu altérée: 'Pourquoi? Il faut que vous me le disiez. Pourquoi?' Je me taisais toujours.
>
> … … … … … … … … … … … … … … … … … …
>
> Je me suis levé et comme j'avais envie de parler, j'ai dit, un peu au hasard d'ailleurs, que je n'avais pas eu l'intention de tuer l'Arabe. Le président a répondu que c'était une affirmation, que jusqu'ici il saisissait mal mon système de défense et qu'il serait heureux, avant d'entendre mon avocat, de me faire préciser les motifs qui avaient inspiré mon acte. J'ai dit rapidement, en mêlant un peu les mots et en me rendant compte de mon ridicule, que c'était à cause du soleil. [79]

On the two central questions: Why did Meursault pause between shots? Why exactly did he kill the Arab? silence is maintained, the answer to the latter question being, to the court at any rate, a non-reply.

The want of introspection detectable in Meursault is a measure of the distance at which *L'Étranger* is situated from first-person narratives of the traditional variety. John Cruickshank has shown that the traditional attributes of the first-person narrator (such as "a high degree of self-knowledge" and "a privileged insight into the thoughts and motives of his fellow-characters") are lacking in Meursault, who is "the

---

[79] *Ibid.*, pp. 100, 151.

direct opposite of his counterpart in nineteenth-century fiction." [80]
In another important way — in the almost total absence of verbal
embellishment — the narrative technique of *L'Étranger* marks a rupture with tradition. Here again John Cruickshank, referring to "the
anti-rhetorical style of writing which marks the work of such differently endowed authors as Hemingway, Greene, Camus and Sartre,"
has made some valuable comments:

> Their dislike and distrust of abstractions has inclined them
> towards economical and unadorned prose. All of them are so
> consciously anti-rhetorical, however, that they have really pro-
> duced what amounts to a laconic counter-rhetoric of their
> own. [81]

The counter-rhetoric of *L'Étranger*, and the avoidance of the protracted analysis of personality, motives and sentiments place the novel
within the movement away from *littérature* in the novel, a movement
which, in the drama, had already been executed by Bernard's theatre
of the unexpressed.

Robbe-Grillet's work continues this movement. Even more marked
than in *L'Étranger* are the absence of self-reflection and the refusal
of analysis in *La Jalousie*. To the much treated situation of the
domestic triangle Robbe-Grillet applies the idiom of the unexpressed,
muting the words that would directly translate the sentiments round
which the entire 'narrative' revolves. As Olga Bernal notes,

> Le personnage de *La Jalousie* ne se répète pas 'je suis jaloux';
> ce qu'il se répète ce sont les images formées par la présence
> de sa femme à côté d'un homme. [82] Il est tout entier jalousie
> parce que sa conscience n'est rien d'autre qu'un cycle tou-
> jours recommencé d'une même série d'images.
>
> ... ...
>
> Il n'y a dans ce texte aucun mot qui *signifie* obsession, soup-
> çon, crainte, tourment, jalousie. [83]

---

[80] John Cruickshank, *Albert Camus and the Literature of Revolt*, London,
Oxford University Press, 1959, pp. 151-152.

[81] *Ibid.*, p. 9.

[82] Cf. Bernard's use of images in *L'Invitation*, pp. 146-148 above.

[83] Olga Bernal, *Alain Robbe-Grillet: Le roman de l'absence*, Paris, Gallimard, 1964, pp. 170, 188.

This basically psychological novel, then, is differentiated from its traditional models by its disregard for the interpretative and explanatory rôles of the Word, and by its motions towards the realms of unmediated emotion and sensation. The implicitly proposed equation between the eye peering through the slats of the blind and the lenses of a camera serves the author's endeavour to confront the reader with pictures and to create immediate visual impressions.

La Jalousie strains away from discourse (the novel's paucity of dialogue is worth underlining) and the language of analysis towards the speaking silence of the image. This movement betrays a nostalgia for the pictograph, a yearning for a system of writing based on pictorial symbols in preference to a system based on characters representing the syllables of spoken words. [84] No one who reads *La Jalousie* could fail to notice that while the language might be alphabetical in form, it is pictographic in spirit and in effect. The novel is a stage for the presentation of tableaux in which speech is telegraphic, in which characters do not seek to unfold their inmost preoccupations, and in which the gestural mode of expression predominates. Not everyone might subscribe to the proposition that *La Jalousie* missed its real destiny, which was to be an 'unexpressed' play; but such a proposition has at least the merit of highlighting the link between two authors writing at different times and operating in different genres. *La Jalousie* is an extreme manifestation of the feeling that the artist should confine himself to the direct presentation of experience, and should leave interpretation to his public; it stands as a witness to the distaste for authoritative telling in much of twentieth-century fiction; it is, in short, veined with the intuitions and premisses on which Bernard's theatre of the unexpressed was based.

La Jalousie might be considered as a novel which missed being an 'unexpressed' play; but there is perhaps just as much justification for viewing it as a film *manqué*. Robbe-Grillet's passage from novel to cinema becomes, then, an inevitable transition to his true medium. There seems, also, to be a definite correlation between his nostalgia for the pictograph and the persistence in the twentieth-century mind of the cinematographic image. We were speculating earlier on the

---

[84] A useful comparison may be made here with Artaud's preference for a system of acting based on the ideogram, his advocacy of a "pantomime non pervertie." See *Le Théâtre et son Double*, Paris, Gallimard, 1964, p. 57.

effect the early cinema's use of silence and image might have had on Bernard, and were remarking on his apparent envy for the film's resources. [85] The development of the film is, we submit, largely responsible for the prevailing trend which Martin Esslin sees in this century's art:

> The dominant tendency of our own age might be described as an aspiration of all the arts to attain the condition of *images*. [...] Certainly the contemporary novel tends toward a mosaic of strongly imagined snapshot images. So does the theatre of our day. [86]

The withdrawal from the regions of *la bonne littérature* is, of course, also effected by the various poets who, forgoing punctuation, syntax and logical order, join the quest for new musical, incantatory and pictorial qualities. It should by now be clear too that Bernard's questioning of the right of the literary language to a place of prominence in the theatre ("Le théâtre n'a pas de pire ennemie que la littérature.") [87] forms part of a wider challenge to literature that has been issued by men of letters repeatedly and insistently since the second half of the nineteenth century. The disintegration of language which the Dadaists proposed, the hostile mistrust which the Surrealists showed towards the literary language were after all only later and more extreme manifestations of an attitude of which there had been hints in Mallarmé. The latter's construction of a new, condensed, elliptical language on the ruins of the old, his suspicious attitude towards language and his fight against the temptation to renounce its use reflected an ambivalence, to which Roland Barthes has drawn attention:

> Tout l'effort de Mallarmé a porté sur une destruction du langage, dont la Littérature ne serait en quelque sorte que le cadavre.
>
> ... ...
>
> Ce langage mallarméen, c'est Orphée qui ne peut sauver ce qu'il aime qu'en y renonçant, et qui se retourne tout de même un peu; c'est la Littérature amenée aux portes de la

---

[85] See above, pp. 24 ff.
[86] Martin Esslin, *Brief Chronicles*, London, Temple Smith, 1970, p. 166.
[87] Bernard, 'Le silence au théâtre,' *La Chimère. Bulletin d'Art Dramatique,* mai (2) 1922, p. 67.

Terre promise, c'est-à-dire aux portes d'un monde sans littérature, dont ce serait pourtant aux écrivains à porter témoignage. [88]

The ambivalent contemplation by the man of letters of his instrument
has led progressively to a negation by a number of poets, novelists
and playwrights of what used to be meant by 'poem,' 'novel' and
'play.' In this context, Maurice Blanchot's reply to the question:
"Où va la littérature?" is, however disturbing its implications, especially apposite:

> La littérature va vers elle-même, vers son essence qui est la
> disparition. [89]

This situation reflects a transformation in the writer's attitude to
the tools of his trade. There was a time when the writer regarded
these tools with confident deference, secure in his belief in the authority, integrity and usefulness of language; the person who lacked
this faith and respect was by definition a non-writer. To be sure, the
reversal has not been universal; but it can no longer be considered
an idiosyncrasy of isolated deviationists. Such a breach of the writer-
language covenant is symptomatic of what George Steiner has called
"The Retreat from the Word." [90] The retreat, as Steiner shows, is
visible not only in literature, but also in philosophy, mathematics,
economics, art and music, and has kept pace with the decline of the
belief "that all truth and realness — with the exception of a small,
queer margin at the very top — can be housed inside the walls of
language." [91] The sharpened sensitivity to this aspect of the Word's
insufficiency affords, then, one explanation for the critical contemplation of language. A full discussion of all the possible explanations
would evidently lead too far afield; nevertheless, three other explanations come to mind which can be set forth briefly: a widening
impression of the instability and lubricity of words; [92] an ever-

---

[88] Roland Barthes, *Le degré zéro de l'écriture* suivi de *Nouveaux essais
critiques*, Paris, Seuil, 1972, pp. 9, 55.

[89] Maurice Blanchot, *Le Livre à venir*, Paris, Gallimard, 1959, p. 237.

[90] George Steiner, *Language and Silence*, London, Faber and Faber, 1967,
pp. 30-54.

[91] *Ibid.*, p. 32.

[92] As Eliot phrased it, "words strain, / Crack and sometimes break, under
the burden, / Under the tension, slip, slide, perish, / Decay with imprecision,

increasing apprehension of the power of words to distort and mystify, of the deceptive gaps between *signifiant* and *signifié*; a growing feeling that thought and speech are a secular agglomerate of identical formulas.

The obvious complement of Steiner's predication that "the world of words has shrunk" [93] is that the world of silence has expanded. No longer is silence principally associated with mysticism and religious worship. Still important in ordinary social relationships, it also belongs to the arts of administration and diplomacy; the ability to interpret political silences has passed into the journalist's stock-in-trade. In literature the dilemma of the poet dangerously poised between language and silence, struggling in the land of the ineffable to bypass the impasse of silence, has since Mallarmé become an endemic addiction. It comes as no surprise, in view of the amount of consideration being given in literary, linguistic, philosophical and political fields to the subject of silence, that there has been a reiteration of the concepts underlying the theatre of the unexpressed — as with Sartre's "Se taire ce n'est pas être muet, c'est refuser de parler, donc parler encore." [94]

Bernard's *théâtre de l'inexprimé*, then, has been prophetic in its commitment to the business of language and silence, the silence of language, and the language of silence. It is a reflector of a number of currents of twentieth-century feeling within and outside the drama. In particular, it manifests the *esprit contestataire* that has so comprehensively embraced so much of this century. Bernard, having chosen the drama as his medium, showed a reluctance to accept all its obligations, or, more accurately, he refused to admit that certain presumed obligations were in fact obligations. His revolt, however, was not marked by overweening self-righteousness; his 'unexpressed' plays were experimental probes rather than tyrannical assertions. Nowhere did he preach the absolute superiority of silence over words; what he urged was a delicately ordered interpenetration that would allow both words and silence to gain in resonance. With austerely economical means he was able to create a texture of considerable

---

will not stay in place, / Will not stay still." 'Burnt Norton,' *Four Quartets* in *The Complete Poems and Plays of T. S. Eliot*, London, Faber and Faber, 1969, p. 175.

[93] *Language and Silence*, p. 43.

[94] Jean-Paul Sartre, *Qu'est-ce que la littérature?*, Paris, Gallimard, 1948, p. 32.

density and dramatic intensity. Yet he would have been the last to vituperate the whole of Western drama, and seek to brush aside the fact that excellent works of theatre have emerged from the tradition; nowhere did he preach the absolute inferiority of the methods of the predominantly verbal tradition to his verbally economical manner. His eagerness to introduce new notes and harmonies, without attempting a total destruction of the existing gamut, is summed up in his own words:

> Je ne prétends nullement que les instruments nouveaux que je cherche à apporter doivent supplanter des instruments usés. Je ne veux pas m'opposer à qui que ce soit. L'effort de chacun de nous est comme le complément, plus ou moins fructueux, de tout ce qui a été fait avant lui, de tout ce qui est fait à côté de lui. De l'ensemble des efforts peut naître, un jour, une petite flamme nouvelle. Ce n'est qu'en tremblant d'émotion qu'on ose s'abandonner à l'espoir d'y avoir un peu contribué. [95]

This statement, with its generous attitude to the "instruments usés," looks forward to later phases in Bernard's career. For it is important to bear in mind that his dramatic work was not entirely devoted to the unexpressed. He weighed the individual strengths and weaknesses of various methods, realized that the techniques of the unexpressed were best suited to a particular type of material, and was aware of the danger of trying to use these techniques in every play he wrote. "J'ai toujours pensé," he said, "qu'à chaque sujet de pièce il fallait sa méthode." [96] He saw perpetual renewal as the only permissible formula for his theatre. [97] Admittedly, like so many other writers, he could not completely avoid some measure of self-imitation. But he was too jealous of his liberty as creator, too reluctant after having displaced the old clichés to substitute his own, ever to imply unswerving fidelity to the techniques he had employed in *Martine*. He reserved for himself the right to develop along different lines, even along traditional lines — as he did on approaching the ideological in

[95] Bernard, 'Quelques précisions, après deux récentes expériences,' *Comœdia*, 7 avril 1924, p. 2.
[96] *Ibid.*
[97] See Bernard, 'Avant-Propos,' *Théâtre I*, Paris, Albin Michel, 1925, pp. 6-7.

Jeanne de Pantin and *De Tarse, en Cilicie*..., and the historical in
Louise de la Vallière and *Marie Stuart, Reine d'Écosse.*

Yet it is the theatre of the unexpressed which, in our judgement,
embodies Bernard's sterling accomplishments, and which ultimately
has to be regarded as his most solid contribution to the renewal of
twentieth-century French drama; it is on the achievements of this
theatre that his reputation has justifiably been established. By dem-
onstrating the dramatic viability of the unformulated, by allowing
such unusually deep insights into the unspoken and the unconscious
while consistently maintaining psychological plausibility, the *théâtre
de l'inexprimé* was effectively revitalizing the psychological drama.
This is a theatre which underscored certain basic truths about man
and his linguistic behaviour that had been unduly neglected by playwrights; it rehabilitated for use on the stage elements which may be
found in germ in a great diversity of plays, but which had never
before been given such sustained prominence. It is a drama with
which ordinary mortals can easily identify, for it accepts the *status
quo* of being human, acknowledges — rather than protests against —
the limitation and mediocrity of human experience. Replacing the fret
and fury of heroic drama with simplicity and restraint, showing pathos
to be the very matter of life, present in the most ordinary and
outwardly undramatic of circumstances, substituting for the characteristically grappling spirit of tragedy a more quietistic one, it was
proposing a new conception of the tragic. Again, the hatred of for-
malism which Bernard displayed in carrying the theatre to the then
outermost limits placed him in the front rank of the dramatic vanguard
after the First World War; in helping to spread the concept of theatre
as an autonomous art, not as a mere adjunct of written literature, in
helping to widen the frontiers of the theatre and rescue French drama
from the thraldom of convention, he was helping to pave the way for
today's avant-garde. It is all these factors, all the merits with which
Bernard's theatre of the unexpressed is so economically packed, that
combine to give it its abiding fascination, and an enduring place in
modern French drama.

APPENDIX A

BIOGRAPHICAL SKETCH AND LIST OF
IMPORTANT DATES

JEAN-JACQUES BERNARD — educated: Lycée Carnot, Paris; Sorbonne; Collège de France — Quondam President of *La Société des Auteurs et Compositeurs Dramatiques,* of *Le Comité International des Fédérations Théâtrales d'Amateurs de langue française,* and Vice-President of *La Confédération des travailleurs intellectuels* — Officier de la Légion d'honneur; Commandeur des Palmes Académiques.

1888 30 July: Birth of Jean-Jacques Bernard at Enghien-les-Bains (Seine-et-Oise). Son of Tristan Bernard.

1909 22 March: Première of *Le Voyage à Deux* (one act), first play to be performed.

1912 8 March: Première of *La Joie du sacrifice* (one act).

1919 5 Nov.: Première of *La Maison épargnée* (three acts).

1921 9 June: Première of *Le Feu qui reprend mal* (three acts).

1922 9 May: Première of *Martine* (produced by Gaston Baty). Major event of the theatrical season. Theoretical considerations on the use of silence and the value of the unexpressed in drama.

1924 15 Feb.: Première of *L'Invitation au voyage* (produced by Gaston Baty).

1924 19 March: Première of *Le Printemps des autres* (produced by Lugné-Poe).

1926 12 Jan.: Première of *L'Ame en peine* (produced by Georges Pitoëff) in Monaco.

1926 6 June: Première of *Le Secret d'Arvers.*

1926   14 June: London première of *Le Printemps des autres* (produced by Irene Hentschel) at the Everyman Theatre.

1926   20 June: London première of *Le Feu qui reprend mal* at the Academy Theatre.

1928   22 Jan.: London première of *L'Ame en peine* (produced by Irene Hentschel) at the Apollo Theatre.

1928   April: New York première of *Martine* at the American Laboratory Theatre.

1928   October: New York première of *L'Invitation au voyage* at the Civic Repertory Theatre.

1929   18 Oct.: First performance at the *Comédie-Française* of *Le Feu qui reprend mal*.

1929   4 Dec.: London première of *Martine* at the Gate Theatre.

1930   Jan.: London première of *L'Invitation au voyage* at the Everyman Theatre.

1934   12 Nov.: First performance at the *Comédie-Française* of *Martine*. Madeleine Renaud as Martine.

1935   23 Sep.: Première of *Nationale 6* in Prague.

1935   18 Oct.: Paris première of *Nationale 6*.

1935   29 Oct.: London première of *Nationale 6*.

1939   12 April: Première of *Le Jardinier d'Ispahan*.

1941   12 Dec.: Bernard arrested by the Germans. Interned at Compiègne camp for Jews.

1942   13 March: Bernard released by the Germans.

1957-59   President of *La Société des Auteurs et Compositeurs Dramatiques*.

1959   June: Represented France in Helsinki at the Eighth Congress of the International Theatre Institute.

1961   June: Represented France in Vienna at the Ninth Congress of the International Theatre Institute.

1972   12 Sep.: Death of Jean-Jacques Bernard.

TELEVISION PRODUCTIONS OF BERNARD'S PLAYS IN FRANCE AND BRITAIN

FRENCH TELEVISION:

23 February 1957: *Martine.*
16 September 1958: *L'Ame en peine.*
26 May 1962: *Nationale 6.*

B.B.C. TELEVISION:

22 May 1947: *Martine.*
10 October 1948: *Le Printemps des autres.*
11 May 1952: *Martine.*
21 June 1953: *Nationale 6.*
15 June 1958: *Le Feu qui reprend mal.*

INDEPENDENT TELEVISION:

26 July 1956: *Martine.*
13 November 1957: *Le Printemps des autres.*

BIBLIOGRAPHY

I. WORKS BY JEAN-JACQUES BERNARD

PLAYS:

Le Voyage à Deux, Paris, Librairie Théâtrale, 1910.
La Joie du sacrifice in *L'Illustration Théâtrale*, no. 217, 8 juin 1912.
La Maison épargnée, Paris, Librairie Théâtrale, Artistique et Littéraire, 1920.
Théâtre I (Le Feu qui reprend mal, Martine, Le Printemps des autres, L'Invitation au voyage), Paris, Albin Michel, 1925.
L'Invitation au voyage (Version nouvelle) in *Masques. Cahiers d'Art Dramatique*, 8ᵉ cahier, 1928.
Théâtre II (Le Secret d'Arvers, Denise Marette, L'Ame en peine), Paris, Albin Michel, 1927.
Théâtre III (A la recherche des cœurs, Les Sœurs Guédonec, La Louise), Paris, Albin Michel, 1932.
Théâtre IV (Jeanne de Pantin, Le Roy de Malousie), Paris, Albin Michel, 1934.
Théâtre V (Nationale 6, Les Conseils d'Agathe, 8 Chevaux, 4 Cylindres... et pas de truites!, Deux Hommes), Paris, Albin Michel, 1936.
Théâtre VI (Louise de la Vallière, Le Jardinier d'Ispahan), Paris, Albin Michel, 1946.
Théâtre VII (Marie Stuart, Reine d'Écosse, Richelieu), Paris, Albin Michel, 1949.
Théâtre VIII (Notre-Dame d'en haut, La Route de France), Paris, Albin Michel 1952.
La Grande B.A., Paris, Albin Michel, 1930.
Molière in *L'Age nouveau*, no. 11, janv. 1939, pp. 168-171.
L'Impromptu du Téléphone (Typescript), Paris, 1946. [1]
La Librairie Jalin in *La Revue Théâtrale*, no. 16, avril-juin 1951, pp. 51-78.
La Leçon de français in *L'Avant-Scène*, no. 155, 1957, pp. 45-47.
De Tarse, en Cilicie..., Paris, Albin Michel, 1961.
Martine (Translated and introduced by John Leslie Frith), London, H. F. W. Deane & Sons, 1932.
The Unquiet Spirit (L'Ame en peine), (Translated and introduced by John Leslie Frith), London, H. F. W. Deane & Sons, 1932.
The Poet's Secret (Le Secret d'Arvers), pp. 1-23 in *Modern One-Act Plays from the French* (by Jean-Jacques Bernard et al.), Collected and translated by Virginia and Frank Vernon, London, Allen and Unwin, 1935.

---

[1] I am indebted to M. Nicolas Bernard for this donation.

The Sulky Fire (*Le Feu qui reprend mal, Martine, Le Printemps des autres, L'Invitation au voyage, L'Ame en peine* — translated and introduced by John Leslie Frith), London, Jonathan Cape, 1939.

OTHER PUBLICATIONS:

L'Épicier, Paris, Ollendorff, 1914.
Les Enfants jouent..., Paris, Bernard Grasset, 1919.
Les Tendresses menacées, Paris, Albin Michel, 1924.
Le Roman de Martine, Paris, Flammarion, 1929.
Madeleine Landier & *New-Chicago*, Paris, Albin Michel, 1933.
Témoignages, Paris, Coutan-Lambert, 1933.
Le Camp de la mort lente (Compiègne 1941-42), Paris, Albin Michel, 1944.
The Camp of Slow Death (Translated by Edward Owen Marsh), London, Victor Gollancz, 1945.
Le Pain Rouge, Paris, Albin Michel, 1947.
Marie et le vagabond, Paris, Albin Michel, 1949.
Mon père Tristan Bernard, Paris, Albin Michel, 1955.
Mon Ami le Théâtre, Paris, Albin Michel, 1958.
Saint Paul ou la fidélité, Tours, Maison Mame, 1962.

ARTICLES:

'Le silence au théâtre,' *La Chimère. Bulletin d'Art Dramatique*, no. 5, mai[2] 1922, pp. 66-68.
'Le Théâtre de Demain' (Réponse à une enquête), *La Revue Mondiale*, no. 5, 1er mars 1923, pp. 6-10.
(Réponse à une) 'Enquête sur le renouvellement du décor et de la mise en scène et l'évolution du théâtre,' *La Revue Critique des idées et des livres*, no. 213, 23 juin 1923, pp. 357-361.
'Sur le Présent et l'Avenir prochain du Théâtre en France' (Réponse à une enquête), *Comœdia*, no. 3877, 30 juillet 1923, p. 1.
'L'Invitation au voyage,' *Le Journal*, no. 11451, 23 fév. 1924, p. 4.
'Quelques précisions, après deux récentes expériences,' *Comœdia*, no. 4129, 7 avril 1924, pp. 1-2.
'La rénovation théâtrale en France,' *Le Monde Nouveau*, no. 3, 15 mai 1928, pp. 188-192.
'Les Auteurs d'aujourd'hui: mil neuf cent trente,' *Bravo*, 3 janv. 1930, p. 7.
'La "Théorie du Silence",' *La Revue Théâtrale*, no. 6, juin-juillet-août 1947, pp. 278-281.
'Le Drame et le théâtre radiophonique,' *The Listener*, no. 985, 11 Dec. 1947, pp. 1013-14.
'Gaston Baty professeur d'enthousiasme,' *Arts*, no. 382, 24-30 oct. 1952, p. 3.
'Réflexions sur le théâtre. De la suggestion et de l'artifice,' *Le Théâtre Contemporain* (*Recherches et Débats du Centre Catholique des Intellectuels Français*), nouvelle série no. 2, oct. 1952, pp. 43-54.
'Art and Artifice' (Translated by Mary Glasgow), *Drama*, no. 27, Winter 1952, pp. 14-17.
'Théâtre 1959,' *La Revue Théâtrale*, no. 40, 1959, pp. 6-8.

Films:

1922: *L'Absolution*, Scenario by Bernard.
1931: *Le Rêve*, Dialogue by Bernard.
1934: *La Fille de Madame Angot*, Dialogue by Bernard.
1938: *Katia*, Dialogue by Bernard, in collaboration with Lucile Decaux.
1941: *Caprices*, Dialogue by Bernard.

II. WORKS BY OTHER AUTHORS

Amiel, Denys, *Théâtre I (Le Voyageur, Le Couple, Café-Tabac)*, Paris, Albin Michel, 1925.
——, *Théâtre II (L'Engrenage, Monsieur et Madame Un Tel)*, Paris, Albin Michel, 1928.
Amiel (Denys) & Obey (André), *Théâtre (La Carcasse, La Souriante Madame Beudet)*, Paris, Albin Michel, 1926.
Arvers, Alexis-Félix, 'Mon âme a son secret...,' p. 387 in *The Oxford Book of French Verse* (ed. P. Mansell Jones), Oxford at the Clarendon Press, 1968.
Baudelaire, Charles, *Les Fleurs du Mal* (eds. Jacques Crépet, Georges Blin, Claude Pichois), Paris, José Corti, 1968.
Beckett, Samuel, *En attendant Godot*, Paris, Éditions de Minuit, 1952.
——, *Fin de partie* suivi de *Acte sans paroles I*, Paris, Éditions de Minuit, 1957.
——, *Oh les beaux jours*, Paris, Éditions de Minuit, 1963.
——, *Comédie et actes divers*, Paris, Éditions de Minuit, 1966.
Becque, Henry, *Théâtre Complet II (Les Honnêtes Femmes, Les Corbeaux, La Parisienne)*, Paris, Charpentier, 1890.
Bolt, Robert, *Three Plays (Flowering Cherry, A Man for all Seasons, The Tiger and the Horse)*, London, Mercury Books, 1963.
Camus, Albert, *L'Étranger*, Paris, Gallimard (Le Livre de Poche), 1957.
Chekhov, Anton, *Four Plays (The Seagull, Uncle Vanya, The Three Sisters, The Cherry Orchard)*, Translated by David Magarshack, London, Allen and Unwin, 1970.
——, *Théâtre* (Traduit et commenté par Elsa Triolet), Paris, Club des amis du Livre progressiste, 1963.
Corneille, *Le Cid* (ed. N. Scarlyn Wilson), London, Harrap, 1959.
——, *Cinna* (ed. Marcel Barral), Paris, Bordas (P.C.B.), 1967.
D'Annunzio, Gabriele, *Le Martyre de Saint Sébastien* in *L'Illustration Théâtrale*, no. 181, 17 mai 1911.
Eliot, T. S., *The Complete Poems and Plays*, London, Faber and Faber, 1969.
Flaubert, Gustave, *Madame Bovary*, Paris, Garnier Frères, 1951.
Ford, John, *'Tis Pity She's a Whore* (ed. N. W. Bawcutt), London, Edward Arnold, 1966.
Genet, Jean, *Œuvres Complètes IV* (Includes *Le Balcon, Les Bonnes*), Paris, Gallimard, 1968.
Géraldy, Paul, *Christine* in *La Petite Illustration*, Théâtre no. 312, 31 déc. 1932.

Géraldy, Paul, *Tragédies Légères I* (*Les Noces d'Argent, Les Grands Garçons, Aimer*) Paris, Julliard, 1950.

————, *Tragédies Légères II* (*Robert et Marianne, Duo*), Paris, Julliard, 1952.

————, *Toi et Moi* suivi de *Vous et Moi*, Paris, Stock (Le Livre de Poche), 1960.

Giraudoux, Jean, *Siegfried* (Version définitive suivie de *Fin de Siegfried*), Paris, Bernard Grasset, 1949.

Hardy, Thomas, *The Dynasts* (An epic-drama of the war with Napoleon, in three parts, nineteen acts, & one hundred & thirty scenes, the time covered by the action being about Ten Years), London, Macmillan, 1910.

Hugo, Victor, *Hernani* (ed. Alexandre Beaujour), Paris, Bordas (P.C.B.), 1964.

————, *Œuvres Poétiques I* (ed. Pierre Albouy), Paris, Gallimard (Bibliothèque de la Pléiade), 1964.

Ibsen, Henrik, *Volume V* (*Pillars of Society, A Doll's House, Ghosts*), Translated by James Walter McFarlane, London, Oxford University Press, 1961.

————, *Volume VII* (*The Lady From The Sea, Hedda Gabler, The Master Builder*), Translated by Jens Arup and James Walter McFarlane, London, Oxford University Press, 1966.

Ionesco, Eugène, *Théâtre I* (Includes *La Cantatrice chauve, La Leçon, Les Chaises*), Paris, Gallimard, 1954.

————, *Macbett*, Paris, Gallimard (Le Manteau d'Arlequin), 1972.

Lenormand, Henri-René, *Théâtre Complet II* (*Le Simoun, Le Mangeur de rêves*), Paris, G. Crès et Cie., 1922.

Maeterlinck, Maurice, *Théâtre I* (*La Princesse Maleine, L'Intruse, Les Aveugles*), Paris, Fasquelle, 1929.

————, *Théâtre II* (*Pelléas et Mélisande, Alladine et Palomides, Intérieur, La Mort de Tintagiles*), Paris, Fasquelle, 1929.

————, *Théâtre III* (*Aglavaine et Sélysette, Ariane et Barbe-Bleue, Sœur Béatrice*), Paris, Fasquelle, 1930.

Mallarmé, Stéphane, *Œuvres Complètes* (eds. Henri Mondor & G. Jean-Aubry), Paris, Gallimard (Bibliothèque de la Pléiade), 1945.

Musset, Alfred de, *Comédies et proverbes II*, Paris, Société Les Belles Lettres, 1952.

O'Neill, Eugene, *Mourning Becomes Electra*, London, Jonathan Cape, 1932.

Pellerin, Jean-Victor, *Têtes de rechange* & *Intimité*, Paris, Calmann-Lévy, 1929.

Pinter, Harold, *The Birthday Party and Other Plays*, London, Methuen, 1960.

————, *The Collection and The Lover*, London, Methuen, 1964.

————, *The Caretaker*, London, Methuen, 1965.

Pirandello, Luigi, *Three Plays* (*Six Characters in Search of an Author, Henry IV, Right You Are! (If You Think So)*), Translated by Edward Storer and Arthur Livingston, London, Dent, 1936.

Racine, *Bajazet* (ed. Eugène Berest), Paris, Bordas (P.C.B.), 1965.

————, *Bérénice* (ed. Gabriel Spillebout), Paris, Bordas (P.C.B.), 1967.

————, *Britannicus* (ed. Maurice Martin), Paris, Bordas (P.C.B.), 1970.

————, *Mithridate* (eds. Jean Boullé & Claude Labrosse), Paris, Bordas (P.C.B.), 1965.

————, *Phèdre* (ed. Jean Salles), Paris, Bordas (P.C.B.), 1970.

Renard, Jules, *Théâtre Complet* suivi de *Propos de Théâtre* et de *La Semaine Théâtrale* (ed. Gilbert Sigaux), Paris, Gallimard, 1959.

Robbe-Grillet, Alain, *La Jalousie*, Paris, Éditions de Minuit, 1957.

Sand, George, *François le Champi*, Paris, Nelson-Calmann-Lévy, 1937.
Shakespeare, *Complete Works* (ed. W. J. Craig), London, Oxford University Press, 1971.
Sophocles, *Volume I (Oedipus the King, Oedipus at Colonus, Antigone)*, Translated by F. Storr, London, Heinemann, 1962.
———, *Volume II (Ajax, Electra, Trachiniae, Philoctetes)*, Translated by F. Storr, London, Heinemann, 1961.
Strindberg, August, *The Plays. Volume One* (Translated by Michael Meyer), London, Mercury Books, 1964.
Vigny, Alfred de, *Œuvres Complètes I* (ed. F. Baldensperger), Paris Gallimard (Bibliothèque de la Pléiade), 1950.
Vildrac, Charles, *Madame Béliard*, Paris, Émile-Paul Frères, 1928.
———, *Théâtre I (Le Paquebot Tenacity, Poucette, Trois mois de prison)*, Paris, Gallimard, 1943.
———, *Théâtre II (Michel Auclair, Le Pèlerin, L'Air du Temps)*, Paris, Gallimard, 1948.
———, *Livre d'Amour* (Édition augmentée), Paris Éditions de Minuit, 1946.

III. SECONDARY SOURCES

BOOKS:

Agate, James, *The Contemporary Theatre: 1926*, London, Chapman & Hall, 1927.
———, *The Contemporary Theatre: 1944 and 1945*, London, Harrap, 1946.
Anders, France, *Jacques Copeau et le Cartel des Quatre*, Paris, A. G. Nizet, 1959.
Andrieu, Jean-Marie, *Maeterlinck*, Paris, Éditions Universitaires, 1962.
Antoine, André, *Le Théâtre (La Troisième République. De 1870 à nos jours)*, Paris, Éditions de France, 1932.
Arnold, Morris Le Roy, *The Soliloquies of Shakespeare. A Study in Technic*, New York, Columbia University Press, 1911.
Artaud, Antonin, *Le Théâtre et son Double* suivi de *Le Théâtre de Séraphin*, Paris, Gallimard, 1964.
Auerbach, Erich, *Mimesis. The Representation of Reality in Western Literature* (Translated by Willard Trask), New York, Doubleday Anchor Books, 1957.
Azaïs, Marcel, *Le Chemin des Gardies*, Paris, Nouvelle Librairie Nationale, 1926.
Barthes, Roland, *Le degré zéro de l'écriture* suivi de *Nouveaux essais critiques*, Paris, Seuil, 1972.
Baty, Gaston, *Rideau Baissé*, Paris, Bordas, 1949.
Beigbeder, Marc, *Le Théâtre en France depuis la libération*, Paris, Bordas, 1959.
Bernal, Olga, *Alain Robbe-Grillet: Le roman de l'absence*, Paris, Gallimard, 1964.
Bishop, Thomas, *Pirandello and the French Theatre*, London, Peter Owen, 1961.
Bissell, Clifford H., *Les Conventions du théâtre bourgeois contemporain en France: 1887-1914*, Paris, Presses Universitaires de France, 1930.

Blanchart, Paul, *Jean-Jacques Bernard* (*Masques. Cahiers d'Art Dramatique,* 11ᵉ cahier), Paris, Coutan-Lambert, 1928.

Blanchot, Maurice, *Le Livre à venir,* Paris, Gallimard, 1959.

Bloch, Jean-Richard, *Destin du théâtre,* Paris, Gallimard, 1930.

Bonnefoy, Claude, *Entretiens avec Eugène Ionesco,* Paris, Pierre Belfond, 1966.

Bouquet (Georges) & Menanteau (Pierre) (eds.), *Charles Vildrac,* Paris, Pierre Seghers (Poètes d'aujourd'hui), 1959.

Brisson, Pierre, *Le Théâtre des années folles,* Genève, Éditions du Milieu du Monde, 1943.

Carlyle, Thomas, *Sartor Resartus* (ed. Rev. James Wood), London, Dent, 1902.

Chandler, Frank W., *Modern Continental Playwrights,* New York-London, Harper and Brothers, 1931.

Chiari, J., *Landmarks of Contemporary Drama,* London, Herbert Jenkins, 1965.

Clark, Barrett H., *A Study of the Modern Drama,* New York-London, D. Appleton-Century Company, 1938.

Clark (Barrett H.) & Freedley (George) (eds.), *A History of Modern Drama,* New York-London, D. Appleton-Century Company, 1947.

Claudel, Paul, *Mes idées sur le théâtre* (eds. Jacques Petit & Jean-Pierre Kempf), Paris, Gallimard, 1966.

Cogniat, Raymond, *Cinquante ans de spectacles en France. Les décorateurs de théâtre,* Paris, Librairie Théâtrale, 1955.

Coindreau, Maurice Edgar, *La Farce est jouée. Vingt-cinq ans de théâtre français: 1900-1925,* New York, Éditions de la Maison Française, 1942.

Copeau, Jacques, *Souvenirs du Vieux-Colombier,* Paris, Nouvelles Éditions Latines, 1931.

Corneille, Pierre, *Trois discours sur le Poème dramatique* (Texte de 1660) (ed. Louis Forestier), Paris, Société d'Édition d'Enseignement Supérieur, 1963.

Craig, Edward Gordon, *On the Art of the Theatre,* London, Heinemann, 1929.

Crémieux, Benjamin, *Inquiétude et Reconstruction. Essai sur la littérature d'après-guerre,* Paris, Corrêa, 1931.

Cruickshank, John, *Albert Camus and the Literature of Revolt,* London, Oxford University Press, 1959.

Daniels, May, *The French Drama of The Unspoken,* Edinburgh at the University Press, 1953.

Deloffre, Frédéric, *Une Préciosité nouvelle. Marivaux et le Marivaudage,* Paris, Société d'Édition Les Belles Lettres, 1955.

Dickinson, Thomas H. (ed.), *The Theatre in a Changing Europe,* London, Putnam, 1938.

Diderot, Denis, *Lettre sur les sourds et muets* (ed. Paul Hugo Meyer), *Diderot Studies VII,* Genève, Librairie Droz, 1965.

Doisy, Marcel, *Le Théâtre Français Contemporain,* Bruxelles, Éditions 'La Boétie,' 1947.

Dubech, Lucien, *Les Chefs de File de la Jeune Génération,* Paris, Plon, 1925.

———, *La crise du théâtre,* Paris, Librairie de France, 1928.

Dullin, Charles, *Souvenirs et Notes de travail d'un acteur,* Paris, Odette Lieutier, 1946.

Ellis-Fermor, Una, *The Frontiers of Drama,* London, Methuen, 1964.

Esslin, Martin, *The Theatre of the Absurd* (Revised and enlarged edition), Harmondsworth, Penguin Books, 1968.
——, *Brief Chronicles*, London, Temple Smith, 1970.
——, *The Peopled Wound. The Plays of Harold Pinter*, London, Methuen, 1970.
Gascoigne, Bamber, *Twentieth-century Drama*, London, Hutchinson University Library, 1963.
Gautier, Jean-Jacques, *Théâtre d'aujourd'hui*, Paris, Julliard, 1972.
Gide, André, *Journal: 1889-1939*, Paris, Gallimard (Bibliothèque de la Pléiade), 1955.
Giraudoux, Jean, *Littérature*, Paris, Bernard Grasset, 1941.
Gouhier, Henri, *L'Essence du théâtre*, Paris, Aubier-Montaigne, 1968.
Guicharnaud, Jacques (in collaboration with June Beckelman), *Modern French Theatre from Giraudoux to Beckett*, New Haven, Yale University Press, 1961.
Guilhou, Étienne, *Quelques tendances du théâtre d'après-guerre en France*, Paris, Boivin & Cie., 1926.
Henriot, Émile, *Les Romantiques*, Paris, Albin Michel, 1953.
Hesnard, A., *L'Œuvre de Freud et son importance pour le monde moderne*, Paris, Payot, 1960.
Hobson, Harold, *The French Theatre of To-day*, London, Harrap, 1953.
Jouvet, Louis, *Témoignages sur le théâtre*, Paris, Flammarion, 1952.
Kiehl, Jean, *Les Ennemis du Théâtre*, Neuchâtel, Éditions de la Baconnière, 1951.
Knowles, Dorothy, *La Réaction idéaliste au théâtre depuis 1890*, Paris, Librairie E. Droz, 1934.
——, *French Drama of the Inter-War Years 1918-39*, London, Harrap, 1967.
Lalou, René, *Le Théâtre en France depuis 1900*, Paris, Presses Universitaires de France (Que sais-je?), 1951.
Lecat, Maurice, *Le Maeterlinckianisme*, Bruxelles, Ancienne Librairie Castaigne, 1937.
——, *La Philosophie de Maeterlinck*, Bruxelles, Ancienne Librairie Castaigne, 1939.
Leclerc, Guy, *Le T.N.P. de Jean Vilar*, Paris, Union Générale d'Éditions, 1971.
Lenormand, Henri-René, *Les Confessions d'un auteur dramatique II*, Paris, Albin Michel, 1953.
Lumley, Frederick, *New Trends in 20th Century Drama*, London, Barrie and Jenkins, 1972.
Maeterlinck, Maurice, *Le Trésor des humbles*, Paris, Société du Mercure de France, 1896.
——, *Le Double Jardin*, Paris, Fasquelle, 1904.
Mignon, Paul-Louis (ed.), *Les Entretiens d'Helsinki ou les tendances du théâtre d'avant-garde dans le monde*, Paris, Michel Brient, 1961.
——, *Les Entretiens de Vienne ou les droits et les devoirs du metteur en scène*, Paris, Michel Brient, 1963.
Mornet, Daniel, *Introduction à l'étude des écrivains français d'aujourd'hui*, Paris, Boivin & Cie., 1939.
Mortier, Alfred, *Quinze ans de théâtre (1917-1932)*, Paris, Albert Messein, 1933.
Nicoll, Allardyce, *Film and Theatre*, London, Harrap, 1936.

Nicoll, Allardyce, *World Drama. From Aeschylus to Anouilh*, London, Harrap, 1949.
——, *The Theatre and Dramatic Theory*, London, Harrap, 1962.
Northam, John, *Ibsen's Dramatic Method. A Study of the Prose Dramas*, London, Faber and Faber, 1953.
——, *Ibsen. A Critical Study*, Cambridge at the University Press, 1973.
Palmer, John, *Studies in the Contemporary Theatre*, London, Martin Secker, 1927.
Parain, Brice, *Recherches sur la nature et les fonctions du langage*, Paris, Gallimard, 1942.
Peacock, Ronald, *The Art of Drama*, London, Routledge & Kegan Paul, 1957.
——, *The Poet in the Theatre*, London, Macgibbon & Kee, 1961.
Peterkiewicz, Jerzy, *The Other Side of Silence: The Poet at the Limits of Language*, London, Oxford University Press, 1970.
Pillement, Georges, *Anthologie du Théâtre Français Contemporain*, Paris, Éditions du Bélier, 1946.
Radine, Serge, *Essais sur le théâtre* (1919-1939), Genève-Annemasse, Éditions du Mont-Blanc, S. A., 1944.
Rageot, Gaston, *Prise de Vues*, Paris, La Nouvelle Revue Critique, 1928.
Raymond, Marcel, *Le Jeu retrouvé*, Montréal, Éditions de l'Arbre, 1943.
Robichez, Jacques, *Le Symbolisme au théâtre. Lugné-Poe et les débuts de l'Œuvre*, Paris, L'Arche, 1957.
Sadoul, Georges, *Le Cinéma Français* (1890-1962), Paris, Flammarion, 1962.
Salomon, Michel, *Charles Nodier et le Groupe Romantique*, Paris, Perrin et Cie., 1908.
Sartre, Jean-Paul, *Qu'est-ce que la littérature?*, Paris, Gallimard, 1948.
Shattuck, Roger, *The Banquet Years*, London, Faber and Faber, 1959.
Simon, Alfred, *Dictionnaire du théâtre français contemporain*, Paris, Larousse, 1970.
Stanislavski, Constantin, *Building a Character* (Translated by Elizabeth Reynolds Hapgood), London, Reinhardt & Evans, 1950.
Steiner, George, *Language and Silence*, London, Faber and Faber, 1967.
Stendhal, *De l'Amour*, Paris, Éditions de Cluny, 1938.
Strindberg, August, *Letters to the Intimate Theatre* (Translated and introduced by Walter Johnson), London, Peter Owen, 1967.
Styan, J. L., *The Elements of Drama*, Cambridge at the University Press, 1960.
Surer, Paul, *Le Théâtre Français Contemporain*, Paris, Société d'Édition d'Enseignement Supérieur, 1964.
Tennant, P. F. D., *Ibsen's Dramatic Technique*, New York, Humanities Press, 1965.
Touchard, Pierre-Aimé, *Dionysos suivi de L'Amateur de Théâtre*, Paris, Seuil, 1968.
Trilling, Lionel, *Sincerity and Authenticity*, London, Oxford University Press, 1972.
Vandérem, Fernand, *Le Miroir des lettres* (2ᵉ série), Paris, Flammarion, 1921.
——, *Le Miroir des lettres* (4ᵉ série), Paris, Flammarion, 1922.
——, *Le Miroir des lettres* (5ᵉ série), Paris, Flammarion, 1924.
——, *Le Miroir des lettres* (7ᵉ série), Paris, Flammarion, 1929.
Veinstein, André, *Du Théâtre Libre au Théâtre Louis Jouvet (Les Théâtres d'Art à travers leur périodique: 1887-1934)*, Paris, Billaudot, 1955.
Vildrac, Charles, *Pages de Journal: 1922-1966*, Paris, Gallimard, 1968.

Virmaux, Alain, *Antonin Artaud et le théâtre*, Paris, Seghers, 1970.

Voellmy, Jean, *Aspects du silence dans la poésie moderne*, Zurich, Otto Altoforer & Co., 1952.

Williams, Raymond, *Drama from Ibsen to Brecht*, London, Chatto & Windus, 1968.

――――, *Drama in Performance*, Harmondsworth, Penguin Books, 1972.

Yeats, William Butler, *Collected Works. Vol. VIII*, Stratford-on-Avon, Shakespeare Head Press, 1908.

ARTICLES AND ESSAYS:

Amico, Silvio d', 'Autour du théâtre du "Silence" et de l'inexprimé,' *Comœdia*, no. 4738, 12 déc. 1925, p. 3.

Amiel, Denys, 'Le Théâtre qui vient,' *Gazette des Sept Arts*, no. 1, 15 déc. 1922, p. 6.

――――, 'Le Voyageur,' *Bonsoir*, no. 1544, 28 avril 1923, p. 3.

――――, 'Les Œuvres par Leurs Auteurs,' *Gazette des Sept Arts*, nos. 6-7, 10 mai 1923, pp. 3-4.

――――, 'Sur le Présent et l'Avenir prochain du Théâtre en France' (Réponse à une enquête), *Comœdia*, no. 3867, 20 juillet 1923, p. 1.

――――, (Réponse à une) 'Enquête sur le renouvellement du décor et de la mise en scène et l'évolution du théâtre,' *La Revue Critique des idées et des livres*, no. 215, 25 août 1923, pp. 476-477.

Anon., 'A World of Elusive Things' (Review of *The Sulky Fire*, John Leslie Frith's translation of *Le Feu qui reprend mal, Martine, Le Printemps des autres, L'Invitation au voyage* and *L'Ame en peine*), *The Times Literary Supplement*, no. 1982, 27 Jan. 1940, p. 41.

Anon., 'Footnotes to Fascism. The Camp of Slow Death' (Review of Edward Marsh's translation of Bernard's *Le Camp de la mort lente*), *The Times Literary Supplement*, no. 2296, 2 Feb. 1946, p. 52.

Anon., '*Notre-Dame d'en haut* devant la critique,' *France Illustration. Supplément théâtral et littéraire*, no. 102, 8 mars 1952, not paginated.

Anon., 'Obituary: M. J.-J. Bernard. Intimate theatre,' *The Times*, no. 58583, 19 Sep. 1972, p. 15.

Baignères, Claude, 'L'adaptation des pièces anglo-saxonnes peut-elle résoudre la crise du théâtre français?', *Le Figaro littéraire*, no. 1380, 28 oct. 1972, p. vi.

Barthes, Roland, 'A l'avant-garde de quel théâtre?', *Théâtre populaire*, no. 18, 1ᵉʳ mai 1956, pp. 1-3.

Baty, Gaston, 'Le programme des *Compagnons de la Chimère,' La Chimère. Bulletin d'Art Dramatique*, no. 1, fév. 1922, pp. 3-4.

――――, 'Un Comité de Lecture,' *La Chimère. Bulletin d'Art Dramatique*, no. 3, avril 1922, pp. 33-34.

――――, 'Le rôle du décor,' *La Chimère. Bulletin d'Art Dramatique*, no. 4, mai 1922, pp. 49-51.

――――, 'Le Texte,' *La Chimère. Bulletin d'Art Dramatique*, no. 6, oct. 1922, pp. 82-89.

――――, 'La Baraque de la Chimère ferme ses portes...,' *La Chimère. Bulletin d'Art Dramatique*, no. 13, 1923, pp. 203-204.

Beauplan, Robert de, 'Le Voyageur à la Baraque de la Chimère,' *La Petite Illustration*, Théâtre, nouvelle série no. 100, 18 août 1923, not paginated.

Beauplan, Robert de, 'L'Invitation au voyage au théâthe de l'Odéon,' La Petite Illustration, Théâtre, nouvelle série no. 116, 29 mars 1924, not paginated.

——, 'Le Printemps des autres au Théâtre Fémina,' La Petite Illustration, Théâtre, nouvelle série no. 125, 2 août 1924, not paginated.

——, 'Le Secret d'Arvers sur la Petite Scène,' La Petite Illustration, Théâtre no. 167, 31 juillet 1926, not paginated.

——, 'Les Sœurs Guédonec au Studio des Champs-Élysées,' La Petite Illustration, Théâtre no. 287, 26 déc. 1931, not paginated.

——, 'Christine à la Comédie-Française,' La Petite Illustration, Théâtre no. 312, 31 déc. 1932, not paginated.

——, 'Nationale 6 au théâtre de l'Œuvre,' La Petite Illustration, Théâtre no. 376, 23 nov. 1935, not paginated.

Berton, Claude, 'Les Visages de la Comédie,' Les Nouvelles littéraires, no. 133, 2 mai 1925, p. 7.

——, 'Les Visages de la Comédie,' Les Nouvelles littéraires, no. 180, 27 mars 1926, p. 7.

Bidou, Henry, 'Chronique Dramatique,' Journal des Débats, no. 1473, 19 mai 1922, pp. 840-843.

——, 'La Semaine Dramatique,' Journal des Débats, no. 97, 7 avril 1924, p. 3.

——, 'La Semaine Dramatique,' Journal des Débats, no. 292, 21 oct. 1929, p. 3.

Blanchart, Paul, 'Jean-Jacques Bernard ou l'intelligence de la sensibilité,' Chantecler, no. 110, 28 avril 1928, p. 1.

Bourgeois, André, 'L'Attitude devant la Vie des Auteurs Dramatiques Contemporains — Évasion, Rébellion ou Acceptation,' Le Bayou, no. 53, printemps 1953, pp. 259-265.

Brown, John Russell, 'Dialogue in Pinter and Others,' The Critical Quarterly, vol. 7, no. 3, Autumn 1965, pp. 225-243.

Caillois, Roger, 'Le langage et la littérature moderne,' La Table Ronde, no. 2, fév. 1948, pp. 237-250.

Catalogne, Gérard de, 'Jean-Jacques Bernard ou la psychanalyse au théâtre,' La pensée latine, no. 53, janv. 1925, pp. 5-10.

Clair, René, 'Du Théâtre au Cinéma,' Anthologie du cinéma (ed. Marcel Lapierre), Paris, La Nouvelle Édition, 1946, pp. 264-270.

Copeau, Jacques, 'Un essai de rénovation dramatique. Le Théâtre du Vieux-Colombier,' La Nouvelle Revue Française, no. 57, 1er sep. 1913, pp. 337-353.

——, 'Le Paquebot Tenacity,' L'Art Libre, no. 3, mars 1921, p. 40.

Cor, Laurence W., 'French Views on Language in the Theater,' The French Review, vol. XXXV, no. 1, Oct. 1961, pp. 11-18.

Crémieux, Benjamin, 'Le Théâtre,' La Nouvelle Revue Française, no. 147, 1er déc. 1925, pp. 745-748.

——, 'Chronique Dramatique: L'Impérialisme du Metteur en Scène,' La Nouvelle Revue Française, no. 166, 1er juillet 1927, pp. 96-100.

——, 'Chronique Dramatique,' La Nouvelle Revue Française, no. 169, 1er oct. 1927, pp. 529-533.

Crommelynck, Fernand, 'La crise? ... Tout le mal est venu du metteur en scène,' La Table Ronde, no. 220, mai 1966, pp. 28-30.

Delpit, Louise, 'Paris — Théâtre Contemporain: Rôle Prépondérant des Scènes d'avant-garde depuis trente ans,' Smith College Studies in Modern Languages, vol. VI, nos. 1-2, Oct. 1924-Jan. 1925.

Delpit, Louise, 'Paris — Théâtre Contemporain: Tableau du Mouvement Dramatique en France de 1925 à 1938,' *Smith College Studies in Modern Languages,* vol. XX, nos. 1-2, Oct. 1938-Jan. 1939.

Deval, Jacques, 'A travers les théâtres,' *Revue des Deux Mondes,* 15 juin 1928, pp. 938-947.

Doumic, René, 'Revue Dramatique,' *Revue des Deux Mondes,* 15 déc. 1921, pp. 943-946.

———, 'Revue Dramatique,' *Revue des Deux Mondes,* 15 mars 1924, pp. 466-469.

Dubech, Lucien, 'Le Théâtre: L'École du silence,' *La Revue Universelle,* vol. XVII, no. 3, 1ᵉʳ mai 1924, pp. 379-383.

———, 'Chronique Dramatique: L'École du silence,' *L'Action Française,* no. 284, 11 oct. 1925, p. 2.

———, 'Le Théâtre,' *La Revue Universelle,* vol. XXV, no. 3, 1ᵉʳ mai 1926, pp. 380-383.

———, 'Le Théâtre,' *La Revue Universelle,* vol. XXVI, no. 8, 15 juillet 1926, pp. 253-255.

———, 'Les écoles dans l'art dramatique en 1926,' *La Revue Universelle,* vol. XXVI, no. 10, 15 août 1926, pp. 508-511.

George, André, 'La Vie Théâtrale,' *Les Lettres,* no. 1, janv. 1926, pp. 115-127.

Hommel, Luc, 'Le Théâtre de Jean-Jacques Bernard,' *La Revue Générale,* 15 mai 1925, pp. 592-597.

Hunt, Hugh, 'Droits et Devoirs du metteur en scène,' *World Theatre,* vol. X, no. 3, automne 1961, pp. 199-212.

Ionesco, Eugène, 'Expérience du théâtre,' *La Nouvelle Nouvelle Revue Française,* no. 62, 1ᵉʳ fév. 1958, pp. 247-270.

Jamati, Georges, 'Charles Vildrac dramaturge de la vie intérieure,' *Les Primaires,* no. 5, fév. 1928, pp. 208-216.

Kanters, Robert, 'De l'art de la mise en scène considéré comme un assassinat,' *La Table Ronde,* no. 1, janv. 1948, pp. 133-138.

Kern, Edith, 'Drama Stripped for Inaction: Beckett's *Godot,*' *Yale French Studies,* no. 14, Winter 1954-55, pp. 41-47.

Lakich, John J., 'The Ideal and Reality in the French Theater of the 1920's,' *Modern Language Quarterly,* vol. 31, no. 1, March 1970, pp. 64-77.

Lamb, Charles, 'On the Tragedies of Shakespeare, Considered with Reference to their Fitness for Stage Representation,' *English Critical Essays: Nineteenth Century* (ed. Edmund D. Jones), London, Oxford University Press, 1971, pp. 81-101.

Lemonnier, Léon, 'Le Théâtre de M. Jean-Jacques Bernard,' *Choses de théâtre,* no. 15, mars 1923, pp. 268-272.

———, 'Le Théâtre de Jean-Jacques Bernard,' *La Revue Mondiale,* no. 15, 1ᵉʳ août 1925, pp. 292-296.

Lenormand, Henri-René, 'L'Inconscient dans la littérature dramatique,' *La Chimère. Bulletin d'Art Dramatique,* no. 5, mai² 1922, pp. 74-80.

Marcel, Gabriel, 'Le Théâtre français entre les deux guerres,' *Les Nouvelles littéraires,* no. 1000, 3 oct. 1946, p. 12.

———, 'Le Théâtre,' *Les Nouvelles littéraires,* no. 1026, 1ᵉʳ mai 1947, p. 10.

———, 'Adieu à Jean-Jacques Bernard,' *Les Nouvelles littéraires,* no. 2348, 25 sep.-1ᵉʳ oct. 1972, p. 22.

Maulnier, Thierry, 'Le Théâtre,' *La Revue de Paris,* nov. 1965, pp. 134-137.

Mauriac, François, 'Les Spectacles,' *La Nouvelle Revue Française*, no. 148, 1er janv. 1926, pp. 122-123.

Orna, Adolphe, 'Sur le Présent et l'Avenir prochain du Théâtre en France' (Réponse à une enquête), *Comœdia*, no. 3889, 11 août 1923, pp. 1-2.

Pellerin, Jean-Victor, 'A propos d'*Intimité*,' *La Chimère. Bulletin d'Art Dramatique*, no. 5, mai[2] 1922, pp. 70-71.

Peyre, Henri, 'Paul Claudel (1868-1955),' *Yale French Studies*, no. 14, Winter 1954-55, pp. 94-97.

Pietrkiewicz, Jerzy, 'Introducing Norwid,' *The Slavonic and East European Review*, no. 68, Dec. 1948, pp. 228-247.

Pinter, Harold, 'Writing for the Theatre,' *Evergreen*, no. 33, August-September 1964, pp. 80-82.

Rageot, Gaston, 'Le Théâtre: Une nouvelle forme du théâtre psychologique,' *Revue Bleue*, no. 17, 3 sep. 1921, pp. 557-559.

——, 'Le Théâtre: Une fantaisie caricaturale,' *Revue Bleue*, no. 11, 2 juin 1928, pp. 345-346.

——, 'Le Théâtre: La Révolution à l'Odéon,' *Revue Bleue*, no. 23, 2 déc. 1933, pp. 728-729.

Rambaud (Henri) & Varillon (Pierre), 'Enquête sur les maîtres de la jeune littérature: Les Auteurs dramatiques' (Replies of Denys Amiel, Jean-Jacques Bernard, Jacques Copeau, Gabriel Marcel *et al*), *La Revue Hebdomadaire*, no. 50, 16 déc. 1922, pp. 328-352.

Renaud, Luc, 'Notre Giraudoux,' *Paris-Théâtre*, no. 67, déc. 1952, pp. 7-12.

Reynolds, George F., 'Plays as Literature for an Audience,' *University of Colorado Studies* (Series in Language and Literature), no. 4, July 1953, pp. 1-51.

Rouveyre, André, 'Théâtre,' *Mercure de France*, no. 668, 15 avril 1926, pp. 415-421.

Salvan, J. L., 'L'Esprit du Théâtre Nouveau,' *The French Review*, vol. XIV, no. 2, Dec. 1940, pp. 109-117.

Sarraute, Nathalie, 'Conversation et sous-conversation,' *La Nouvelle Nouvelle Revue Française*, no. 37, 1er janv. 1956, pp. 50-63 & no. 38, 1er fév. 1956, pp. 233-244.

Savitzky, Ludmila, 'Charles Vildrac et le théâtre contemporain,' *Mercure de France*, no. 596, 15 avril 1923, pp. 289-305.

Sée, Edmond, 'Le Théâtre et la Vie,' *La Revue de France*, no. 4, 15 fév. 1934, pp. 719-720.

Séverin-Mars, 'Le théâtre du silence,' *Anthologie du cinéma* (ed. Marcel Lapierre), Paris, La Nouvelle Édition, 1946, pp. 130-133.

Sorbets, Gaston, '*Le Feu qui reprend mal*, au théâtre Antoine,' *La Petite Illustration*, Roman-Théâtre, nouvelle série no. 47, 6 août 1921, not paginated.

——, '*Martine*, au théâtre des Mathurins,' *La Petite Illustration*, Théâtre, nouvelle série no. 74, 22 juillet 1922, not paginated.

Vannier, Jean, 'Langages de l'avant-garde,' *Théâtre populaire*, no. 18, 1er mai 1956, pp. 30-39.

Vildrac, Charles, 'Sur le Présent et l'Avenir prochain du Théâtre en France' (Réponse à une enquête), *Comœdia*, no. 3860, 13 juillet 1923, pp. 1-2.

——, 'Réflexions sur le théâtre,' *Théâtre* (ed. Paul Arnold), Paris, Éditions du Pavois, 1945, pp. 21-33.

——, 'Jacques Copeau,' *Hommes et Mondes*, no. 42, janv. 1950, p. 103.

PRESS CUTTINGS (CONTAINING REVIEWS OF PLAYS) IN THE 'COLLEC-
TION RONDEL' OF THE 'BIBLIOTHÈQUE DE L'ARSENAL':

Le Jardinier d'Ispahan, Shelf-mark: R. Supp. 470.
Louise de la Vallière, Shelf-mark: R. Supp. 1604.
Martine, Shelf-mark: R. Supp. 1609.
Martine, Shelf-mark: R. Supp. 2307.
Martine (pièce lyrique en cinq tableaux, livret de Jean-Jacques Bernard, mu-
sique d'Henri Rabaud), Shelf-mark: R. Supp. 2308.
Notre-Dame d'en haut, Shelf-mark: R. Supp. 3756.

IV. MISCELLANEOUS

LETTERS TO THE AUTHOR FROM:

Amiel, Denys, 14 January 1972.
Bernard, Nicolas, 17 January 1972.
Bernard, Nicolas, 19 April 1972.
Bernard, Raymond, 10 March 1972.
Gautier, Jean-Jacques, June 1972.
Géraldy, Paul, January 1972.
Mignon, Paul-Louis, 21 August 1972.
Pinter, Harold, August 1972.
Touchard, Pierre-Aimé, August 1972.

INTERVIEW:

With Henri Crémieux, 22 January 1972.